SERVICE SHEETS
B31-B32-B33-B34
1945-1960
Including: Gold Star and Competition Models

A Floyd Clymer Publication
Published in 2021 by VelocePress.com

INTRODUCTION

Welcome to the world of digital publishing ~ the book you now hold in your hand was printed using the latest state of the art digital technology. The advent of print-on-demand has forever changed the publishing process, never has information been so accessible and it is our hope that this book serves your informational needs for years to come. If this is your first exposure to digital publishing, we hope that you are pleased with the results. Many more titles of interest to the classic automobile and motorcycle enthusiast, collector and restorer are available via our website at www.VelocePress.com. We hope that you find this title as interesting as we do.

NOTE FROM THE PUBLISHER

The information presented is true and complete to the best of our knowledge. All recommendations are made without any guarantees on the part of the author or the publisher, who also disclaim all liability incurred with the use of this information.

TRADEMARKS

We recognize that some words, model names and designations, for example, mentioned herein are the property of the trademark holder. We use them for identification purposes only. This is not an official publication.

INFORMATION ON THE USE OF THIS PUBLICATION

This manual is an invaluable resource for those interested in performing their own maintenance. However, in today's information age we are constantly subject to changes in common practice, new technology, availability of improved materials and increased awareness of chemical toxicity. As such, it is advised that the user consult with an experienced professional prior to undertaking any procedure described herein. While every care has been taken to ensure correctness of information, it is obviously not possible to guarantee complete freedom from errors or omissions or to accept liability arising from such errors or omissions. Therefore, any individual that uses the information contained within, or elects to perform or participate in do-it-yourself repairs or modifications acknowledges that there is a risk factor involved and that the publisher or its associates cannot be held responsible for personal injury or property damage resulting from the use of the information or the outcome of such procedures.

WARNING!

One final word of advice, this publication is intended to be used as a reference guide, and when in doubt the reader should consult with a qualified technician.

BSA 'SERVICE SHEETS'

UNDERSTANDING AND INTERPRETING THE 1945 AND ONWARDS PUBLICATIONS

In 1945, after the war had ended, BSA resumed production of their civilian line of motorcycles. However, they continued their pre-war practice of publishing repair, overhaul and technical information in the form of individual 'Service Sheets'. It should be noted that BSA never intended that these service sheets would be distributed to the general public, they were 'dealer only' publications and, as such, the print quality was at times somewhat questionable. It was not until the early 1960's that BSA eventually started publishing model specific workshop manuals that were available to the general public. Consequently, these 'Service Sheets' were the only publications available for the maintenance and repair of BSA models that were manufactured through the early 1960's.

At some point in the 1930's, BSA adopted the practice of identifying their various model types by 'groups' and the models manufactured from 1945 through the mid 1960's were in Groups A, B, C, D and M. The service sheets that were associated to a particular group were identified numerically and, while there were some exceptions due to overlapping data between models, in general terms the numbers relate to a particular model group. They are as follows: The 200 series of service sheets were applicable to Group A models, the 300 series to Group B, the 400 series to Group C, the 500 series to Group D and the 600 series to Group M. In addition, there were a 700 series applicable to mechanical maintenance and an 800 series for electronic service and wiring diagrams. Both the 700 and 800 series of service sheets contained information that was not model specific but was applicable across multiple model groups. Finally, there were a 900 series for the BSA Dandy and a 1000 series for the BSA Sunbeam and Triumph Tigress scooter.

Unfortunately, as these service sheets were issued individually and at random times, the numbering sequence within any group is, at times, illogical and not necessarily consecutive. Consequently, assembling those individual sheets into a publication that serves as a model specific workshop manual is a somewhat difficult task and owners of BSA motor cycles are subjected to considerable confusion surrounding the appropriate selection from the multitude of reprints that have recently flooded the on-line marketplace. Many of the reprints found on internet websites are from 'bedroom sellers' at enticingly low prices by individuals that really have no idea what they are selling. Many are nothing more than poor quality comb-bound photocopies that are scanned and printed complete with greasy pages and thumbprints and, as such, are deceptively described as 'pre-owned', 'used' or even 'refurbished'! In addition, they are often advertised for the incorrect series and/or model years of motorcycles.

The most complete compilation of the 1945 and onwards service sheets was issued by BSA in the form of a 'dealer only' ring binder that contained all of the individual service sheets totaling to almost 500 pages, it is extremely scarce and difficult to find. It is this ring bound publication that was used to create this 'Service Sheet' manual'.

'B' GROUP SERVICE SHEET MANUAL 1945-1960

This manual contains 59 service sheets (190 pages) extracted from that 'dealer only' publication, which cover the 1945 to 1960 pre-unit, rigid, plunger and swing arm B31, B32, B33 and B34 plus Gold Star and Competition models. Please note that service sheets other than those in the 300 series that are included in this publication may also contain data that is applicable to 'other' model groups, as that was the original intention.

For additional information the reader is directed to **'The Book of the BSA 250cc, 350cc, 500cc & 600cc OHV & SV singles 1945 to 1959'** (ISBN 9781588502292) which covers the B31, B32, B33, B34, C10, C11, C11DL, M20, M21 & M33 models. For later models see **'The Book of the BSA OHV Singles 350cc & 500cc 1955-1967'** (ISBN 9781588501561) which covers the B31, B32, B33, B34 & Star B40 & SS90

GENERAL INDEX

PAGE	SHEET	SUBJECT	PAGE	SHEET	SUBJECT
3	212A	Brakes	78	702	Technical Data
5	212B	Brakes	80	703	Technical Data
7	212C	Brakes	82	704	Technical Data
9	212D	Brakes	84	705	General Maintenance
11	212E	Brakes	85	706	Front Forks
16	213	Rear Suspension	89	707	Gold Star 350 & 500
18	301	Engine	90	708	Carburetter
19	302	Gearbox	98	708B	Carburetter
20	302A	Gearbox	99	709	Fault Diagnosis
21	302B	Gearbox	100	710	Chain
23	302C	Gearbox	102	710X	Frames by model
24	303	Engine	119	711	Special Tools
28	304	Engine	127	711A	Special Tools
32	305	Engine	131	711B	Special Tools
36	306	Gearbox	138	712X	Flywheel
40	307	Gearbox	140	713	Steering
42	308	Clutch	141	714	Spokes
44	309	Hubs	145	802	MagDyno
46	310	Clutch	153	804	Regulator
48	311	Gearbox	157	804A	Control Box
51	312	Tech	161	805	Battery
52	313	Rear Suspension	165	806	Lights
54	314	Gearbox	168	807	Horn
56	315	Clutch	170	808	Wiring Diagrams
57	602A	Gearbox	172	808A	Wiring Diagrams
58	603	Lube	174	808F	Wiring Diagrams
66	604	Engine	176	808H	Wiring
70	608	Gearbox	177	809	Generator
74	612	Brakes	185	813	Alternator
76	701	Technical Data			

BSA SERVICE SHEET No. 212A

Reprinted December 1967

A, B AND M GROUP MODELS
(for A7 models before engine number ZA7-101—see Service Sheet 212)

ADJUSTMENT, DISMANTLING AND RE-ASSEMBLY OF FRONT HUB AND BRAKE (7 in. Brake)

Wheel Removal and Replacement

To remove the front wheel, first disconnect the brake cable, then slacken the pinch bolt (*A*) Fig. A31A. Insert a tommy bar in the hole in the head of the spindle at (*B*) and unscrew the spindle, noting that it has a left-hand thread and therefore unscrews in a clockwise direction. With the spindle withdrawn the bush (*C*) should be pulled out to its fullest extent. This will leave the wheel free to be pulled away from the right-hand fork leg and withdrawn from the machine.

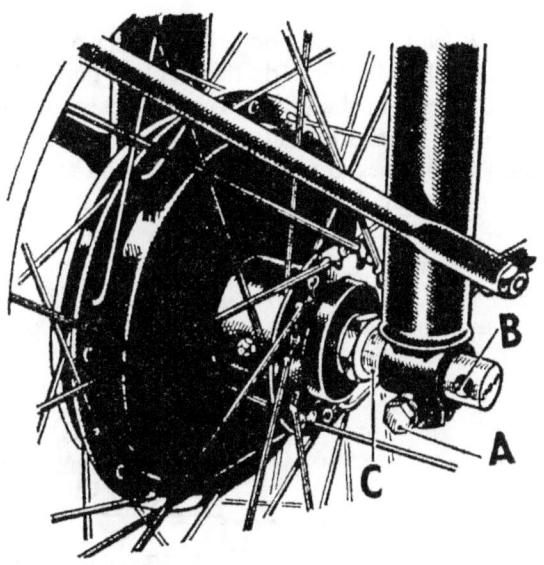

Fig. A31A. *Wheel removal.*

The wheel is replaced in the reverse order, noting that the brake plate stop must be located in its recess at the rear of the right-hand fork leg. It is most important that after the spindle has been tightened and before the pinch bolt is tightened, the forks are depressed once or twice to enable the left-hand fork end to position itself on the distance bush. If this precaution is not observed, the fork leg may be clipped out of position and will not function correctly.

Dismantling and Reassembly of the Hub

This is fitted with ball journal bearings and therefore no adjustment is necessary or provided for. The only attention required is periodical grease gun lubrication.

If it becomes necessary to replace the bearings unscrew the nut retaining the brake anchor plate and remove the plate together with the brake mechanism.

Unscrew the cap (*A*) Fig. A32A, noting that this has a left-hand thread and therefore unscrews in a clockwise direction. Using a hide mallet from the brake drum side, drive out the hollow spindle (*B*) which will carry with it the nearside ballrace (*C*), dust cap (*D*), and distance piece (*E*).

Only the offside ballrace (*F*) now remains in the hub and this should be driven out with the aid of a soft drift.

B.S.A. Service Sheet No. 212A (contd.)

During reassembly ensure that the ballrace (*F*) is fully home and that the retaining collar (*A*) is quite tight.

Brake Relining
To remove the brake shoes lay the drum cover plate flat on a bench and lever the shoes upwards. They can then be drawn over, and free of the cam and fulcrum pin. If the cam pads show excessive wear the brake shoes should be renewed.

When the brake shoes are removed the linings can be replaced as described in Service Sheet 612.

When new linings or new shoes have been fitted, the brakes must be centralised after refitting the wheel. To do this, replace the brake cover plate, complete with shoes, fulcrum pin and cam in the brake drum. Slacken the fulcrum pin nut, and turn the cam so as to open the brake shoes in the normal manner. The fulcrum pin will then move in its slot until both shoes are pressing equally on to the drum. Tighten the fulcrum pin nut firmly and release the brake.

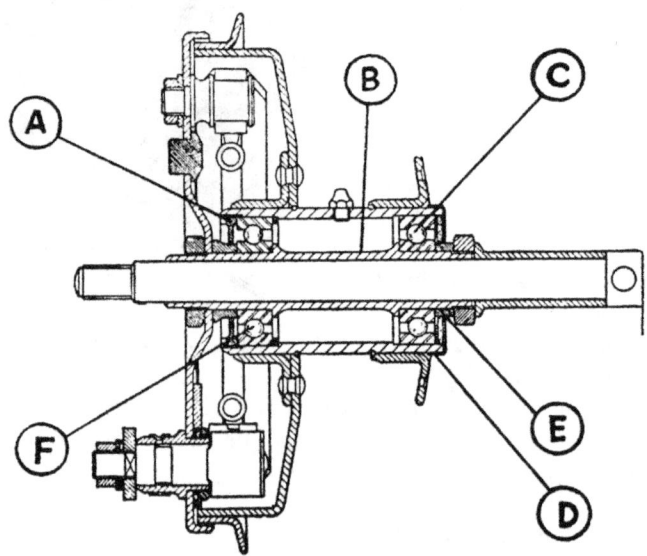

Fig. A32A. *Section of front hub (7 in. brake).*

B.S.A. MOTOR CYCLES LTD., Service Department, Armoury Road, Birmingham 11.
PRINTED IN ENGLAND—B.S.A. PRESS

BSA SERVICE SHEET No. 212B

"A", "B" AND "M" GROUP MODELS
ADJUSTMENT, DISMANTLING AND RE-ASSEMBLY OF FRONT HUB AND BRAKE (8 in. Brake)

Wheel Removal and Replacement

To detach the wheel, first disconnect the brake cable by pushing it out of the brake clip at (E) and unscrewing it from the bracket at (F). Remove the torque arm nut (C) and undo the pinch bolt (A). Insert a tommy bar in the hole in the head of the spindle at (B) and unscrew the spindle, noting that it has a left-hand thread and therefore unscrews in a clockwise direction. Support the wheel as the spindle is withdrawn, and when it is clear the wheel can be pulled away from the right-hand fork leg and removed from the machine.

After removal do not let the wheel fall on to the bush which projects from the brake drum side of the hub. Although the bush is pressed in, it may, if subjected to a sharp blow, be forced back into the hub. If this should happen the bush can be retrieved and re-positioned with the aid of the wheel spindle.

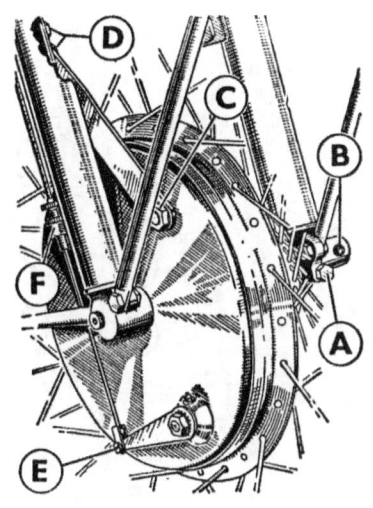

Fig. A31b. *Wheel Removal.*

The wheel is replaced in the reverse order to that for removal. It is most important that after the spindle has been tightened and before the pinch bolt is tightened, the forks are depressed once or twice to enable the left-hand fork end to position itself on the spindle shank. If this precaution is not observed, the fork leg may be clipped out of position and will not function correctly.

Dismantling and Reassembly of the Hub

Withdraw the brake plate which is a push-fit on the bush (B) Fig. A32b. Remove the locking split pins and unscrew the bearing retaining collars (C) and (D), which have normal right-hand threads. Replace the spindle and drive out the brake side ballrace (E) together with the bush (B) by striking the end of the spindle with a hide mallet. Only the ballrace (F) now remains in the hub and can be removed with a suitable soft drift.

Before replacing the bearing retaining collars ensure that the rubber oil seals in them are in good condition. The collars should be done up quite tight and if necessary fresh holes should be made for the locking split pins.

B.S.A. Service Sheet No. 212B (contd.)

Brake Relining

To remove the brake shoes lay the drum cover plate flat on a bench and lever the shoes upwards. They can then be drawn over, and free of the cam and fulcrum pin. If the cam pads show excessive wear the brake shoes should be renewed.

When the brake shoes are removed the linings can be replaced as described in Service Sheet No. 612.

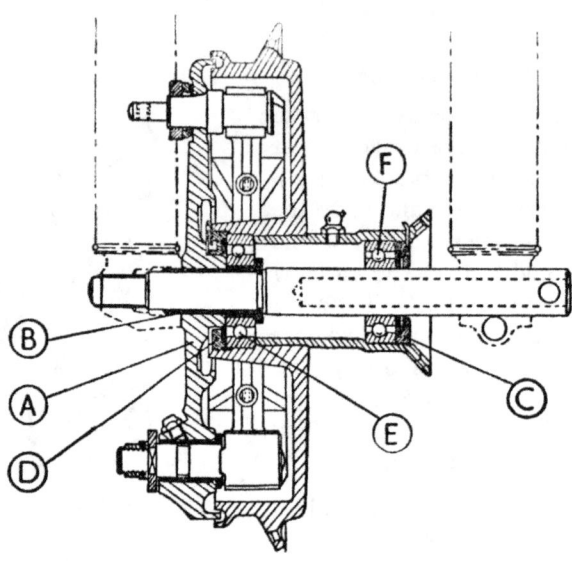

Fig. A32b. *Section of Front Hub (8 in. brake).*

B.S.A. MOTOR CYCLES LTD., Service Department, Armoury Road, Birmingham 11.
Printed in England
B.S.A. Press.

BSA SERVICE SHEET No. 212C

Reprinted December 1967

'A', 'B' AND 'M' GROUP MODELS
(with plunger-type rear suspension)

ADJUSTMENT, DISMANTLING AND RE-ASSEMBLY OF REAR HUB AND BRAKE

Rear Wheel Removal and Replacement

Remove the smaller outer nut (*C*) Fig. A31c, on the left-hand side of the rear wheel spindle, and withdraw the spindle (*A*) from the right-hand side of the machine.

The distance bush (*B*) will normally fall clear when the spindle is removed. The wheel should then be pulled towards the right-hand side of the machine until it is free from the spline engaging it with the brake drum. When the hub is free from the drum the wheel can be dropped out. To replace

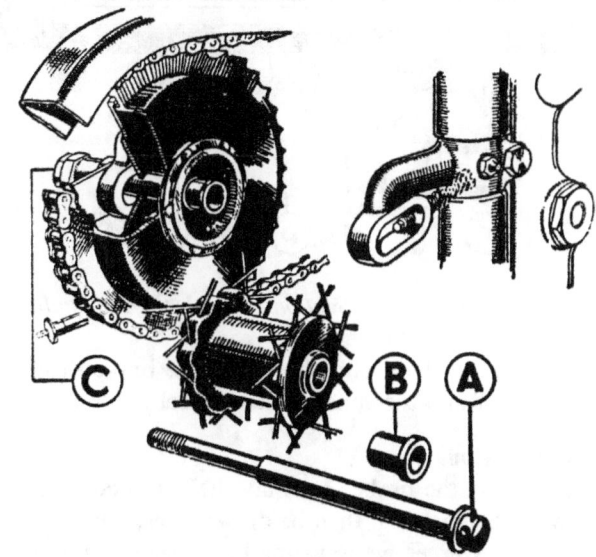

Fig. A31c. *Rear wheel removal (spring frame).*

the wheel the operations are carried out in the reverse order. When detaching the rear wheel, it is quite unnecessary to touch the larger of the two hexagonal nuts on the left-hand side of the spindle.

Dismantling and Reassembly of the Rear Hub

The hub is fitted with two ballraces which are a light press-fit in the hub shell. Remove the dust cap (*A*) Fig. A32c. Unscrew and remove the two screwed rings (*C*) and (*M*). These rings are left-hand threaded, and therefore unscrew clockwise. Remove distance piece (*F*).

Place the wheel spindle through the hub from the offside. Using a hide mallet tap the head of the spindle so as to drive the offside ballrace toward the centre of the hub shell. By this means the brake drum side race will be driven out, after which the distance pieces (*D*) and (*H*) can be removed.

The only part now remaining in the shell will be the offside ballrace which can be driven out with a soft drift.

Removal and Dismantling of the Brake Drum

After removal of the rear wheel the brake drum is held in position in the wheel by nut (*J*) see Fig. A32c. To remove the drum disconnect the chain and rear brake rod, remove nut (*J*) and withdraw the drum.

With the brake drum removed from the frame, the brake drum cover plate, to which are attached the brake shoes, can be withdrawn, together with their fulcrum pin and operating arm.

B.S.A. Service Sheet No. 212C (contd.)

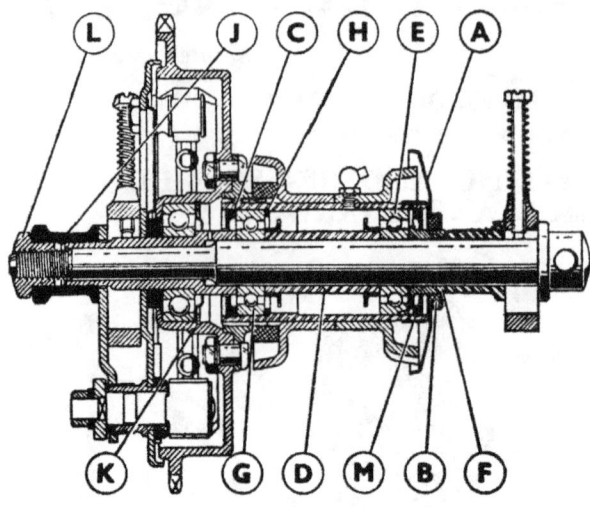

Fig. A32C. *Section through the rear hub.*

The brake drum ballrace is held in position in its housing by means of a spring circlip (*K*), which can be removed with the aid of a screwdriver. The replacement ballrace should be well greased before fitting the washer in place to prevent grease entering he brake drum.

If examination of the brake drum shows that the teeth have become worn and the braking surface scored, a new drum must be fitted. The drum must not be machined to produce a new braking surface. To do so is only a temporary cure and further attention would be required later. The spline bolted to the brake drum should be replaced if there is any play between it and the spline on the wheel hub.

Brake Relining

To remove the brake shoes lay the drum cover plate flat on a bench, and lever the shoes upwards. They can then be drawn over, and free of the cam and fulcrum pin. If the cam pads show excessive wear the brake shoes should be renewed. When the brake shoes are removed the linings can be replaced as described in Service Sheet No. 612.

Rear Chain Adjustment

Put the machine on its stand. The rear wheel must be at its lowest point in the suspension unit when the adjustment is made. Undo nut (*A*) Fig. A33C, several turns and slacken nut (*B*) just sufficient to allow the wheel to move.

Screw in the adjusters (*D*) to tighten the chain. There should be a total up and down movement of half an inch at the centre of the chain span. See that the wheel spindle is up against the adjusters and that the wheels are in line. Check the alignment by means of a taut piece of string, which should be equidistant from the front and rear of each wheel.

Tighten the large hexagon nut (*B*) very firmly, followed by the smaller nut (*A*). Re-adjust the rear brake.

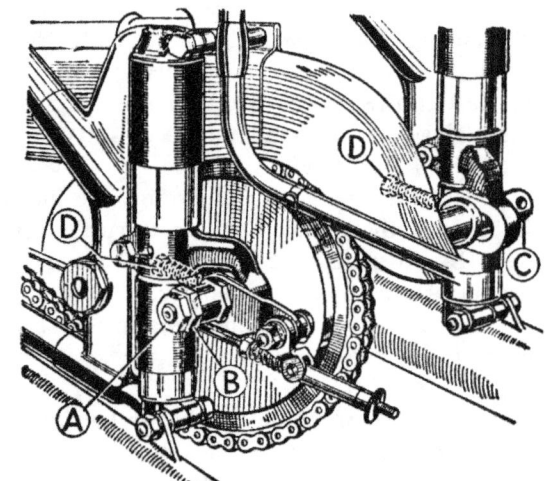

Fig. A33C. *Rear chain adjustment.*

B.S.A. MOTOR CYCLES LTD., Service Department, Armoury Road, Birmingham 11.
PRINTED IN ENGLAND — B.S.A. PRESS

BSA SERVICE SHEET No. 212D

"A" AND "B" GROUP MODELS
(with Welded Type Frame)
ADJUSTMENT, DISMANTLING AND RE-ASSEMBLY OF REAR HUB AND BRAKE

Wheel Removal

Removal of the wheel does not affect the chain or brake adjustment. Remove the spindle (B) Fig. A31d, it has a normal right-hand thread and therefore unscrews in an anticlockwise direction. The distance bush (E) falls clear when the spindle is removed and the wheel can then be pulled away from the brake drum and withdrawn from the machine.

When detaching the rear wheel it is quite unnecessary to touch the hexagon nut (A) on the left-hand side.

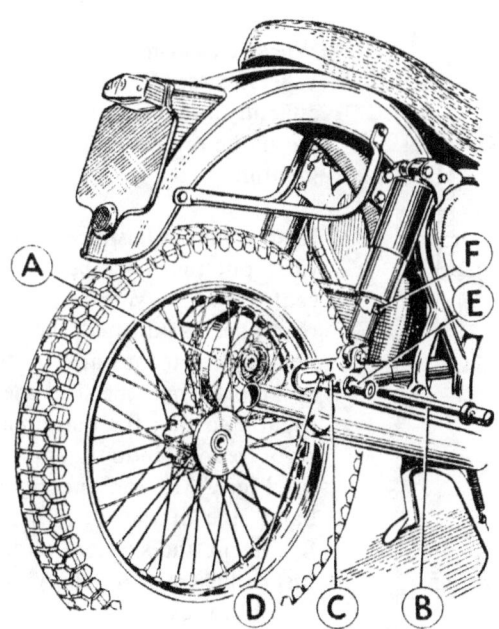

Fig. A31d. *Rear wheel removal.*

Hub Dismantling and Reassembly

The hub is fitted with two ballraces which are a light press-fit on the hollow spindle and in the hub shell. Remove the dust cap (A) Fig. A32d, and felt washer (B). Unscrew the ballrace retaining ring (C). This ring has a left-hand thread and therefore unscrews in a clockwise direction.

With the aid of a suitable soft drift applied to the brake drum end of the hollow spindle (D), drive out the spindle and ballrace (E). Then tap the spindle from the bearing, as the spindle comes away the distance bush (F) will be released. The only parts remaining in the hub are the ballrace (G) and the spacing washer (H), and these need not be disturbed unless the ballrace is suspected of being faulty. Wash it thoroughly in paraffin to remove all trace of grease when any play will be immediately detected. If it is decided to replace the race it can be driven from the hub shell with the aid of a soft drift. During reassembly ensure that this bearing is fully home and that the locking ring (C) is quite tight.

Removal and Dismantling of the Brake Drum

After removal of the rear wheel the brake drum is held in position by the nut (J) and by the nut securing the brake anchor strap. To remove the drum, first disconnect the rear chain and brake rod, then remove the nut (J) and the nut retaining the torque arm to the brake plate. The brake drum can then be pulled away from the brake plate and removed

B.S.A. Service Sheet No. 212D (contd.)

from the machine. Pivot the brake plate support strap on the cam lever boss so that the brake plate is free to be withdrawn from the fork leg.

To remove the brake shoes lay the brake plate on a bench (shoes uppermost) and lever the shoes upwards. They can then be drawn over and free of the cam and fulcrum pin. The operating cam and fulcrum pin should be inspected but it is unlikely that more than greasing will be necessary. If the cam pads on the brake shoes show excessive wear then new shoes should be fitted. To replace the shoes, attach the springs and push the shoes over the cam and pivot by reversing the dismantling procedure.

If examination of the brake drum shows that the teeth have become worn and the braking surface scored, a new drum must be fitted. The drum must not be machined to produce a new braking surface. To do so is only a temporary cure and further attention would be required later.

The brake drum ballrace, which is totally enclosed in the drum, should not normally require attention. The ballrace is held in position in its housing by a dished washer and a spring circlip (K), which can be removed with the aid of a screwdriver. The replacement ballrace should be well greased before fitting the dished washer which prevents the entry of grease into the brake drum.

Brake Shoe Relining

After removal of the brake shoes (see "Dismantling of Brake Drum") the old lining can be removed as described in Service Sheet No. 612.

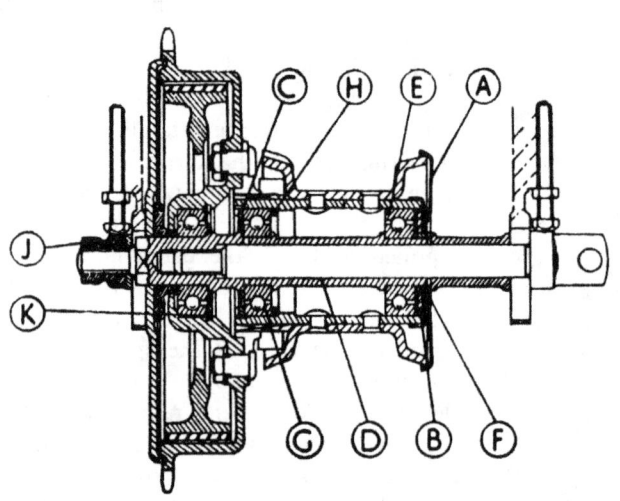

Fig. A32d. *Section through the rear hub.*

Wheel Reassembly

Wheel reassembly involves no difficulty and should be carried out in the reverse order to dismantling.

Rear Chain Adjustment

First put the machine on its centre stand. Whenever the rear wheel is adjusted, the nut securing the torque arm to the brake plate must be slackened slightly so that the plate may pivot freely. Undo the spindle (B) Fig. A31d, on the right-hand side of the machine, a few turns, and slacken nut (A) just sufficiently to allow the wheel to move.

Slacken the locknuts (C) and screw out the adjusters (D) to tighten the chain. With the wheel in its lowest position there should be a total up and down movement of $1\frac{1}{4}$ in. in the centre of the chain at its tightest point. Ensure that the wheel spindle is against the adjusters and that the wheels are in line. Check the alignment by means of a taut piece of string which should be equidistant from the front and rear of each wheel.

Tighten the nut (A), the spindle (B) and the nut securing the torque arm to the brake plate. Re-check the chain adjustment and the wheel alignment.

B.S.A. MOTOR CYCLES LTD., Service Department, Armoury Road, Birmingham 11.

BSA SERVICE SHEET No. 212E

"A" and "B" Group Models
(with Full Width Hubs)

ADJUSTMENT, DISMANTLING AND RE-ASSEMBLY OF HUBS AND BRAKES

FRONT WHEEL REMOVAL AND REPLACEMENT

To remove the wheel, place the machine on both front and centre stands, take out the two bolts securing the brake anchor strap to the fork leg, and unscrew the large nut from the right-hand side of the wheel spindle. Disconnect the brake cable completely from the brake plate. If sufficient slack cannot be obtained by screwing down the cable adjuster, the outer casing may be released from its holder at the handlebar end.

Next, slacken the pinch bolt in the left-hand fork leg and draw out the spindle by inserting a tommy bar in the hole provided, and using a pulling and twisting motion. At the same time support the weight of the wheel to avoid damaging the bush which projects through the brake plate and partly enters the right-hand fork leg. Should this bush be pushed inadvertently back inside the hub, it can be re-positioned by inserting the wheel spindle from the left-hand side.

There is no distance piece fitted outside the hub, location being maintained by means of a shoulder formed on the spindle meeting the bush already referred to. Once the spindle has been removed, the wheel can be pulled away from the right-hand fork leg and withdrawn.

Refitting is carried out by reversing the procedure for removal, except that tightening the pinch bolt must be left until the machine has been taken off the stands. The forks should then be fully depressed and released several times to ensure that the left-hand leg takes up the correct position on the wheel spindle. The inner edge of the tommy bar hole should be approximately level with the outer face of the fork leg. Finally, tighten the pinch bolt and check the tightness of all other bolts and nuts which have been disturbed.

FRONT WHEEL REMOVAL AND REPLACEMENT (models with Frame prefix letters FA or FB)

To remove the wheel, place the machine on the stand, disconnect the brake cable by removing the split pin and clevis pin on the brake arm. Unscrew the four bolts holding the fork end caps when the wheel will then drop to the ground. Note that there is a register at each end of the spindle to clear the bolts, these also serve to locate the wheel in the forks.

REFITTING

This is simply the reverse of the above procedure but care must be taken to locate the lug on the right-hand leg in the groove on the brake cover plate.

Do not omit the split pin when re-connecting the brake cable.

B.S.A. Service Sheet No. 212E (contd.)

REAR WHEEL REMOVAL AND REPLACEMENT

Place the machine on the centre stand, and remove the right-hand silencer. Unscrew the four nuts securing the sprocket to the hub. Where the rear chain is totally enclosed, access to these nuts is gained by removing the rearmost of the two rubber plugs in the chaincase. Disconnect the brake cable completely from the brake plate. It may be necessary to disengage the ferrule of the outer casing from the frame lug, in order to obtain enough slack in the inner cable. Take off the brake anchor strap by removing the nut holding it to the brake plate, and loosening the bolt fixing the forward end to the swinging arm fork.

Next, unscrew and take out the wheel spindle from the right-hand side, and extract the distance piece. The large nut on the left-hand fork end should not be disturbed as this holds the fixed spindle of the sprocket which remains in position. The wheel can now be pulled away from the sprocket. By standing on the left-hand side of the machine and tilting it in that direction, the wheel can be taken out. If the rear part of the wheel is brought clear of the mudguard first, this is a simple operation.

The wheel is replaced by reversing the order of the instructions given for removal. Make sure that the four sprocket retaining nuts are fully and evenly tightened, and that the washer beneath the head of the wheel spindle has not been omitted.

REAR CHAIN ADJUSTMENT

The chain must be adjusted while the machine is on the centre stand, with the swinging arm fork at the lower limit of its travel. When a chaincase is fitted, access to the chain is gained by removing the foremost of the two rubber plugs. Rotate the wheel several times to find the position in which the chain is tightest. The total up and down movement in the centre of the top run should be 1¼ in. If the setting varies appreciably from this, the chain should be re-adjusted as follows:—

Slacken the wheel spindle and the fixed spindle nut. Release the two locknuts and screw the adjusting screws in or out as required. Take care that both are turned an equal amount to avoid putting the wheel out of line.

When the tension is correct, secure the locknuts, press the wheel forward in the fork ends and tighten, first the fixed spindle nut and finally the wheel spindle.

B.S.A. Service Sheet No. 212E (contd.)

WHEEL ALIGNMENT

It is advisable to check the aligneent of the wheels periodically, particularly after the chain, has been adjusted. A long straight-edge is placed alongside and close to, the two wheels and supported as high up from the ground as possible. The distances from the straight-edge to the rims, measured at the front and rear of each wheel, should all be equal.

Tyres are unreliable guides in checking wheel alignment, since tyres of different section will give the appearance of error when, in fact, everything is in order.

BRAKE ADJUSTMENT

A fulcrum type adjuster is provided on each brake (except those models with engine prefix letters FA or FB, where adjustment is carried out by screwing in or out, as required, the finger adjusters on the brake cables), in addition to the usual cable adjuster. The adjusting pin should be turned in a clockwise direction until it will turn no further, then slackened off until the wheel rotates freely. The adjusters have a click action, each click representing one-twelfth of a turn.

The brake shoes must not be allowed to bind even slightly, as this may generate sufficient heat to distort the drum, or cause the grease to melt and impregnate the linings.

BRAKE SHOE RECONDITIONING

After the brake plate has been taken from the hub, the adjusting pin should be slackened right off, and the plate laid flat with the shoes uppermost. They can then be levered up at right angles to the plate, pivoting on their ends, until the tension of the springs has been relieved.

Should new linings be required, full instructions for fitting are contained in Service Sheet No. 612

SPROCKET ASSEMBLY—REMOVING AND DISMANTLING

Before the sprocket assembly can be removed, the chaincase must first be taken off. The rear section is held by two hexagon-headed set screws, while the top and bottom sections are secured by two bolts in each, passing through lugs on the swinging arm fork. The large nut on the fixed spindle must also be loosened.

If a chainguard instead of a chaincase is fitted, the four bolts holding it to the swinging arm fork can be taken out to allow the guard to be raised sufficiently to clear the sprocket.

After parting the chain at the spring link, the large nut on the end of the fixed spindle is screwed off. The sprocket can then be dismounted and the spindle tapped out. The bearing and the grease retainer are pressed in, and may be driven out with a suitable drift.

When reassembling note that there should be a large washer between the sprocket and the fork end, and also a smaller washer between the fork end and the fixed spindle nut.

B.S.A. Service Sheet No. 212E (contd.)

HUB DISMANTLING AND REASSEMBLY

The front hub contains two ball journal bearings which require no adjustment. They are secured by locking rings on the outside, and are located by circlips in the hub shell on the inside. Both locking rings have a right-hand thread, the one on the brake drum side being split-pinned to the hub for additional security. A special peg spanner (part number 61–3542), is used to unscrew the locking rings, which incorporate felt grease seals. Early models had separate seals and steel retainers, the concave sides of which should face the bearings. The bearings themselves are pressed into the hub shell, and can be tapped out with a soft metal drift, taking care not to damage the circlips.

When reassembling, make sure that the circlips are properly seated in their grooves before refitting the bearings. Do not omit the bush from the right-hand bearing, as this has a shoulder on the inner end and cannot be replaced from outside the hub. Note that the locking rings have different sized centre holes, the larger being for the right-hand side.

The rear hub carries only one bearing, on the right-hand side, which is held by a locking ring and split pin in exactly the same way as already described for the front hub. It is removed and replaced in a similar manner.

On the left-hand side is a pressed in grease retainer. There is also a loose distance piece inside the hub.

If the bearing locking rings have been renewed it will be necessary to drill fresh split pin holes.

The other rear wheel bearing is housed in the sprocket itself. All four bearings are identical, the part number being 89–3022. No grease nipples are provided on these hubs; the bearings are packed with grease during assembly and they should be re-packed at intervals of 10,000 to 15,000 miles.

The brake cam spindle housings have grease nipples, but these should be used sparingly to avoid forcing grease into the brakes.

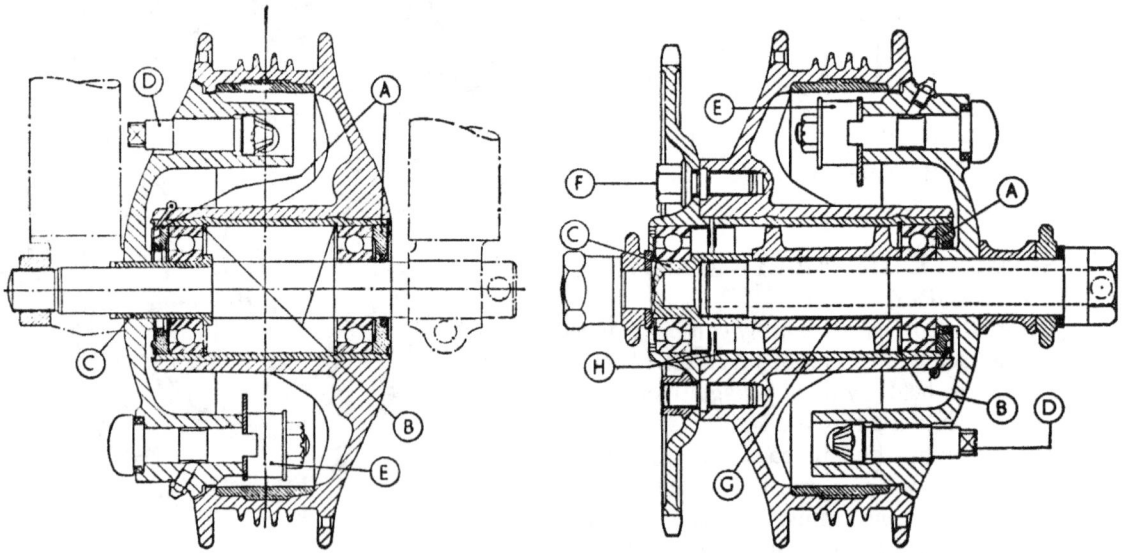

B.S.A. Service Sheet No. 212E (contd.)

HUB DISMANTLING AND REASSEMBLY (models with engine prefix letter FA or FB)

The front hub has two bearings part number 42-5819, the right-hand side can be driven out from the left-hand side using the spindle as a drift, after the brake cover plate and bearing lock-ring have been removed.

To remove the left-hand side bearing, take out the circlip and dust cover and drive out the bearing from the right-hand side using the spindle reversed.

When replacing the bearings do not omit the ring behind the bearing on the right-hand side.

REAR HUB

The rear hub is similar to the earlier type except that there is only one grease retainer on the sprocket side (bearing number 89-3022) and the right-hand bearing is part number 42-5819, no split pin being used to secure the lock-ring.

There is a smaller grease retainer midway along the centre distance tube.

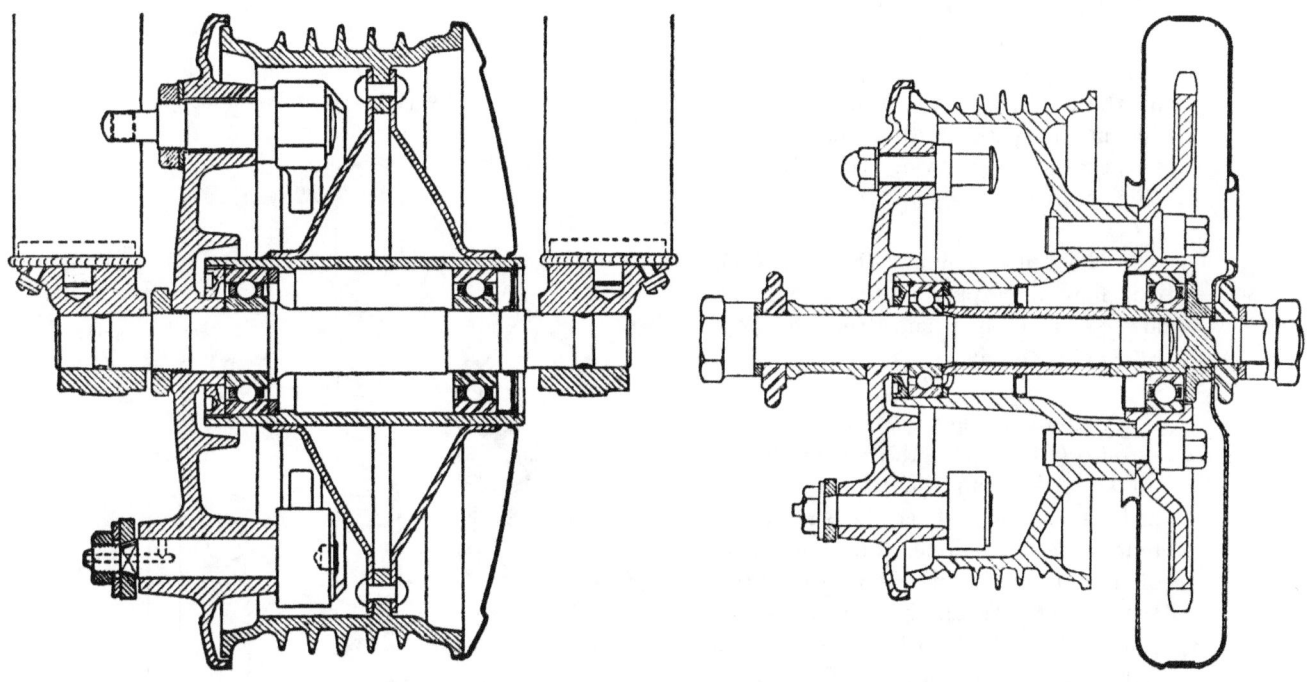

B.S.A. MOTOR CYCLES LTD., Service Department, Armoury Road, Birmingham 11.

B.S.A. PRESS

BSA SERVICE SHEET No. 213

"A," "B" and "M" Group Models

March 1950.
Reprinted Sept. 1961.

THE SPRING FRAME

The B.S.A. rear suspension is entirely automatic, and no adjustment is required or provided for. The only maintenance necessary is lubrication by grease gun every thousand miles.

TO DISMANTLE.

First remove the rear wheel (see Service Sheet No. 212A), detach the silencers by removing the nuts (A), Fig. A35, and slacken the clip bolts to the exhaust pipes. Take off the nuts (B), spring washers (C) and remove the pinch bolts (D). Remove plug (E) and in the space vacated, screw in the formed end of Service Tool 61-3222 (Fig. A36).

The centre column (F) Fig. A35, can now be tapped out through the lower frame lug and Service Tool 61-3222 withdrawn.

Grip the top and bottom suspension shrouds (G) and press the bottom shroud up and out from the frame lugs. A kick is experienced as the suspension unit leaves the frame, and a firm grip on the shrouds is necessary to control the springs. When the bottom of the column is clear the whole unit can be removed from the frame, and placed on the bench for complete dismantling. The inner and outer shrouds, springs (J), washers (K), if fitted, and locating pieces (L) may be withdrawn, carefully noting their respective positions for subsequent reassembly.

The wheel spindle brackets (M) together with the bearing sleeves (N), to which they are attached, form the spring plunger, and can be separated from the sleeves when the pinch bolts (O) are withdrawn. Note that each

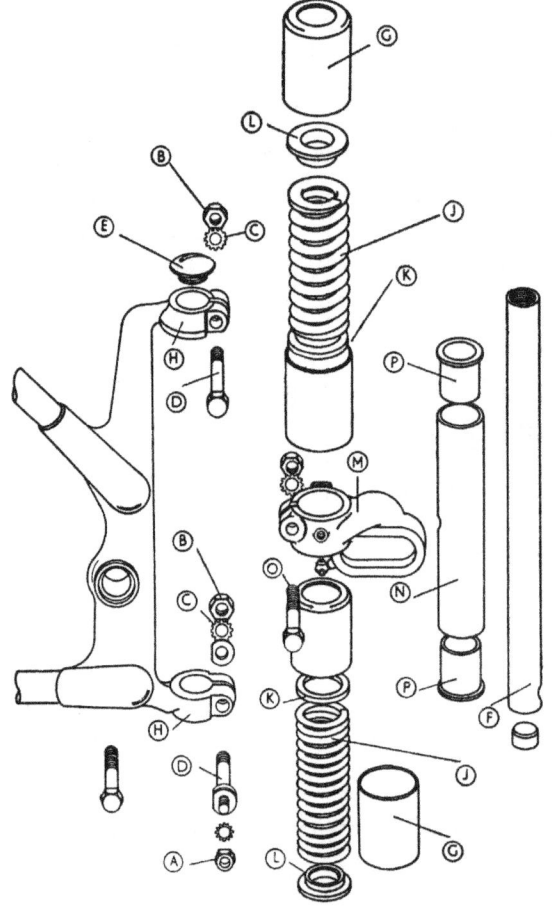

FIG A35   THE SUSPENSION COLUMN (EXPLODED VIEW)

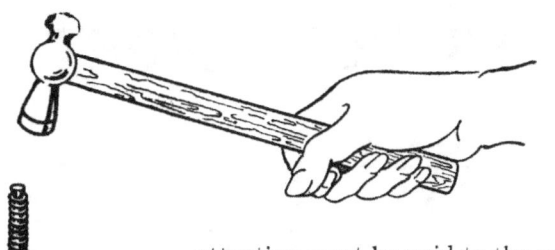

pinch bolt engages in a notch in the bearing sleeve, and also that the bottom bolts (D) similarly engage in notches in the centre column. Particular attention must be paid to the correct alignment of these notches on reassembly.

REASSEMBLY.

Reassemble all units of the suspension column, except the centre column (F) in the same order in which they were dismantled. Pass Service Tool 61-3222 through the assembly and position the top and bottom slotted plates (Fig. A37). Pass the distance piece down the shaft of the tool on to the top plate, and screw up the nut, at the same time supporting the two plates so that they do not come out of position. The nut must be screwed down until the column with the tool in position can be passed up through the top lug of the frame and the bottom of the tool dropped vertically into the bottom lug.

Now unscrew the nut until the top and bottom slotted plates are in contact with the frame lugs. Pass a tommy bar through the holes in the plates and withdraw them. As the plates come away the column will spring into position.

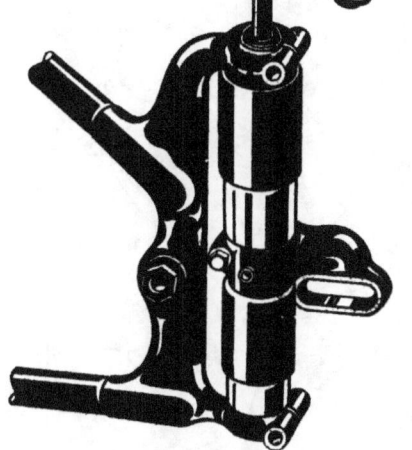

Fig. A36. Removing the centre column with Service Tool 61-3222.

Withdraw Service Tool 61-3222 from the top to ensure alignment of the suspension unit with the frame lugs.

Replace the centre column in the reverse order to that for dismantling. Refit and tighten the pinch bolts.

Replace the cap (C) and the silencers.

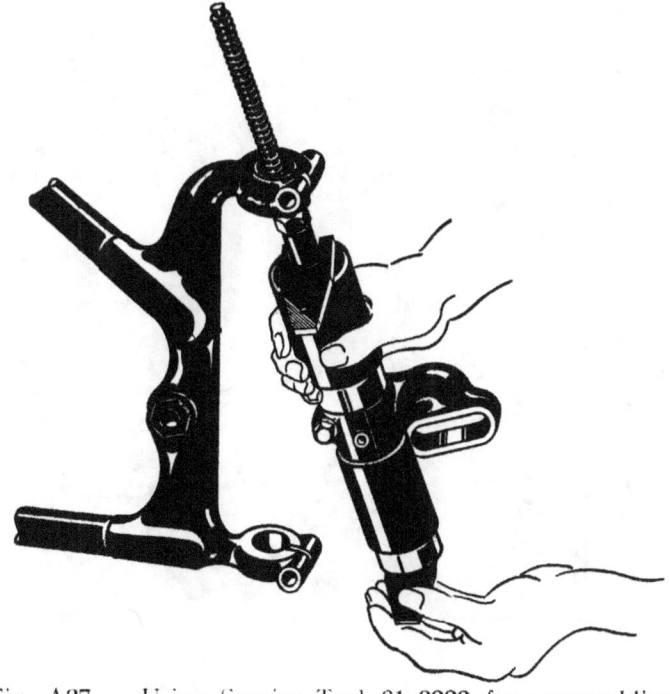

Fig. A37. Using Service Tool 61-3222 for reassembling.

B.S.A. MOTOR CYCLES LTD., Service Dept., Waverley Works, Birmingham, 10.

BSA SERVICE SHEET No. 301

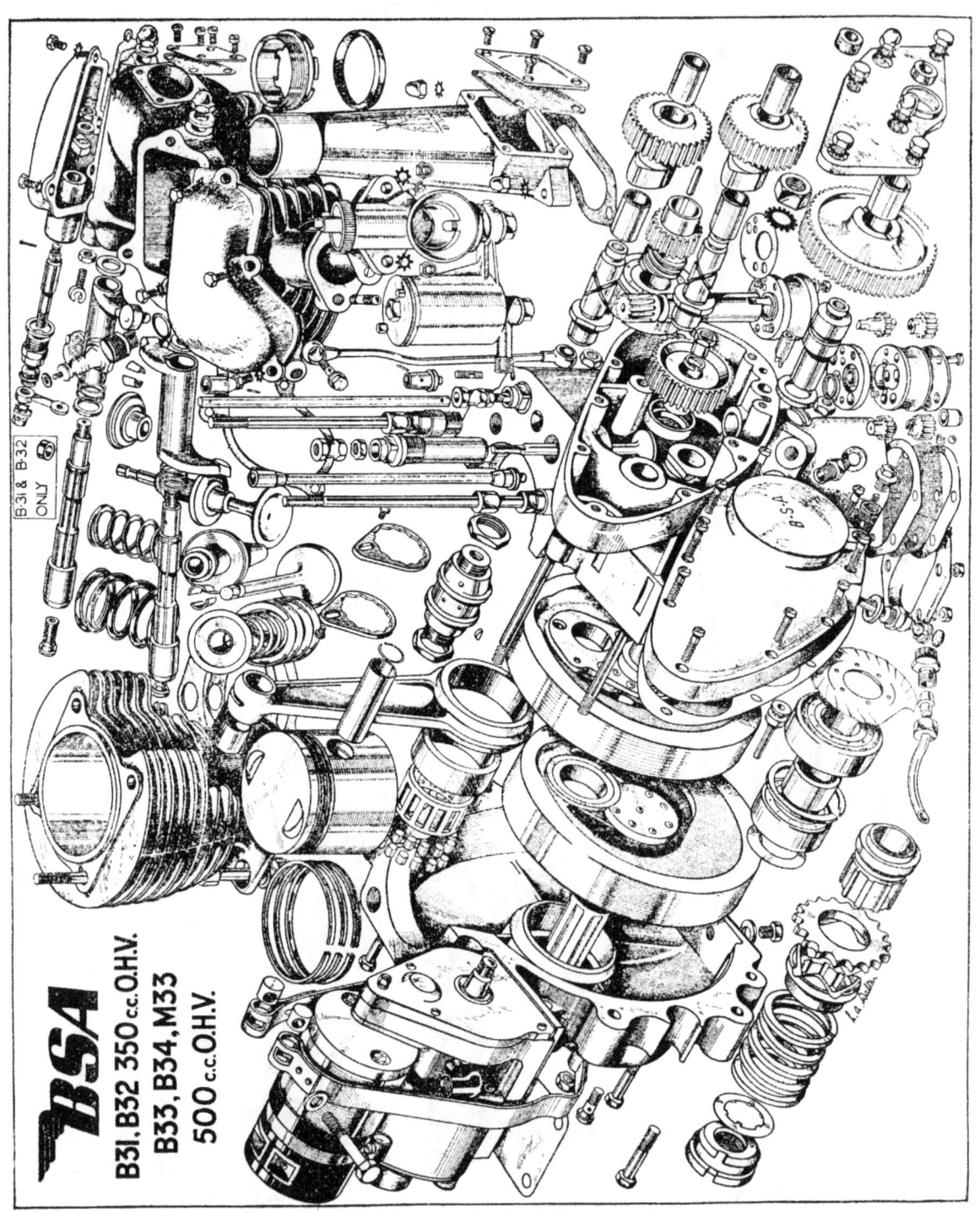

Fig. B1. The "B" Group Engine (Except "G.B." Series) (Exploded View)

B.S.A. MOTOR CYCLES LIMITED, Service Dept., Armoury Road, Birmingham, 11.
(PRINTED IN ENGLAND)

BSA SERVICE SHEET No. 302

Reprinted Oct., 1961.

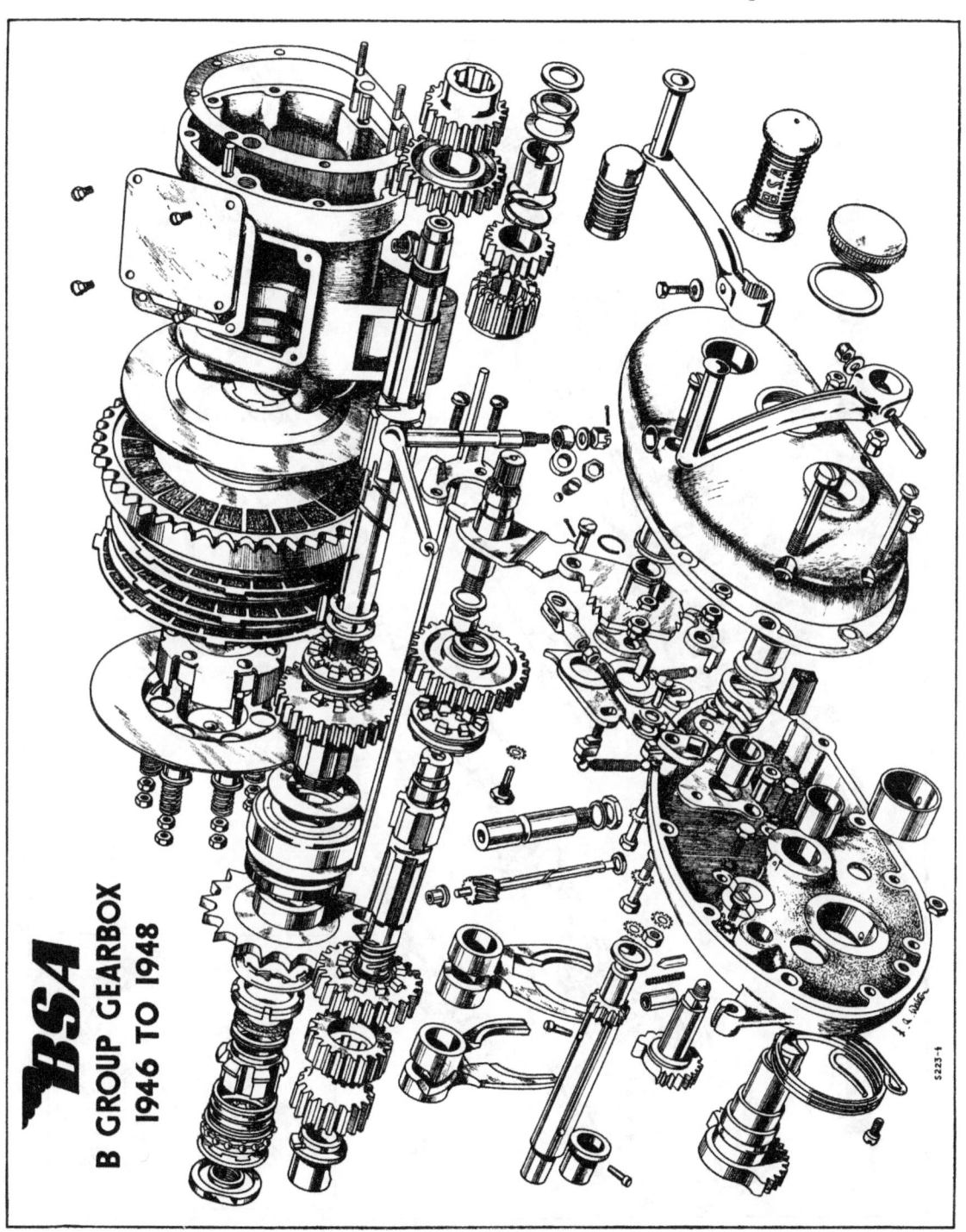

B GROUP GEARBOX 1946 TO 1948

B.S.A. MOTOR CYCLES LIMITED, Service Dept., Waverley Works, Birmingham, 10. (PRINTED IN ENGLAND)

BSA SERVICE SHEET No. 302A

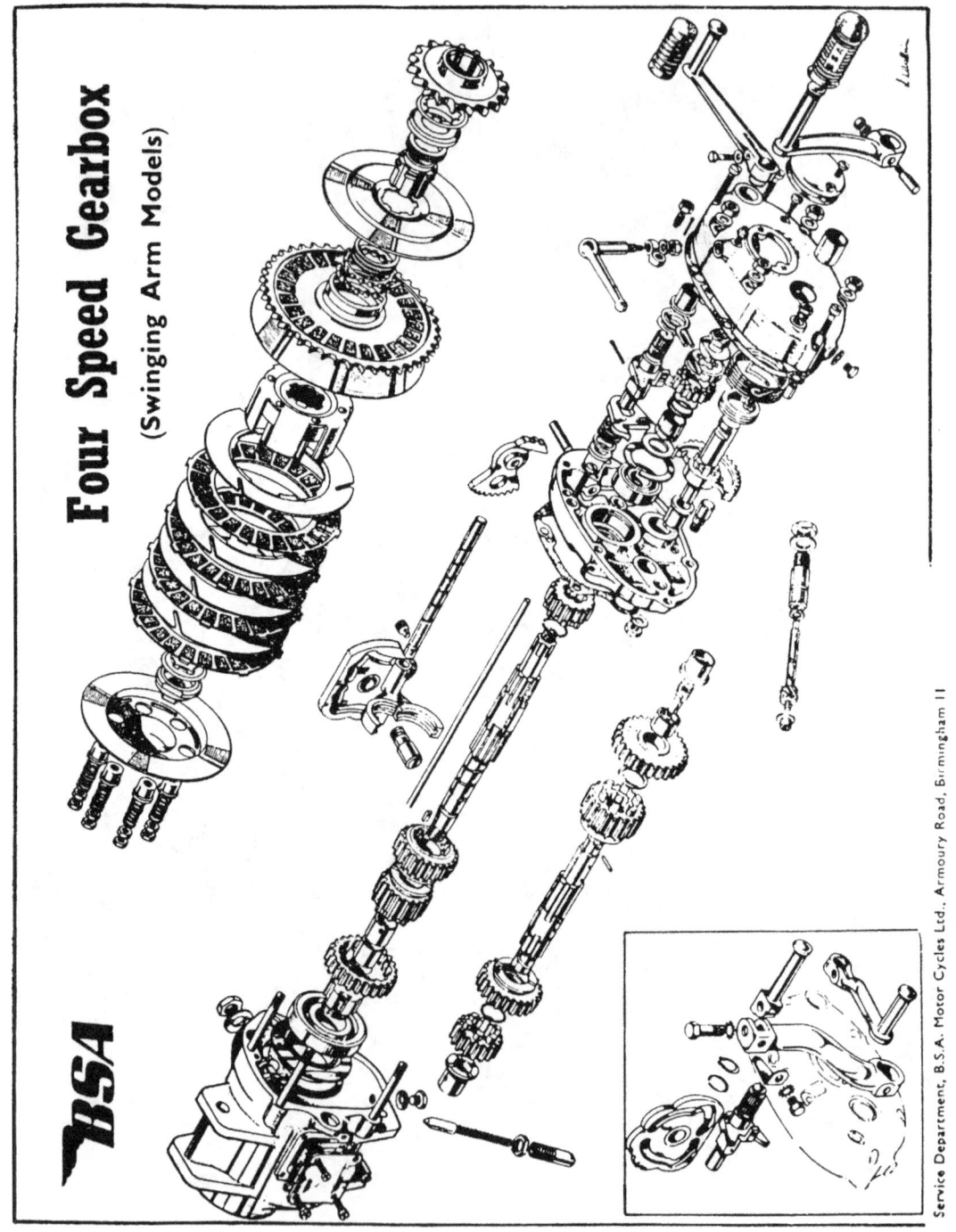

Four Speed Gearbox (Swinging Arm Models)

BSA SERVICE SHEET No. 302B

INTERNAL GEARBOX RATIOS FOR SWINGING ARM FRAME MODELS

The following gearbox ratios are available for models fitted with swinging arm type frame

Description	Marking	Top	Third	Second	Bottom
Extra Close Ratio	R.R.(T2)	1	1.099	1.326	1.754
Extra Close Ratio	R.R. or R.R.(T)	1	1.099	1.326	1.929
Close Ratio	DAY or DAY(T)	1	1.101	1.460	2.124
Scrambles	SC. or SC.(T)	1	1.325	1.754	2.343
Standard	STD. or STD.(T)	1	1.210	1.758	2.580
Wide Ratio (Trials)	TRI. or TRI.(T)	1	1.459	2.339	3.167
Standard	STB or ST. BT.	1	1.325	1.754	2.877

Marking suffix (T) denotes needle roller layshaft bearings. Suffix (T32) denotes needle roller mainshaft and layshaft bearings.

The part numbers and number of teeth for the relative pinions are listed overleaf.

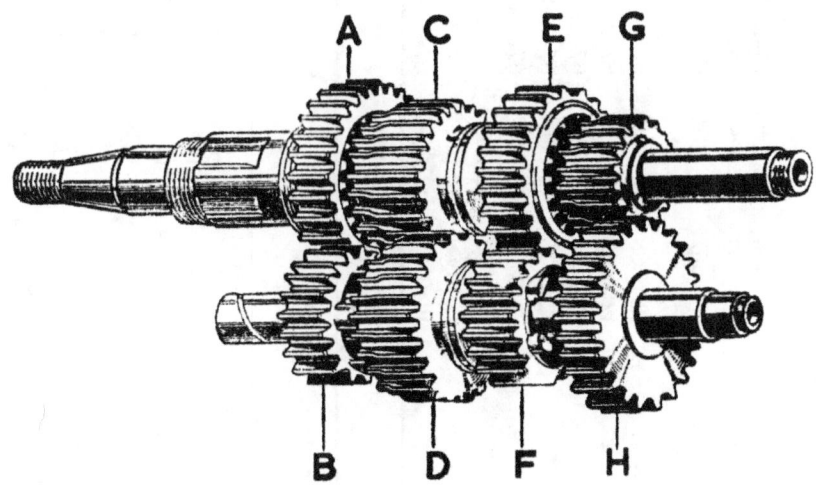

B.S.A. Service Sheet No. 302B (contd.)

PART NUMBERS

Ratios	A	B	C	D	E	F	G	H	M/shaft	Layshaft
R.R.	67-3184	42-3022	67-3361	42-3026	67-3187	67-3198	67-3221	67-3216	67-3330	42-3019
R.R.(T)	67-3184	42-3086	67-3361	42-3026	67-3187	67-3198	67-3221	42-3087	67-3330	42-3094
R.R.(T2)	42-3133	42-3086	67-3361	42-3026	42-3136	67-3198	42-3137	42-3138	42-3131	42-3094
DAY	67-3207	42-3020	67-3361	42-3026	67-3223	67-3226	67-3221	67-3216	67-3330	42-3019
DAY(T)	67-3207	42-3081	67-3361	42-3026	67-3223	67-3226	67-3221	42-3087	67-3330	42-3094
SC.	42-3088	42-3022	67-3302	42-3024	67-3305	67-3212	67-3191	42-3097	67-3315	42-3019
SC.(T)	42-3088	42-3086	67-3302	42-3024	67-3305	67-3212	67-3191	42-3210	67-3315	42-3094
STD.	67-3192	42-3020	67-3201	42-3023	67-3202	67-3198	67-3191	42-3097	67-3330	42-3019
STD.(T)	42-3076	42-3081	67-3201	42-3023	67-3202	67-3198	67-3191	42-3210	67-3330	42-3094
TRI.	67-3309	42-3020	67-3301	42-3025	67-3210	67-3212	67-3313	67-3213	67-3313	42-3019
TRI.(T)	42-3091	42-3081	67-3301	42-3025	67-3210	67-3212	67-3313	42-3093	67-3313	42-3094
ST.B	42-3088	42-3022	67-3302	42-3024	67-3210	67-3212	67-3313	67-3213	67-3313	42-3019
ST. BT.	42-3088	42-3086	67-3302	42-3024	67-3210	67-3212	67-3313	42-3093	67-3313	42-3094

NUMBER OF TEETH

Ratios	A	B	C	D	E	F	G	H	Speedo. Gears Driving	Driven
R.R. & R.R.(T)	25	18	22	21	24	19	18	25	42-3033	42-3032
R.R.(T2)	25	18	22	21	24	19	19	24	42-3033	42-3032
DAY & DAY(T)	26	17	22	21	25	18	18	25	67-3088	67-3175
SC. & SC.(T)	25	18	19	24	22	21	16	27	67-3088	67-3175
STD. & STD.(T)	26	17	20	23	24	19	16	27	67-3088	67-3175
TRI. & TRI.(T)	26	17	17	26	22	21	14	29	67-3088	67-3175
ST. B	25	18	19	24	22	21	14	29	42-3033	42-3032
ST. BT.	25	18	19	24	22	21	14	29	42-3303	42-3032

The forward footchange cam plate is part number 67-3332. The reverse footchange cam plate is part number 42-3011.

B.S.A. MOTOR CYCLES LTD., Service Department, Armoury Road, Birmingham 11.

Printed in England.

BSA SERVICE SHEET No. 302C

Reprinted December 1961.

GEAR RATIOS B and M GROUP (RIGID and PLUNGER)

MODELS B 32 & B 34 — MEDIUM CLOSE (Scrambles)

	PART No.	No. of TEETH
A	15—4165	28
B	66—3212	25
C	65—3435	18 x 22
D	24—4221	17 x 20
E	65—3437	23
F	65—3439	27
MODEL	B32	B34
ENGINE SPROCKET Part No.	15—1568	15—1567
ENGINE SPROCKET No. of Teeth	16	17
GEAR BOX SPROCKET Part No.	65—3504	65—3504
GEAR BOX SPROCKET No. of Teeth	16	16
Gear Ratios with the Combination of Pinions and Sprockets above — Top	7.06	6.63
Third	9.3	8.74
Second	12.15	11.41
First	17.44	16.37

MODELS B 32 & B 34 — EXTRA CLOSE (Road Racing)

	PART No.	No. of TEETH
A	66—3219	26
B	66—3212	25
C	65—3436	19 x 23
D	66—3220	19 x 20
E	66—3266	22
F	65—3441	26
MODEL	B32	B34
ENGINE SPROCKET Part No.	15—1566	15—1564
ENGINE SPROCKET No. of Teeth	18	20
GEAR BOX SPROCKET Part No.	65—3503	65—3503
GEAR BOX SPROCKET No. of Teeth	19	19
GEAR RATIOS with the Combination of Pinions and Sprockets above. — Top	5.28	4.75
Third	5.77	5.19
Second	6.9	6.22
First	9.86	8.88

STANDARD (TRIALS)

			A	B	C	D	E	F
		PART No.	15—4165	66—3212	24—4231	24—4221	66—3215	66—3209
		No. of TEETH	28	25	20 x 16	20 x 17	25	29
MODEL	B31	B32 and Goldstar	B33	B34 and Goldstar	M20 Solo	M21, M33 Solo	M20, M21 S/Car	M33 S/Car
ENGINE SPROCKET Part No.	15—1567	15—1568	15—1565	15—1564	15—1566	15—1564	15—1568	15—1567
ENGINE SPROCKET No. of Teeth	17	16	19	20	18	20	16	17
GEARBOX SPROCKET Part No.	65—3503	65—3504	65—3503	65—3504	65—3503	65—3503	65—3503	65—3503
GEARBOX SPROCKET No. of Teeth	19	16	19	16	19	19	19	19
Gear Ratios with the Combination of Pinions and Sprockets above. — Top	5.6	7.06	5.0	5.64	5.28	4.75	5.94	5.59
Third	7.38	9.3	6.59	7.44	6.95	6.25	7.82	7.37
Second	11.5	14.5	10.3	11.59	10.87	9.77	12.2	11.5
First	16.7	21.1	14.9	16.81	15.76	14.15	17.7	16.72

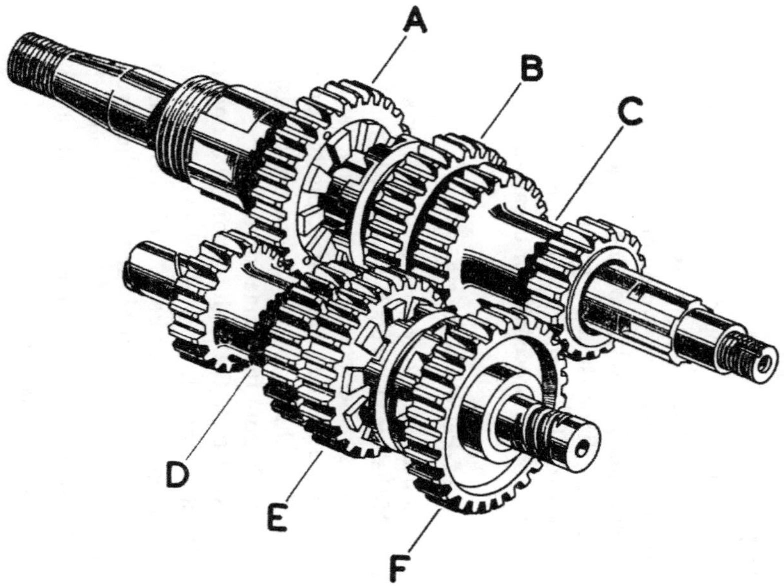

SERVICE DEPARTMENT, B.S.A. MOTOR CYCLES LTD., WAVERLEY WORKS, BIRMINGHAM 10, ENGLAND

BSA SERVICE SHEET No. 303

October 1948

Reprinted April, 1965

"B" GROUP AND M33 MODELS

ENGINE DISMANTLING FOR DECARBONISING

Symptoms which indicate that Decarbonising is necessary

Decarbonising and "top overhaul" of an engine is extremely simple, but it should only be carried out when the engine really needs it, which normally should be only at periods over 2,000 miles. The usual symptoms are an increased inclination to "pink" (a metallic knocking when under heavy load) due to the building-up of carbon on the top of the piston and inside the cylinder head; a general falling-off of power noticeable mainly on hills, and a tendency for the engine to run hotter than usual.

The correct procedure for decarbonising is described by stages.

Removal of Petrol Tank, etc.

It is first necessary to remove the petrol tank. Turn off the petrol tap and detach the petrol pipe. If the speedometer is mounted in the tank, disconnect the speedometer drive by releasing the strainer bolt under the tank, raising the speedometer clear of the tank and unscrewing the knurled nut connecting the drive to the instrument. If the speedometer is mounted on the fork yoke it need not be disturbed. Remove the tank securing bolts and lift the tank from the frame top tube.

Next detach the high-tension lead and remove the sparking plug. Disconnect the steady-stay from the rear of the cylinder to the frame, and then take off the carburetter by removing the flange bolts. Take care not to damage the carburetter flange washer. By unscrewing the ring nut at the top of the carburetter, the slide can be pulled right out and tied up to the top tube out of the way, while the main body of the instrument can be completely removed. By unscrewing the exhaust pipe and silencer clips to the frame, the pipe and silencer can be removed complete.

Removing Cylinder Head

Disconnect the oil feed pipe from the rocker spindles and the return pipe from the inlet rocker box. Note that the union screw plugs for the oil pipe to the rockers have a much smaller hole in the side than the union for the return pipe—a point to remember when reassembling.

The exhaust valve lifter cable can either be disconnected, or the exhaust rocker box cover removed leaving the cable intact. Remove the inlet valve rocker box cover. Slacken the castellated gland nut securing the push-rod cover tube to the cylinder head (a special "C" spanner is provided for this). Detach the tappet inspection cover at the base of the tube and undo the two acorn nuts clamping the base of the tube to the crankcase.

Lastly unscrew the four long bolts holding the cylinder head and barrel to the crankcase, applying the spanner to the top, or smaller diameter, hexagon. The larger diameter hexagon screws the bolt sockets into the crankcase and should not be touched unless it becomes necessary to replace a holding-down bolt, when the complete assembly of bolt and socket must be fitted.

B.S.A. Service Sheet No. 303 (contd.)

The cylinder head, complete with push-rod cover tube, should now be raised, the push-rods lifted off the tappets and dropped to the crankcase face. The head and push-rod cover tube can now be lifted upwards and forwards clear of the barrel. Note that the head has plain ground joint to the barrel, no gasket being used. If the head shows a tendency to stick, a few light taps with a wooden mallet under the exhaust port will loosen it. With the head clear of the machine, the push-rod cover tube can be detached.

Decarbonising

Rotate the engine by means of the kickstarter until the piston is at the top of its stroke, and scrape off the carbon deposit with an old penknife, taking care not to damage the piston crown.

All traces of carbon must be cleaned from the cylinder head in a similar manner. This is preferably done after the valves have been removed (see below) in which case care must be taken to avoid damaging the valve seats.

Grinding-In Valves

It is not necessary to remove the rockers in order to take out the valves and spring, but if it is decided to strip the head completely, it is only necessary to undo the acorn nuts on the rocker spindles and tap these out, preferably using a small centre punch so as not to damage the threads on the spindle ends. Careful note should be kept of the rocker assembly for replacement—i.e. the spring, followed by the steel washer, and finally the aluminium oil seal washer.

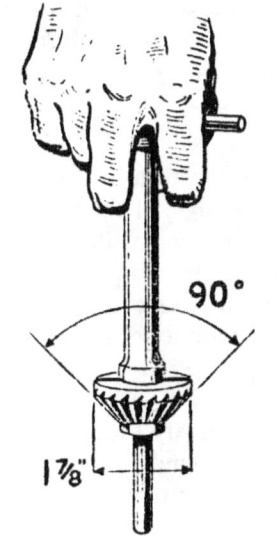

Fig. B3. *The Valve Seat Cutter.*

To remove the valves place a wooden block, of a size which will fit inside the cylinder head, on a bench, and then lay the head over the block with the valve heads resting on it. Lift off the hardened end caps if fitted from the valve ends, and then compress the valve springs until the split collets can be removed. When the collets are out, the valve springs and top collar can be lifted off.

Valve grinding should only be attempted if the seatings are not pitted. If badly pitted the seats must be re-cut, and a special tool 61–3305 is available for this operation Fig. B3. Attempts at grinding-in in this case will result in wear of the valve seats, and the valves may become pocketed.

Smear a small quantity of grinding compound (obtainable from any garage or accessory shop) over the face of the valve, and return the valve to its seat. Hold the valve with the special tool provided and rotate the valve backwards and forwards whilst maintaining a steady pressure. The valve should be raised and turned to a new position after every few

B.S.A. Service Sheet No. 303 (contd.)

strokes. Grinding should be continued until the valve seat and face show a uniformly polished surface all round. It is most important that valves should be ground-in on their correct seats. Both valves are marked, one "IN" and the other "EX", for identification purposes.

Before replacing the valves and springs, all traces of grinding compound must be removed from both faces and seats, and the valve stems smeared with engine oil.

Replacing Valve Guides

If new valve guides are to be fitted, the removal of the original ones is quite a simple operation, and necessitates the use of a valve guide punch (Fig. B4) and a hammer to drive the guides out of the cylinder head.

For B31, B32 and Gold Star inlet guides use Service Tool number 61–3265, the dimensions of which are (A) ½ in. diameter, (B) .310 in. diameter.

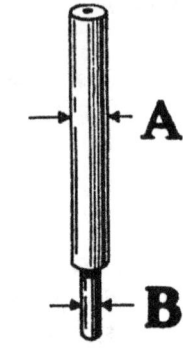

Service Tool number 61–3268, (A) ½ in. diameter, (B) .350 in. diameter should be used for B31, B32 and Gold Star exhaust valve guides and for inlet guides on models B33-34 and M33.

For exhaust guides on B33-34 and M33 use Service Tool number 61–3263 (A) ½ in. diameter, (B) .370 in. diameter.

Fig. B4.

Valve Springs

After a period of several thousand miles it may be desirable to renew the valve springs as these tend to lose their efficiency due to heat. If the springs are renewed while decarbonising, it will save dismantling specially to replace them at a later date.

Piston and Ring

While the engine is dismantled, it is advisable to examine the piston, rings and cylinder barrel. Lift the barrel upwards and forwards into the front angle of the frame, and as the piston emerges from the barrel it should be steadied to prevent possible damage. When the barrel is removed, cover the mouth of the crankcase with rag to prevent dust and grit falling in. To remove the piston from the connecting rod it is first necessary to take out one of the gudgeon pin circlips. This is best accomplished with a pointed instrument such as the tang end of a file suitably ground.

Before the gudgeon pin can be withdrawn it may be necessary to heat the piston with the aid of rags immersed in hot water, wrung out, and held round the piston. Then, supporting the piston, tap the gudgeon pin through using a light hammer and a punch.

When the piston is free, mark the inside of the piston skirt at the back, so that it can be replaced the correct way.

If the rings are stuck in the grooves they will need to be carefully prised free and removed from the piston. All carbon deposit should be carefully scraped from the grooves and the inside edges of the rings. If either of the rings shows brown patches on the face, replace with a new ring.

B.S.A. Service Sheet No. 303 (contd.)

Check the piston ring gap by inserting the piston in the barrel and sliding each ring independently up to the skirt of the piston. Check the gap with feeler gauges; this should not be less than .008 in. or more than .012 in. Fit new rings if the gap exceeds the figure stated. It is advisable to check the gap of new rings before fitting, and if the gap is less then .008 in. the ends of the rings should be carefully filed to the correct limit.

It should be noted that piston rings are very brittle, and unless handled very carefully are easily broken.

Reassembly

Reassembly is carried out in the reverse order and points to note are as follows:—

When assembling the piston it is advisable to heat it as explained in "dismantling" in order that the gudgeon pin can be fitted easily (if a degreaser is available the required temperature can be reached by a few seconds immersion). Make sure that the piston is fitted the correct way round and that the gudgeon pin circlips are firmly located. The piston ring gaps should be "staggered" around the piston circumference and the piston oiled liberally before the barrel is fitted.

Remember that it is essential that the valves are fitted to their correct seats.

Before fitting the cylinder head place the push-rod cover tube in position, but do not screw up the gland nut. Place the push-rods inside the tube and lift the head into position, keeping the head raised until the rods are located on the tappet, then position them on the rockers. Lower the head into position and replace the acorn nuts securing the push-rod tube. Screw up the long cylinder head and barrel bolts in diagonal order until they are tight. The push-rod cover gland nut can now be tightened up and the tappets adjusted as described in Service Sheet No. 604. Connect up the oil feed pipes to the rockers and replace the engine steady stay.

The fitting of the exhaust pipe, valve lifter cable and fuel tank are perfectly straightforward and should present no difficulty.

B.S.A. MOTOR CYCLES LTD., Service Department, Armoury Road, Birmingham 11.
Printed in England

BSA SERVICE SHEET No. 304

"B" GROUP MODELS
REMOVING ENGINE FROM FRAME AND COMPLETE DISMANTLING

Procedure for removal of the engine from the frame will commence from the point reached on Service Sheet No. 303 where the cylinder head and barrel had been removed.

Drain the oil tank, and disconnect the oil pipes. Detach the leads to the dynamo, and the earth wires situated on the magneto near the contact breaker housing. Then disconnect the ignition control cable at the handlebar end.

Models with Engine Prefix Letters G.B.
After draining the oil tank disconnect the leads to the **alternator** and the contact breaker.

Chaincase Removal
The chaincase and primary transmission should be removed as described in Service Sheets 307 or 310 on primary transmission (on models fitted with alternator refer to Service Sheet No. 315).

Engine Removal
Remove the bolts securing the engine plates to the crankcase and then unbolt and remove the front engine plates. Slacken the gearbox bolts as these tend to clamp the rear engine plates together. The engine is now ready to be lifted from the frame.

Dismantling the Engine
It is advisable, before commencing to dismantle the engine, to construct a simple jig as shown in the accompanying diagram, on which the engine can be mounted (see Fig. B.5). Alternatively one of the crankcase lugs can be clamped in a vice, with the weight of the crankcase being taken by a suitable support.

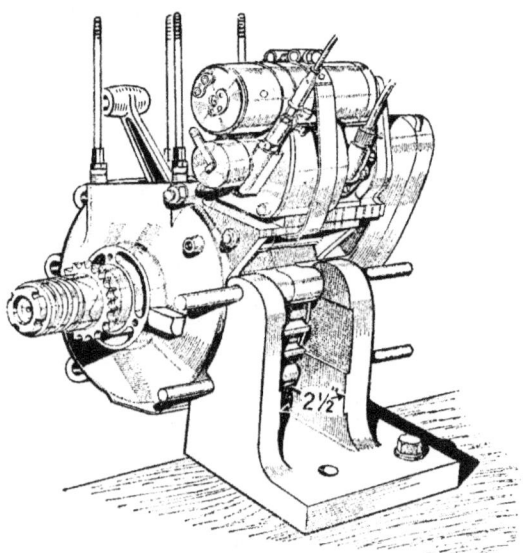

FIG. B.5. *Angle bracket for mounting engine.*

B.S.A. Service Sheet No. 304 (contd.)

Place a tray underneath the engine to catch any oil which may drip, and then remove the timing cover. Removal of the timing cover screws will be greatly facilitated if a comparatively large screwdriver is used.

Some difficulty may be experienced in removing the timing cover owing to the adhesion of the sealing compound, and in this case the lugs at the end of the cover should be tapped gently to break the joint.

Care should be taken to ensure that the small nozzle in the timing cover which feeds oil to the big-end is not damaged or distorted in any way, as it may subsequently foul the mainshaft and get broken off, and thus starve the big-end and cylinder barrel of lubrication.

Removing Magneto Pinion

This pinion locked on to the magneto shaft by its taper, and after removing the nut, an extractor (61-1903) must be applied to the threads on the inside of the pinion to withdraw the pinion. Next slacken off the magdyno strap bolt, and remove the magdyno as a complete unit.

NOTE:—There is a composition oil seal washer behind the magneto pinion, and there may be shims fitted to the base of the magneto. These items must be replaced when rebuilding.

Models with Engine Prefix Letters G.B.

The contact breaker pinion is secured to its shaft by a pin and circlip and need not be disturbed unless the pinion is to be replaced, the unit can be withdrawn complete with the pinion after the three nuts have been removed. A paper gasket is used between the back of the timing case and the contact breaker.

Out-rigger Plate

Remove the engine mainshaft nut, and the six bolts which hold the plate in position. It will be noted that all these bolts are not alike, and they must be replaced in the same position as prior to removal. The plate and all the pinions with the exception of the timing pinion can now be removed, and to withdraw this pinion an extractor (61-3256) should be applied (see Fig. B.6.).

To obviate the possibility of damage to the mainshaft, a plug of suitable dimensions should be placed in the oil hole of the mainshaft. If the pinions are rebushed they should

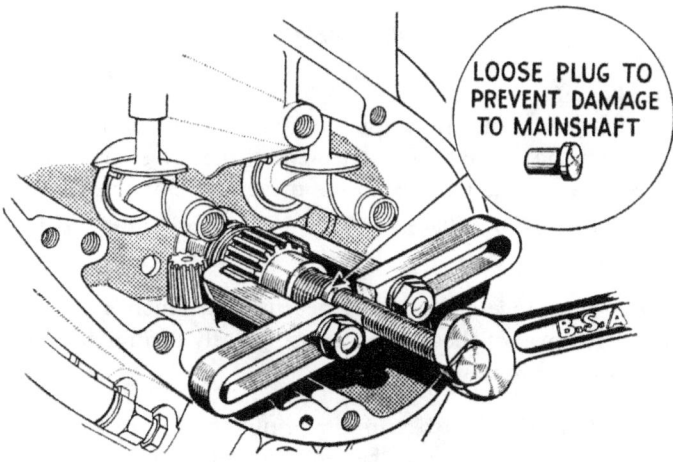

FIG. B.6. *Engine shaft pinion extractor 61-3256.*

B.S.A. Service Sheet No. 304 (contd.)

be reamed out to .6255—.6250 in. for the cams, and .7505—.7495 in. for the idler pinion. The correct size for the bearing in the out-rigger plate is .815—.814 in.

Before the oil pump spindle is released it is necessary to remove the locating plunger which is situated in the timing case. This plunger has an internal thread, and a timing cover screw can be inserted and used to pull out the plunger once the washer has been removed (see Fig. B.7).

Pump Removal

Unscrew the four nuts in the base of the crankcase, and remove the pump cover plate with the filter and joint washers. Now the two bolts holding the pump in position can be removed and the pump, together with the spindle, withdrawn from the crankcase.

NOTE:—The bolts holding the pump on to its seating can be identified by the spring washers under the heads of the bolts. The other bolts, which do not have washers under the head, serve to hold the pump together, and these should not be touched unless the pump is faulty and it is necessary to replace the internal parts.

If it is necessary to replace the cylinder holding-down bolts, the originals should now be removed, and the crankcase will be ready for splitting.

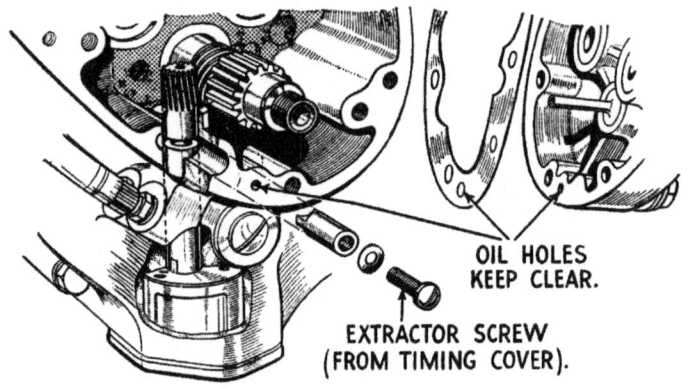

FIG. B.7. *Oil pump spindle locking plunger.*

Splitting the Crankcase

Remove all the bolts around the crankcase joint, and draw each half of the crankcase from the flywheels. It will be noted that the outer races of the drive and gear-side roller bearings will stay in the crankcase. The ballrace in the drive-side crankcase half is held in position by a spring ring, and this ring must be removed before any attempt is made to press out the bearing.

To remove the outer race of the roller bearings, a punch must be applied, as shown in Fig. B.8, and the removal of these races will be greatly facilitated if the crankcase is first heated by immersion in boiling water.

To remove the drive-side ball bearing, take out the distance piece which is normally positioned between the ball and roller bearings, remove the spring ring and use a press tool to press the bearing from its housing.

B.S.A. Service Sheet No. 304 (contd.)

If it is desired to remove the cam pinion spindles they can easily be withdrawn by means of an extractor (61-691), but do not remove these spindles unless it is absolutely necessary. If it is necessary to replace a tappet, of course, the cam spindles must be removed so that the tappets can be drawn out downwards into the timing cover. When removing tappets it is necessary to unscrew the tappet guides in addition to withdrawing the cam spindles, and in the case of the exhaust guide the timing pinion must also be removed.

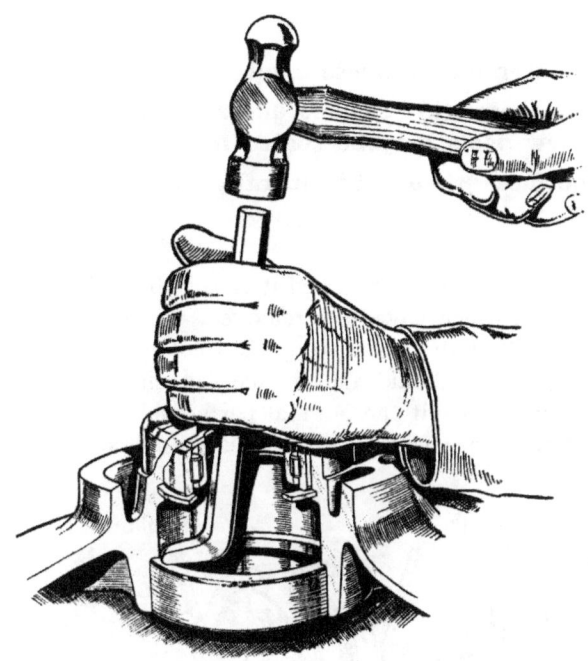

Fig. B.8. *Roller-race extraction (drive-side).*

Parting the Flywheels

Remove the locking plates holding the crankpin nuts, and unscrew the nuts. It will be found that considerable leverage is necessary to unscrew these, and it is suggested that a length of strong tubing of suitable size be applied to the spanner so that the desired leverage may be obtained.

The crankpin is a taper fit in the flywheels, and can be released by being tapped smartly with a mallet.

In the event of big-end wear we do not advise the fitting of oversize rollers, and the whole big-end assembly should be replaced. When a new big-end bearing has been inserted it is necessary for it to be ground out to 1.7702—1.7704 in., as a slight distortion is liable to occur when the bearing is pressed in.

B.S.A. MOTOR CYCLES LTD., Service Department, Armoury Road, Birmingham 11
PRINTED IN ENGLAND. B.S.A. PRESS

BSA SERVICE SHEET No. 305

October, 1948
Reprinted Jan., 1965

"B" Group Models

RE-ASSEMBLING THE ENGINE

The need for extreme cleanliness cannot be over-emphasized.

Parts should be thoroughly cleaned and all trace of any anti-rust preparations with which new parts may be coated must be removed.

All bearing surfaces should be liberally smeared with engine oil when assembling.

Flywheels

If the big-end assembly is to be renewed it is as well to check the weight of the new components against those which have been removed. A slight variation in the weights is inevitable, but provided that the discrepancy does not exceed $1\frac{1}{2}$ ozs. no further action need be taken. This tolerance should not be exceeded, since in the first instance the flywheels have been balanced to suit the original parts, and the balance may be adversely affected if the weight of the new components varies considerably from that of the original ones.

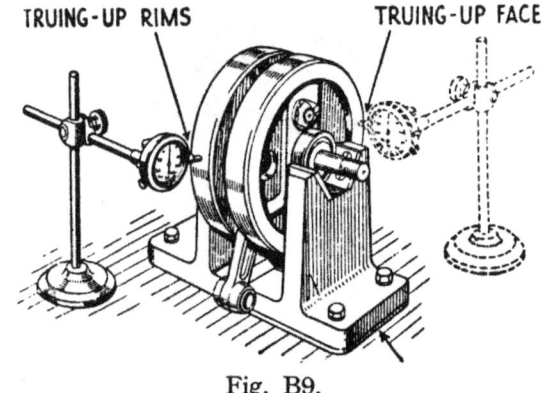

Fig. B9.
Suitable packing under timing side "vee" block to compensate for smaller diameter bearing.

The driving side flywheel should now be fitted to the crankpin (this is the side with the keyway) and the nut tightened up by hand. Fit the timing side flywheel and again tighten the crankpin nut by hand.

In order to tighten the crankpin nuts properly, the whole flywheel assembly must be held rigidly. For this purpose, it should be mounted in a large vice (fitted with lead clamps) with the driving side flywheel uppermost. If a large enough vice is not readily available an alternative method is to fix rigidly to the bench in a vertical position, two $1\frac{1}{16}$ in. diameter posts, the distance between their centres being $3\frac{7}{8}$ in. Midway between the posts a hole of 1 in. diameter should be bored in the bench to receive the mainshaft. The flywheel assembly is mounted on these posts so that they pass through the holes bored in the

B.S.A. Service Sheet No. 305 (contd.)

flywheels, and the driving side flywheel should be uppermost. Tighten the crankpin nut very firmly, using a tubular extension to the spanner as when dismantling, and fit the locking plate and screw.

Now turn the assembly over, so that the gearside flywheel is on top, and tighten the crankpin nut lightly. The grub screw in the end of the crankpin must be riveted over or centre-punched to prevent its unscrewing. If it unscrews, serious damage may result to the engine. Check that the side clearance of the connecting rod in the flywheels does not exceed .012 in. and is not less than .010 in.

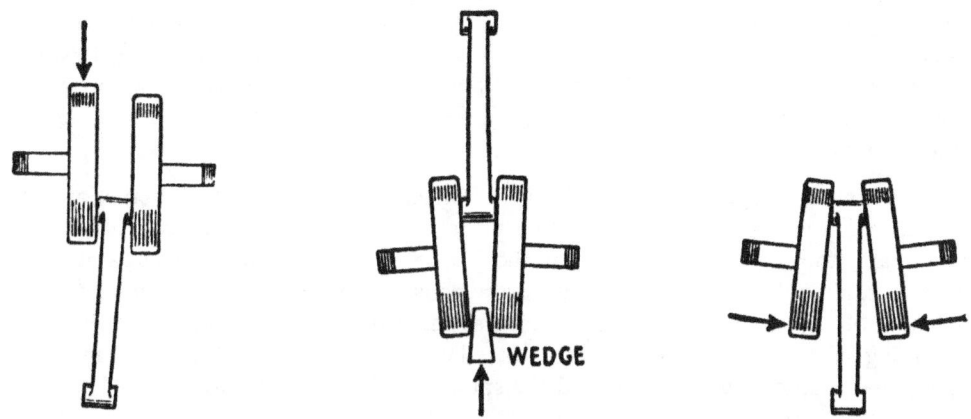

To bring shafts into line, a sharp blow with a mallet on **timing side** flywheel. (indicated by arrow)

To bring flyweels parallel when sides opposite crankpin are converging, insert wedge as shown and deal sharp blow, with mallet.

To bring flywheels parallel a sharp blow with mallet on flywheel rims on opposite side to crankpin

Fig. B10.

The flywheels will now be aligned only very approximately and further steps must be taken to ensure that the wheels are aligned as true as possible. Two of the actual (or similar) bearings to be used in the engine should be fitted to the mainshafts and the latter mounted on vee-blocks. The flywheels must be trued up, both on faces and rims, for which purpose a dial micrometer is necessary (Fig. B9), and after the wheels are trued to within at least .005 in. tighten the timing side crankpin nut fully. A mallet or lead hammer applied to the flywheels will provide a sufficiently heavy blow for final truing, and will not harm the flywheels (Fig. B10). The shafts must not be struck. The shafts should be finally trued to within .002 in. maximum.

Crankcase

Withdraw the bearings from the shaft and press them into their appropriate positions in the crankcase halves. A new washer will be required behind the small drive side bearing and a new retaining ring must be fitted. In the case of single lip roller bearings, only the outer race can be so fitted. Do not omit the retaining ring which holds the driving side bearing in position, and check that the ends of the spacing sleeve between the bearings are parallel to within .002 in. In order that the inner bearing and the sleeve will stay in position, it is advisable to lay the crankcase half on a bench with the outer bearing lowest.

B.S.A. Service Sheet No. 305 (contd.)

Fit the oil flinger washer to the driving side mainshaft and note this washer is bent over in one place to prevent accidental movement when fitting. If a new washer is being used it should be bent in a similar manner to the one which has been removed. Insert the driving shaft carefully into the crankcase, taking care not to disturb the flinger washer. The shaft should fit into the bearing without the use of unnecessary force and although the shaft must be a fairly tight fit in the bearings it should be possible to assemble it by hand. If necessary, ease the shaft with emery cloth, carefully cleaning off any trace of emery afterwards.

It is advisable to attend to the timing side of the crankcase before continuing further. Replace the oil pump driving spindle together with its locating pin (see Fig. B7) and then fit the oil pump in position. The fibre washer between the pump and the crankcase should be smeared with jointing compound, but an excessive amount must not be used, since any surplus will be squeezed out and may find its way into the oil passage. The pins securing the oil pump must not be screwed up too tightly. Check that the pump spindle can be rotated between finger and thumb.

Now replace the tappets and guides, the latter being screwed well home, and insert the cam pinion spindles. These should be pressed home, taking great care to keep them dead square, and must be fitted so that the flat on the spindle shoulder is parallel to the tappet foot, for which it provides clearance and consequently its position is most important.

Assembly of the crankcase will be made easier if the flywheel assembly, together with the driving side portion of the crankcase fitted on as previously explained, is mounted in a vice. Lead clamps must be used and the splined portion of the shaft held.

The mainshaft bearings may now be pressed into the gearside half of the crankcase and the latter replaced on the mainshaft. Bolt up the crankcase and check that the flywheels, etc., spin easily. Fit sprocket centre, tighten up, and verify also that the connecting rod is centrally disposed in the crankcase mouth. Provided that the connecting rod is not visibly out of the centre, there is no necessity for any adjustment to be made. If the connecting rod is out of centre, it will invariably be towards the driving side of the crankcase. In this event a shim will have to be made and inserted between the driving side flywheel and the oil flinger washer. It may also be that the distance sleeve between the driving side bearings has become a little worn on its end faces, and a new component (one specially chosen so that its length is on the maximum limit) will rectify the connecting rod alignment.

When the connecting rod alignment is found correct, remove the gearside half of the crankcase and clean the joint of any compound used previously. Fit the magdyno straps on their hinge pins, smear jointing compound lightly on the crankcase joint face and again bolt up the crankcase. Check that top of crankcase, where cylinder base flange fits, is dead flat.

Timing Gears

Replace the engine shaft pinion, taking special care to note that the worm is engaging properly with the oil pump spindle and that rotation of the flywheels drives the pump.

The cam pinions are interchangeable and consequently the timing marks are duplicated on both pinions. This should not cause any difficulty when timing the valves if it is remembered that the dash mark only is used for the inlet cam and the dot for the exhaust cam (Fig. B11).

B.S.A. Service Sheet No. 305 (contd.)

The magdyno can now be fitted to the crankcase and its straps loosely coupled up. Make sure that the dowels in the base engage properly in their holes in the platform, and that any packing shims are refitted. Refit the idler pinion between the inlet cam pinion and the magdyno pinion, but do not replace the pinion retaining plate at this stage.

Fig. B11. Valve Timing.

An oil sealing washer is fitted behind the magdyno pinion, and this should be temporarily removed. Replace the magdyno pinion on its taper; it need not be driven on very firmly, but just tight enough to prevent slip. Check the backlash between this pinion and the idler. If excessive, the gear will be noisy; if insufficient, a whining noise will result.

In order to adjust the backlash, shims are fitted under the magdyno if necessary, when the engine is first built. If a different magdyno is being fitted, it is essential this backlash be checked carefully, shims of a different thickness being used as required.

Remove the magdyno pinion once more, replace the oil sealing washer and again fit the magdyno pinion loosely in position. It is preferable to leave the setting of the ignition until the barrel and piston are in position, and for this reason the magdyno pinion should not be tightened up. The valve timing can now be set. Replace the pinion retaining plate, noting that the coarse threaded bolts screw into the crankcase bosses, and then fit the lockwasher and nut on the engine mainshaft. Play between the pinions and the retaining plate should be .002—.003 in.

Assembly from this point will be the same as after decarbonising (Service Sheet No. 303).

B.S.A. Motor Cycles Ltd., Service Dept., Armoury Road, Birmingham 11.
B.SA. PRESS.

BSA SERVICE SHEET No. 306

Reprinted May, 1963

B Group Models
(Up to 1948)
REMOVAL, DISMANTLING AND RE-ASSEMBLY OF GEARBOX

The Gearbox described in this sheet is fitted to models up to Engine No. ZB——101. The Gearbox fitted after this number is described in Service Sheet No. 608.

Removal from Frame

To remove the gearbox from the frame the primary chaincase, clutch and cush drive must be removed as described on Service Sheet No. 304 under the heading of Removal of Engine from Frame. The clutch cable rear chain and speedometer drive must also be disconnected.

Withdraw the gearbox bolts and when removing the box from the frame note that the gearbox adjustment bolt which is situated in the rear of the gearbox shell, and moves the gearbox backward or forward to adjust the tension of the primary chain, must be disengaged from the frame lug.

Before dismantling remove the gearbox drain plug so that any oil in the gearbox can be run off.

Disconnect the foot change lever and kick starter lever, and then unscrew the four bolts in the rear of the gearbox cover behind the foot change mechanism, and the screws in the gearbox end cover. The end cover can now be withdrawn, permitting access to the foot change mechanism.

Next remove the pin from the link mechanism, and unscrew the large nut in the rear of the gearbox inner cover, which holds the foot change spindle in position. The gearchange mechanism can now be taken off as a complete unit. Take care not to lose the small plunger which is revealed when the mechanism is withdrawn.

The gearbox inner cover bolts may now be withdrawn, and the inner cover removed, complete with kick starter, quadrant spring, and foot change selector quadrant.

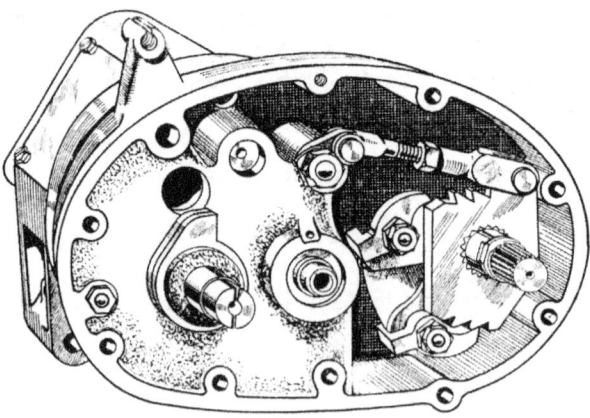

Fig. B.12. Gearbox shewing F/Change mechanism

B.S.A. Service Sheet No. 306 (cont.)

When removing the gearbox inner cover careful note should be made of the positions of the various distance washers on the shafts, as these washers are of varying thickness and are fitted to allow the correct amount of end play in the shafts. This end play should be evident with the end cover bolted in position, but should not exceed .001 in. to .002 in.

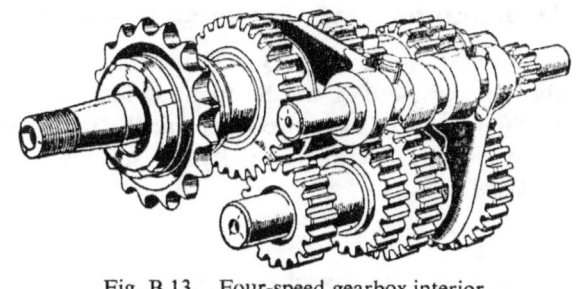

Fig. B.13. Four-speed gearbox interior

Fig. B.14. Selector quadrant

Replacing the Kickstarter return Spring

Should it be necessary to replace the Kickstarter return Spring, remove the screw retaining the Spring and rotate the Kickstarter quadrant to disengage it from the loop in the Spring. The quadrant can now be driven out with a copper hammer and the Spring removed. Note the position of the return stops on the quadrant shaft so that they may be replaced correctly.

If the gear selector quadrant is removed from the inner cover, care must be taken to ensure that the plunger is in position when re-fitting (Fig. B.14).

The gear cluster can now be removed from the gearbox shell, leaving only the pinion sleeve, mainshaft ballrace, and gearbox sprocket in position. These parts should not be removed unless they definitely require attention.

In the event of one of the above mentioned parts needing replacement, the sprocket ring nut washer must be flattened, and if difficulty is experienced in preventing the pinion sleeve from rotating, a piece of wood can be placed under the teeth of the sprocket, and a punch used to tap the ring nut loose.

Examine the various parts for wear, and if the sliding dogs show signs of seizure it is best to replace them. Attempts to erase the seizure marks will result in excessive side-play.

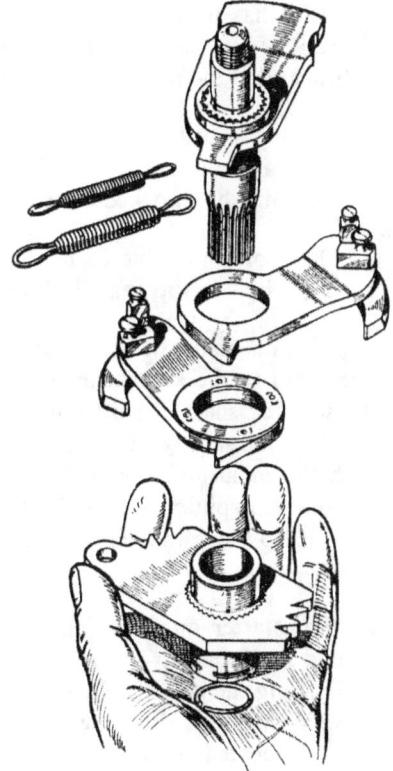

Fig. B.15. Gear change mechanism

B.S.A. Service Sheet No. 306 (cont.)

Dismantling gear change mechanism

It is only necessary to prise the pawl springs off their pegs, and to remove the circlip, then the whole unit can be stripped into its separate components. The only parts likely to show signs of excessive wear are the pawls and the ratchet plate, and these should be replaced as necessary. If the pawl springs show signs of stretching they too, should be replaced.

Removing the Speedometer drive

This should rarely be necessary and the Speedometer drive should not be removed unless obviously needing attention.

Slack off the large nut on the drive and give the end of the drive a tap with a hide mallet. Remove the locating screw.

The large nut can now be used to withdraw the drive, distance pieces being built up behind the nut until the drive is fully withdrawn.

When replacing, after fitting the locating screw, fully tighten the large nut. Do not omit the fibre washer behind the nut or oil leaks may result.

Re-assembly

If it has been decided to fit a new ballrace to the pinion sleeve, make sure that the oil retainer washers are correctly replaced. The flat washer fits between the pinion and ballrace, and the remaining washer fits behind the ballrace, with its face against the bearing.

If the sprocket teeth are worn hook-shaped, a new sprocket must be fitted or rapid chain wear will take place. When the sprocket locknut has been tightened the locking washer must be knocked over into the grooves machined in the nut.

It is only possible to fit the gear cluster into the box when the shafts are assembled (with pinions in top gear position) outside the gearbox, and all inserted together.

Commencing with the layshafts, remove the bottom gear pinion, which is the large one fitted to the kickstarter end of the shaft, and hold the shaft with the left hand. Take the selector shaft and lift the fork at the kick starter end to the dog on the layshaft. Pick up the mainshaft complete, and engage the selector fork at the sprocket end of the shaft with the mainshaft dog. Slide the assembly into the gearbox shell and place the layshaft bottom gear pinion on its shaft. Verify through the inspection cover that the assembly is still in top gear, and replace the various packing washers on their shafts.

The shell is now ready to receive the gearbox inner cover, and after making sure that the kickstarter quadrant and selector quadrant are correctly positioned, a paper washer should be fitted to the cover joint, and the cover replaced. If difficulty is experienced in pushing the cover right home, a *slight* movement of the selector will permit the teeth to mesh. Fitting of the cover will also be simplified if the selector shaft distance washer is liberally coated with grease and positioned around the selector shaft bush on the inside of the cover *before* attempting to replace the cover.

B.S.A. Service Sheet No. 306 (cont.)

The foot change mechanism may now be re-fitted, and the ratchet plates should be held in the left hand with the shortest length of the sleeve uppermost. Fit the pawl carriers and the spindle in the sequence as shown in the diagram so that the pawls engage with the teeth of the ratchet plate. Fig. B.15.

With the aid of a pair of pliers replace the springs on the pawls, and then fit the spindle circlip which holds the ratchet plate in position.

The unit is now ready for re-assembly in the gearbox. Make sure that the spring loaded plunger is in position in the inner cover before the unit is replaced. Couple the link arm to the ratchet plate, and take care to replace the split pin. Before proceeding with the assembly it is advisable to fit the foot change pedal loosely to its operating shaft, and by looking through the inspection hole, check that all the gears are being properly selected. At the same time the foot change mechanism can be tested to ensure that the springs return the pedal to the neutral position after each gear has been selected. If the selector dogs do not appear to go right home when the box is in top or bottom gear a slight adjustment to the length of the foot change link arm will cure this. It is necessary of course, to rotate the gearbox sprocket by hand while operating the gear change lever.

When all is found to be correct remove the gear change pedal while the gear cluster is in the **top** gear position, replace the clutch push rod, and finally put back the gearbox and cover with a new paper washer in position, and bolt into position. Next fit the foot change and kick starter levers to their shafts. Replace the gearbox in the frame, and loosely attach the fixing bolts. Reconnect the speedometer drive. Reassemble the primary chaincase inner half, cush drive, chain, and clutch. Rotate the gearbox adjusting bolt to give the correct tension to the primary chain, and then firmly tighten the gearbox holding bolts.

Note

The primary chain is correctly adjusted when it has $\frac{1}{2}$ in. up and down play midway between the two sprockets

JU/C2308

B.S.A. MOTOR CYCLES LTD.
Service Dept., Armoury Road,
Birmingham, 11
Printed in England.

BSA SERVICE SHEET No. 307

Revised Nov., 1959
Reprinted May, 1963

"B" Group Models
(Except those with engine prefix letters G.B.)
TRANSMISSION

Clutch Adjustment

The main clutch adjustment is enclosed inside the gearbox inner cover, and access is gained by the removal of the knurled oil filler cap.

The nut 'A' locks the adjusting screw 'B' in position, and to adjust the clearance between the ball and the end of the clutch push rod nut 'A' must be unscrewed, and screw 'B' rotated by means of a screwdriver until the necessary clearance is obtained.

Note. It is essential that a very slight clearance is permitted between the ball and the push rod at all times when the clutch is not being operated.

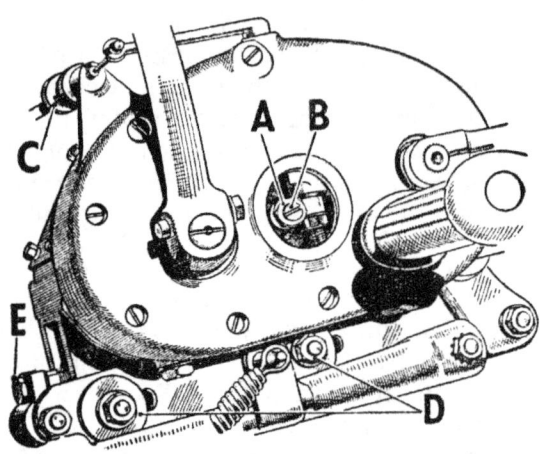

Fig. B16. Clutch adjustment

Further adjustment is provided by the knurled nut 'C' on the top of the gearbox. Remember, however, that some free movement in the control arm is necessary, for if the adjustment is too tight there will be a constant pressure on the clutch, with consequent wear and loss of efficiency.

Primary Chain Adjustment

The front chain tension is adjusted by moving the gearbox backwards or forwards in the frame, and this movement is carried out by slacking off the two large nuts D which attach the gearbox to the rear of the engine plates, and then screwing the adjuster bolt E which is attached to the rear of the gearbox shell either in or out. When the chain is at the correct tension, that is, with ½in. up and down play at the tightest part of the chain, tighten the nuts on the gearbox bolts and re-check the adjustment. Note that after tightening the primary chain the rear chain will be in need of adjustment.

Chain Case Removal

Drain off the oil in the case by removing the drain plug in the rear half. Remove the left hand footrest. The footrests are mounted on splines and may be rather tight. However, a few light blows on the front of the footrest will allow it to be worked clear. Remove the small screws round the rim of the chaincase and pull off the outer half, taking careful note of the positioning of the cork washers and distance pieces to facilitate re-assembly.

To dismantle the cush drive assembly, bend back the cush drive nut locking washer by inserting a small screwdriver through the coils of the spring, and remove the nut. With-

B.S.A. Service Sheet No. 307 (cont.)

draw the locking washer, the spring, and the cush drive sliding sleeve. If any difficulty is experienced in unscrewing the cush drive nut due to the engine rotating, place the machine in gear and apply the back brake.

Remove the clutch in the manner described in Service Sheet 308.

Remove the engine sprocket and pull the cush drive bearing off the mainshaft. Unscrew the three bolts which hold the inner half of the chain case to the crankcase, after breaking the locking wire which passes through the heads of the bolts. There now remains only one nut which holds the rear chainguard to the primary chaincase, and this nut can quite easily be removed if the chaincase is pulled off the crankcase register.

Re-assembly of the primary transmission and chain case should be carried out in the reverse order to dismantling.

Rear Chain Adjustment (Rigid Frame)

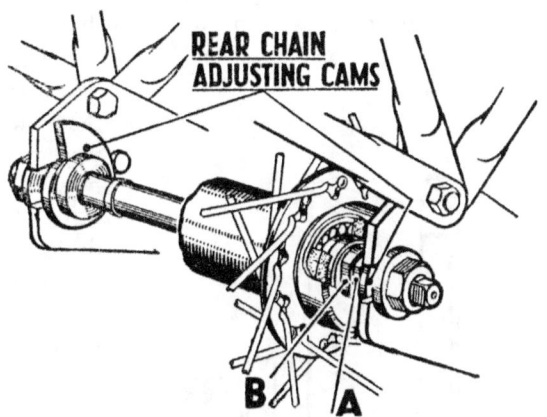

Fig. B17. Chain adjustment

The rear chain is adjusted by means of cams on the rear spindle, which operate against stops on the frame stays (see Fig. B17). To adjust, loosen the spindle nuts, and with a spanner on the end of the spindle, rotate the spindle. The wheel will then slide backwards, increasing the tension on the chain. Rotate the wheel slowly, and check chain tension. This tension is correct when there is ⅜ in. up and down play in the chain at its tightest point. Make sure that both cams are held against their stops, and then tighten up the spindle nuts—first the left hand nut, and then the right hand one. Now check the wheel alignment by means of a straightedge placed alongside the wheels. This straightedge should touch both walls of each tyre if the tyres are the same size.

It is a good plan to remove each chain periodically, thoroughly clean them in paraffin, and then gently warm them in a mixture of grease and graphite. When cool, wipe off excess grease, clean sprockets, and replace chains. Remember when fitting spring links that the closed end of the spring fastener must always face in the direction of travel.

For rear chain adjustment on spring frame models see Service Sheet 212C.

B.S.A. MOTOR CYCLES LTD.
Service Dept., Armoury Road,
Birmingham, 11
Printed in England

JU/C2301

BSA SERVICE SHEET No. 308

'M' GROUP, C10, C11, 'A' GROUP (S.A.), AND 'B' GROUP
(Except those engine with prefix letters G.B. or 'A' Group after engine numbers CA7-8623, CA755-8112 and DA10-13298)

DISMANTLING AND RE-ASSEMBLING THE CLUTCH

Take off the nearside footrest and then undo all the screws round the rim of the chaincase. As the outer half of the chaincase cover is taken off, careful note should be made of the positioning of the washers, etc., for replacement purposes. The joint washer should be carefully preserved.

Remove the six adjusting nuts, the springs and spring cups, and take off the clutch pressure plate so exposing the mainshaft nut which holds the clutch body in position.

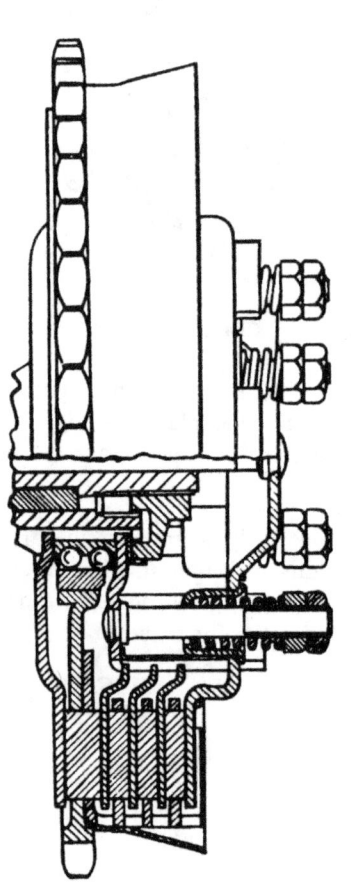

Fig. B18. *Section through clutch.*

The mainshaft nut is prevented from undoing by a locking washer which is turned over a flat on the nut. Flatten out the turned over edge of the washer and remove the nut. The clutch centre can now be withdrawn from the taper on the mainshaft using an extractor (part number 61-3362). Take care that the mainshaft key is not mislaid.

When the clutch is removed from the mainshaft it can be completely dismantled and the various components examined for wear. Special attention should be paid to the slots in which the clutch plates slide and any grooves should be removed with the aid of a fine file. If the grooves are very deep their removal will mean that the plates have excessive clearance and rapid wear will ensue. If the sprocket teeth are worn to a hook shape the sprocket must be replaced, otherwise rapid chain wear will result.

The steel plates should be smooth and if badly scored they should be replaced, while the fabric and cork inserts will require a thorough washing in petrol if there is any trace of oil on them. If the inserts are glazed or saturated in oil they should be replaced.

Finally, examine the balls, ball cages and tracks. If wear on the chainwheel bush or on the bearing boss of the clutch centre exceeds .0015 in. the bush or centre should be replaced (see Service Sheet No. 702 for correct dimensions).

NOTE.—When fitted to certain models this clutch is provided with additional plates, thus necessitating the use of a wider chainwheel and clutch centre, but the method of dismantling and reassembly is unaltered. C10 and C11 models have less plates than shown in the diagram but dismantling and assembly remain the same.

B.S.A. Service Sheet No. 308 (contd.)

Reassembly of the Clutch
The clutch is of straightforward construction and a study of Fig. B18 will show how the parts are assembled. Do not forget the mainshaft key when replacing the clutch centre.

The plates must be fitted in their proper order as follows: drive plate (tongues on inner diameter), fabric insert plates, drive plate, etc. Before refitting the pressure plate it is advisable to smear a small quantity of grease on the centre button at the point of contact with the clutch push rod.

The clutch springs should be replaced if they have shortened appreciably. The spring retaining nuts should be tightened initially until the outer nut (A) Fig. B19, is just fully engaged on its thread.

It is most important that the clutch spring pressure is evenly distributed, and this should be checked by ensuring that the clutch pressure plate does not tilt when the clutch is withdrawn. If the plate does tilt the nuts should be adjusted until the spring pressure is even. Unequal spring pressure may cause clutch drag and noisy gearchange. When the adjustment is complete tighten the locknuts firmly.

Clutch Re-adjustment
After a considerable mileage has been covered it may be necessary to screw the spring retaining nuts in further to allow for wear on the clutch inserts. Release the locknuts (A), and tighten the nuts (B) by a few turns. After the adjustment has been carried out, check that the clutch lifts evenly and then tighten the locknuts.

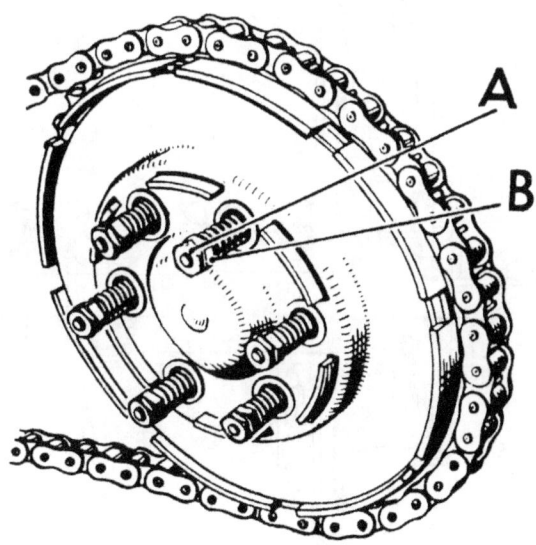

Fig. B19. *Clutch spring adjustment.*

B.S.A. MOTOR CYCLES LTD., Service Department, Armoury Road, Birmingham 11.

BSA SERVICE SHEET No. 309

Oct. 1948.
Reprinted November, 1962.

B and M Group Models
RIGID FRAME MODELS FITTED WITH TELESCOPIC FORKS
ADJUSTMENT, DISMANTLING and RE-ASSEMBLY OF
THE REAR HUB AND BRAKE

Rear Wheel Removal.

The rear wheel is not of the quickly detachable type, and has a riveted up brake drum. To remove the wheel it is necessary to disconnect the rear chain and the rear brake-rod and release the spindle nuts. Next disconnect the tail lamp wire, and remove the detachable portion of the rear mudguard by unscrewing the two bolts adjacent to the rear lifting handle. The wheel can now be pulled out. If a rear wheel drive speedometer is fitted the cable must be disconnected before the wheel can be removed.

Rear Hub.

Taper roller bearings are fitted to the rear hub, and these can be adjusted by loosening the locknut A (Fig. B.21) and tightening or loosening the nut B as required. Both nuts are on the opposite side to the brake drum. Do not overtighten the adjusting nut for it is most important that a very slight amount of side play is permitted in the wheel rim, or very

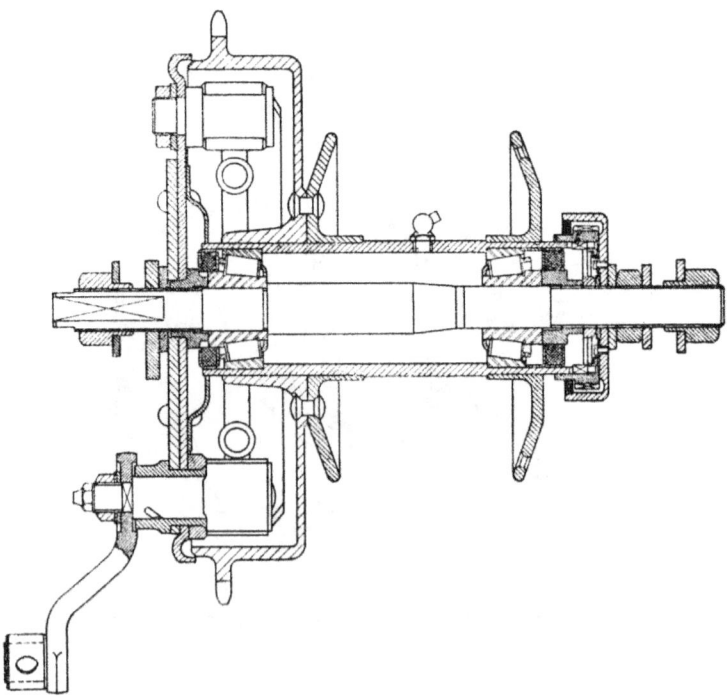

Fig. B20. Section of Rear Hub

B.S.A. Service Sheet No. 309 (cont.)

rapid wear will take place. Adjustment should be made so that $\frac{1}{64}$in. side play is apparent at the rim after the locknut has been finally tightened. It will be noted that, when fitted, the speedometer drive must be removed in order to gain access to the adjusting nut. Some M Group machines have a dust cover fitted in place of the speedometer drive gearbox.

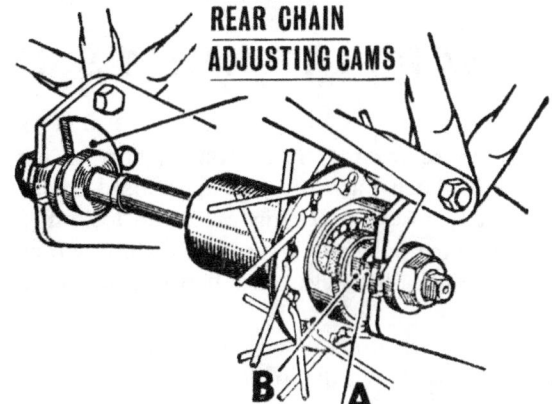

Fig. B21. Hub adjustment.

Hub Dismantling.

Remove the bearing adjusting nut and locknut. Tap the spindle out of the hub, towards the brake drum side, with a hide or copper mallet. The outer bearings may then be removed with the aid of a suitable soft drift.

Hub assembly is carried out in the reverse order to the dismantling. Care should be taken, when replacing the outer bearings to ensure that they are tapped quite home so that they are square in the hub.

Full details of brake adjustment and dismantling are given in Service Sheet 212A.

J.U. B3437

B.S.A. MOTOR CYCLES LTD.
Service Dept., Armoury Road,
Birmingham, 11
Printed in England.

BSA SERVICE SHEET No. 310

A AND B GROUP MODELS
(with welded type frame, except those with engine prefix letters GB)

PRIMARY TRANSMISSION

Clutch Adjustment

Two adjustments are provided for the clutch control arm on the gearbox outer cover. The first of these is at the clutch push rod and is exposed when the inspection plate is removed. It consists of a grub-screw (*H*) Fig. B22, and locknut (*G*). Between the inner end of the screw and the clutch push rod a steel ball is inserted, and the grub-screw must be adjusted so that there is just a little clearance between the ball and push rod.

To carry out this adjustment loosen the locknut and with the aid of a screwdriver adjust the grub-screw. Then retighten the locknut.

The other adjustment is provided by the cable adjuster on top of the gearbox. Remember that some free movement in the control arm is necessary as, if the adjustment is too tight, there will be constant pressure on the clutch with consequent wear and loss of efficiency. The control arm pivot should be greased occasionally by means of the grease nipple (*F*).

Primary Chain Adjustment

Adjustment of the front chain is achieved by pivoting the gearbox backwards and forwards on the bottom support bolt. To adjust the chain, remove the knurled inspection cover on the primary chaincase and slacken the nuts (*A*) and (*B*) Fig. B22, which clamp the top and bottom gearbox lugs in the rear engine plates. An adjuster is attached to the right-hand side of the top gearbox bolt. Slacken the locknut (*C*) and screw the adjuster (*D*) back-

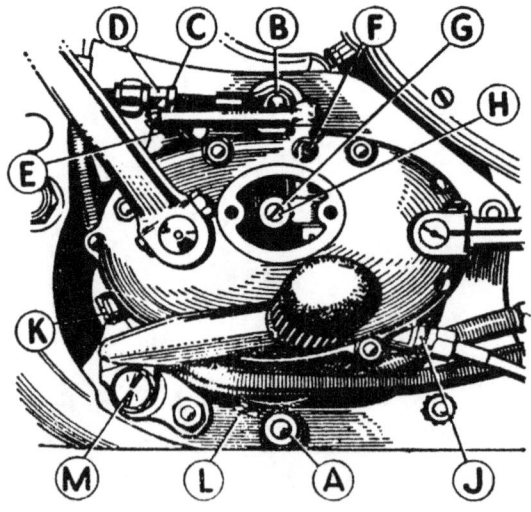

Fig. B22.

B.S.A. Service Sheet No. 310 (contd.)

wards or forwards until the chain tension is correct. This is when the maximum up and down movement of the chain at the tightest point is ½ in. Tighten the gearbox bolt nuts (*A*) and (*B*), also the adjuster locknut, and re-check the adjustment. Note that after re-adjusting the primary chain, the rear chain will be in need of adjustment.

Chaincase Removal

Drain off the oil in the case by removing the drain screw in the lower edge of the primary chaincase. Two of the screws retaining the primary chaincase outer cover have red painted heads. The front one of these is the chaincase oil level screw, and the rear one the drain screw. Remove the left-hand footrest. This may be rather tight, but a few light blows on the front of the footrest should free it. Undo the small screws round the rim of the chaincase and pull off the outer half.

To dismantle the cush drive assembly, bend back the cush drive nut locking washer by inserting a small screwdriver through the coils of the spring, and remove the nut. Withdraw the locking washer, the spring and the cush drive sliding sleeve. If any difficulty is experienced in unscrewing the cush drive nut due to the engine rotating, place the machine in gear and apply the back brake.

Remove the clutch in the manner described in Service Sheet No. 308.

Remove the engine sprocket and pull the cush drive bearing off the mainshaft. Unscrew the bolts which hold the inner half of the chaincase to the crankcase, after breaking the locking wire which passes through the heads of the bolts. There now remains only one bolt which secures the rear of the chaincase to the frame, and its removal will allow the chaincase to be detached.

Reassembly of the primary transmission and chaincase should be carried out in the reverse order to dismantling.

Before replacing the cush drive nut ensure that the lockwasher is correctly located in the splines on the mainshaft.

B.S.A. MOTOR CYCLES LTD., Service Department, Armoury Road, Birmingham 11.

SERVICE SHEET No. 311

Reprinted November, 1966

A and B Group Models
with Swinging Arm Frame

DISMANTLING AND RE-ASSEMBLY
OF GEARBOX AND GEARCHANGE

Gearbox Removal

In most cases it will be found convenient to dismantle the gearbox while it is still in position. However, if attention to the final drive pinion sleeve bearing is required it may be advisable to remove the complete gearbox. The primary transmission, clutch and chaincase must be removed in either case and this should be carried out as described in Service Sheet 310.

To remove the gearbox from the frame, slacken the retaining bolts and remove the two right hand rear engine plates. The gearbox is then free to be withdrawn from the right hand side of the machine.

Dismantling

Remove the clutch and speedometer cables. Move the gears to the neutral position between first and second. Undo the four nuts and three screws round the rim of the outer cover but do not slacken the screw and nut which are not on the edge of the cover as these do not prevent its removal. The outer cover can then be removed complete with the kickstarter, gearchange and clutch lever. As the cover is withdrawn the kickstarter lever will tend to rotate under the action of the return spring and the clutch lever should be pulled out to the fullest extent so that the kickstarter lever may be rested against it, thus preventing the complete release of the spring.

The gearchange mechanism can be dismantled by removing the gearchange lever and the circlip which retains the gearchange spindle in the outer cover. Withdraw the spindle complete with change mechanism which can then be completely dismantled after removing the split pin. Examine the operating claw 'A' for wear and if the ends are no longer well formed the claw should be replaced.

Before the inner cover is removed the clutch push rod should be withdrawn and the single screw to the left of the top right stud, must be undone. The inner cover together with the mainshaft and gearchange rocking lever 'B' can then be withdrawn, leaving the gear cluster in position. To remove the rocking lever the gear lever spindle bush must first be pushed out of the inner cover. This will reveal the end of the rocking lever spindle which is threaded internally $\frac{1}{4}$ in. C.E.I. Screw in a suitable screw or bolt, then use this to pull out the spindle.

If it is necessary to remove the mainshaft from the inner cover the shaft should be held in a soft jawed vice so that the kickstart ratchet nut can be undone after its locking washer has been bent back. The kickstart ratchet, ratchet pinion, spring and bush should

B.S.A. Service Sheet No. 311 (contd.)

then be removed, leaving the shaft free to be pushed from its bearing. This bearing can be removed by pulling out the retaining circlip and then warming the cover in hot water before tapping the bearing from its housing with a suitable soft drift.

The rod 'D' on which the two gear operating claws slide is pressed into the gearbox shell at the clutch end and is secured by a small grub screw on the outside of the case. Release the grub screw and pull out the rod. It is then possible to withdraw the gear cluster and operating claws together with the layshaft so that the only components remaining in the gearbox shell are the final drive pinion sleeve assembly and cam plate 'C'.

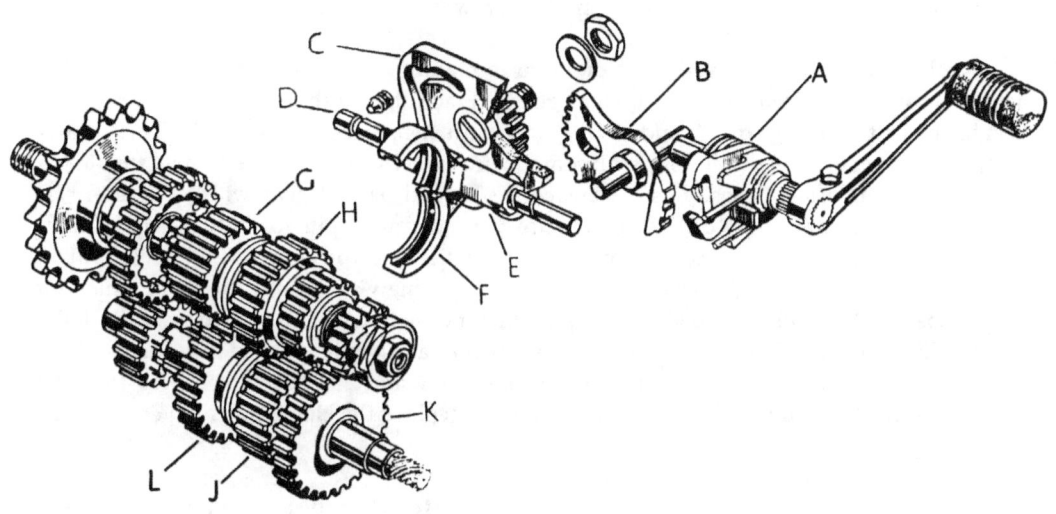

Unscrew the selector plunger housing locknut and remove the plunger housing from the gearbox shell. The gear selector cam plate will now slide from its pivot and the latter can also be removed after unscrewing the retaining nut and warming the case. The layshaft bearings are a press fit in the gearbox and if necessary can be driven out with the aid of a soft punch.

Run a length of old chain round the gearbox sprocket and hold the chain in a vice to prevent the sprocket rotating. Flatten the locking tab washer and undo the retaining nut. Withdraw the sprocket from its spline, then tap the pinion into the gearbox with a soft mallet. To remove the pinion sleeve bearing, prise out the retaining circlip, withdraw the oil seal, then warm the case in hot water before tapping the bearing out of the case. Do not disturb the ballrace unless it is suspected of being faulty. Wash it thoroughly in petrol to remove all traces of oil and any play will then be immediately detected.

Examine the various parts for wear, and if the forks which actuate the sliding pinions show signs of seizure it will be advisable to replace them. Attempts to erase the seizure marks will result in excessive side play.

B.S.A. Service Sheet No. 311 (contd.)

The fixed pinions on the layshaft and mainshaft are pressed on, and new components must be a tight fit. Examine the selector plate for worn cam grooves, and replace if necessary. The rocking arm should be replaced if the teeth show signs of wear as, of course, should pinions with damaged or worn teeth.

Re-assembly

Re-assembly is carried out in the reverse order to dismantling. The aluminium case should always be warmed before a bearing is pressed in. When replacing the gearbox sprocket ensure that the oil seal is in good condition and that the retaining nut locking washer is correctly seated in the spline. Tighten the nut fully and turn the lockwasher over into the slots on the nut. If the teeth on the sprocket are worn to a hook shape a new sprocket must be fitted otherwise rapid chain wear will result.

Replace the cam plate and selector plunger making sure that the plunger is in the neutral position between first and second gear. Place the layshaft in position and then feed in the first pair of gears 'J' and 'L' together with their selector claw 'F.' These claws are interchangeable but if the original components are to be used then they should be replaced in their original positions. Replace the second pair of gear wheels 'G' and 'H' together with selector claw 'E' and make sure that the guide pins of both selector claws are correctly engaged in the cam groove. Replace the selector claw rod and secure it in position by means of its grub screw. Position the spacing washer and the large pinion on the layshaft. Assemble the mainshaft, kickstart ratchet mechanism and rocking lever into the inner cover. The mainshaft and inner cover can then be pushed into the gearbox, but before they are completely home the rocking lever must be correctly set so that the red dots on the lever and on the cover are in line. Replace the single inner cover retaining screw.

Note that when a reverse cam plate 42–3001 is fitted the red dots will not coincide as described above. Correct meshing of the rocking lever must be obtained by trial and error.

Assemble the gearchange and kickstarter mechanism in the outer cover, then push the latter on to the four studs, rotating the kickstarter slightly so that the quadrant does not jam on its stop.

Replace the four nuts and three screws in the outer cover. The gearbox is now completely re-assembled.

B.S.A. MOTOR CYCLES LTD.,
Service Dept., Armoury Road, Birmingham, 11.

BSA SERVICE SHEET No. 312

B Group (Swinging Arm Frame)
USEFUL DATA

ALTERNATOR MODELS

Engine Stroke	88 mm	
Engine Bore	B31 (71 mm.)	B33 (85 mm.)
Engine capacity	B31 (348 c.c.)	B33 (499 c.c.)
Petrol Tank capacity	3½ gallons	2 or 4 gallons
Oil Tank capacity	5 pints	5½ pints
Gearbox capacity	1 pint	
Front Fork capacity (each leg)	⅜ pint (212 c.c.)	
Chaincase capacity	1/7 pint (80 c.c.)	½ pint S.A.E. 20
Tappet clearance (engine cold)	.003 in. inlet and exhaust	
Piston Ring Gap	.010 in.	
Piston Ring side clearance	.002 in.	
Piston clearance (bottom of skirt)	B31 (.0005—.0016in.)	B33 (.0006—.00275in.)
Ignition setting (fully advanced)	$\frac{7}{16}$ in. before T.D.C. ($\frac{3}{8}$ in. B33 model)	
Contact Breaker Gap	.012 in.	
Compression Ratio	B31 (6.5 : 1)	B33 (6.8 : 1)
Sparking Plug	Champion L10S	
Sparking Plug Gap	.018—.020 in.	
Valve Timing: Inlet	Opens 25° before T.D.C.	Closes 65° after B.D.C.
Exhaust	Opens 65° before B.D.C.	Closes 25° after T.D.C.

Carburettor	B31 (Monobloc)	B33 (Monobloc)		
Bore	1 in.	1 in.	1⅛ in.	1 1/16 in.
Main Jet	150	260	200	260
Throttle Valve	6/4	376/3½	29/4	376/3½
Needle Position	3	2	3	3
Needle Jet	.1065	.1065	.1065	.1065

SIDECAR

Gear Ratios	B31	B33	B31	B33
Top	5.6	5.0	6.25	5.59
3rd	6.77	6.05	7.55	6.76
2nd	9.86	8.79	10.95	9.82
1st	14.42	12.90	16.10	14.42
Front Chain ½ × .305 in.	B31 (67 pitches)	B33 (68 pitches)		
Rear Chain ⅝ × ¼ in.	B31 (98 pitches)	B33 (98 pitches)	⅝ × ⅜ in. (97 Solo, 98 Sidecar)	⅝ × ⅜ in. (98 Solo and Sidecar)

Tyres: Front	B31 (3.25 × 19)	B33 (3.25 × 19)
Rear	B31 (3.25 × 19)	B33 (3.50 × 19)
Tyre pressure (Solo)	Front: 16 lbs per sq. in. Rear: 18 lbs per sq. in.	
Total Front Fork movement	5¾ in.	
Rear Suspension movement	4 in.	
Brake Dimension: Front	B31 (7 × 1⅛ in.) B33 (8 × 1⅜ in.)	B31 (7 × 1⅛ in.) B33 (7 × 1⅛ in.)
Rear	B31 (7 × 1⅛ in.)	B31 (7 × 1⅛ in.) B33 (7 × 1⅛ in.)

B.S.A. MOTOR CYCLES LTD., Service Dept., Armoury Road, Birmingham 11.
Printed in England

BSA SERVICE SHEET No. 313

"A" and "B" Group Models
with Swinging Arm Frame

REAR SUSPENSION

REMOVING AND DISMANTLING THE SUSPENSION UNITS

Support the machine on the central stand. Take out the top and bottom bolts securing the suspension units and pull them away from the mounting lugs.

The upper shroud is retained by split collets, and the spring must be compressed before the collets can be removed. The assistance of a second person may be necessary for this operation. Alternatively, Service Tool number 61-3503 can be used, as shown in Fig. B24.

Place the tool in position on the shroud, insert the pin through the top lug and turn the handle until the shroud has been pressed down far enough to allow the collets to be withdrawn. After the tool has been released, the spring and both shrouds can be removed

No further dismantling is possible, and if the damper units are damaged, they must be replaced.

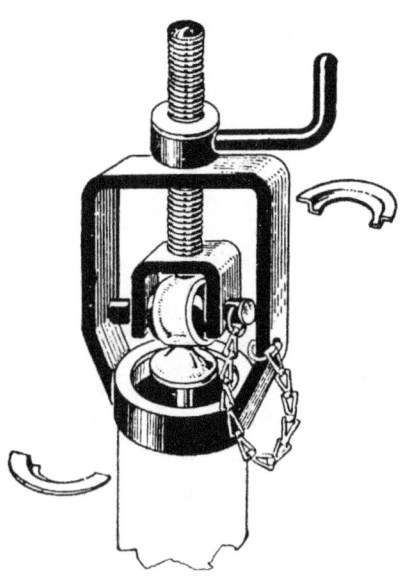

Fig. B24.

B.S.A. Service Sheet No. 313 (contd.)

REMOVING AND REPLACING THE SWINGING ARM FORK

With the machine on the centre stand, take out the rear wheel in the normal manner. Detach the chainguard, or chaincase, and remove the chain and sprocket assembly. Remove the brake pedal and, on 1956 models, withdraw the crossover shaft. Take out the two bottom bolts from the suspension units, and pull these clear of the mounting lugs. Unscrew the large nut on the offside end of the fork spindle, and also the small bolt from the spindle locking plate on the nearside. Drive out the spindle with a suitable drift, taking care not to damage the threaded end.

Now take hold of the two fork ends and twist the whole fork in a clockwise direction. It can then be drawn away towards the rear.

On some models, the rear mudguard extends down between the arms of the fork, behind the pivot. In this case, the mudguard also must be removed before the fork can be taken out.

The "silentbloc" spindle bushes have a very long life, and replacement is rarely necessary.

Reassembly of the fork into the frame is carried out in the reverse order to dismantling, except that the final tighteneing of the spindle nut should be left until all other parts have been refitted. Then, take the machine off the stand and load it with the weight normally carried. Tighten the spindle nut fully so as to clamp the centre sleeves of the bushes to the frame members in the correct position.

B.S.A. MOTOR CYCLES LTD., Service Department, Armoury Road, Birmingham 11.

BSA SERVICE SHEET No. 314

"B" GROUP MODELS
(with engine prefix letters GB)
PRIMARY TRANSMISSION

Clutch Adjustment

Two adjustments are provided for the clutch control arm on the gearbox outer cover. The first of these is at the clutch push rod and is exposed when the inspection plate is removed. It consists of a grub screw (*H*) Fig. B25, and locknut (*G*). Between the inner end of the screw and the clutch push rod a steel ball is inserted, and the grub screw must be adjusted so that there is just a little clearance between the ball and push rod.

To carry out this adjustment loosen the locknut and with the aid of a screwdriver adjust the grub screw. Then retighten the locknut.

The other adjustment is provided by the cable adjuster on top of the gearbox. Remember that some free movement in the control arm is necessary as, if the adjustment is too tight, there will be constant pressure on the clutch with consequent wear and loss of efficiency. The control arm pivot should be greased occasionally by means of the grease nipple (*F*).

Primary Chain Adjustment

Adjustment of the front chain is achieved by pivoting the gearbox backwards and forwards on the bottom support bolt. To adjust the chain, remove the knurled inspection cover on the primary chaincase and slacken the nuts (*A*) and (*B*) Fig. B25, which clamp the top and bottom gearbox lugs in the rear engine plates. An adjuster is attached to the right-hand side of the top gearbox bolt. Slacken the locknut (*C*) and screw the adjuster (*D*) backwards or forwards until the chain tension is correct. This is when the maximum up and down

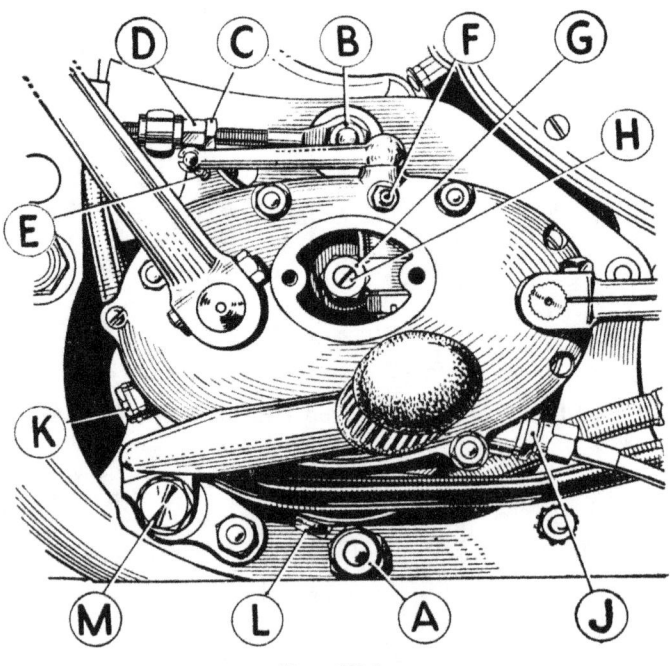

Fig. B25.

B.S.A. Service Sheet No. 314 (contd.)

movement of the chain at the tightest point is ½ in. Tighten the gearbox bolt nuts (*A*) and (*B*), also the adjuster locknut, and re-check the adjustment. Note that after re-adjusting the primary chain, the rear chain will be in need of adjustment.

Chaincase Removal

Drain off the oil in the case by removing the drain screw in the lower edge of the primary chaincase. Two of the screws retaining the primary chaincase outer cover have red painted heads. The front one of these is the chaincase oil level screw, and the rear one the drain screw. Remove the left-hand footrest. This may be rather tight, but a few light blows on the front of the footrest should free it. Undo the small screws round the edge of the chaincase and pull off the outer half.

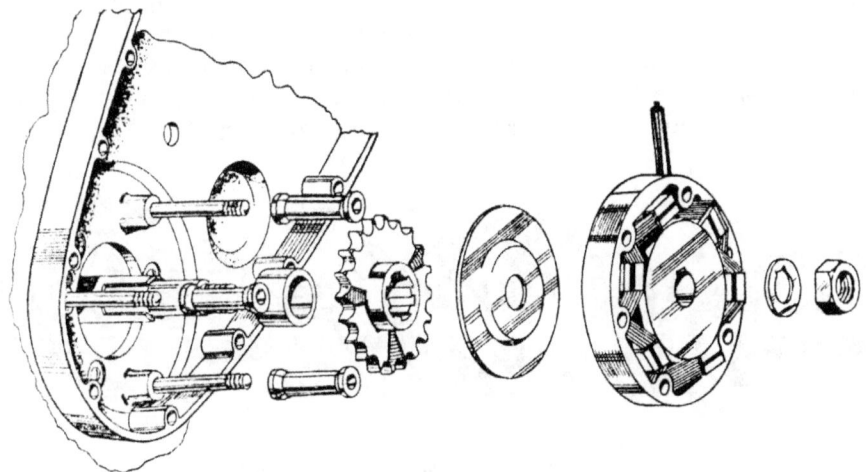

Fig. B26. *Alternator assembly.*

The alternator assembly is dismantled by prising back the tab on the lockwasher and unscrewing the large nut on the end of the engine shaft. If the nut is very tight, engage top gear and apply the rear brake to prevent the engine turning. Next take off the three nuts which retain the coil assembly. Lift this off the studs and withdraw the rotor, which is keyed to the shaft, also the spinner. Should the coil assembly prove difficult to remove, it may be gently prised off with a screwdriver, taking great care not to damage the windings.

Remove the clutch in the manner described in Service Sheet No. 315.

Remove the engine sprocket from the mainshaft. Unscrew the bolts which hold the inner half of the chaincase to the crankcase, after breaking the locking wire which passes through the heads of the bolts. There now remains only one bolt which secures the rear of the chaincase to the frame, and its removal will allow the chaincase to be detached.

Reassembly of the primary transmission and chaincase should be carried out in the reverse order to dismantling.

B.S.A. MOTOR CYCLES LTD., Service Department, Armoury Road, Birmingham 11.
Printed in England.   B.S.A. Press

BSA SERVICE SHEET No. 315

Printed May 1964

"B" GROUP MODELS

(with engine prefix letters GB)

CLUTCH

Dismantling

Remove the chaincase as described in Service Sheet No. 314. Remove the four spring retaining nuts and withdraw the springs and spring cups. The spring pressure plate and other clutch plates can then be removed, and if only attention to these items is required the clutch need not be dismantled further. The steel plates should be smooth, and if badly scored must be replaced, while the cork inserts may require washing in petrol if the oil on them is thick and gummy. If the inserts are burnt or glazed they should be replaced.

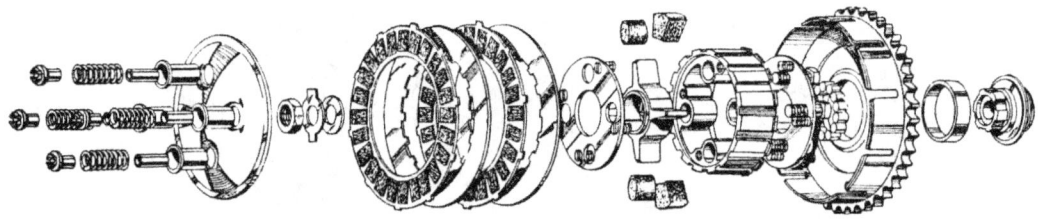

Fig. B27. *Exploded view of clutch.*

To dismantle the remainder of the clutch, turn back the tab washer on the mainshaft and take off the nut which has a right-hand thread, note the position of the plain washer. The complete clutch can now be withdrawn from the mainshaft, making sure that the rollers do not fall out from between the clutch centre and the chainwheel.

Lift the chainwheel from the clutch centre and remove the 20 rollers. The four bolts, eight screws and the two cover plates from the clutch centre can also be removed to expose the vane and shock absorber rubbers. If the rubbers require attention, the vane must be pushed out with the aid of a suitable drift.

Reassembly

Before commencing reassembly examine the roller tracks on the chainwheel bush and clutch centre, and if the wear on either of these components exceeds .0015 in. it should be replaced.

BSA SERVICE SHEET No. 602A

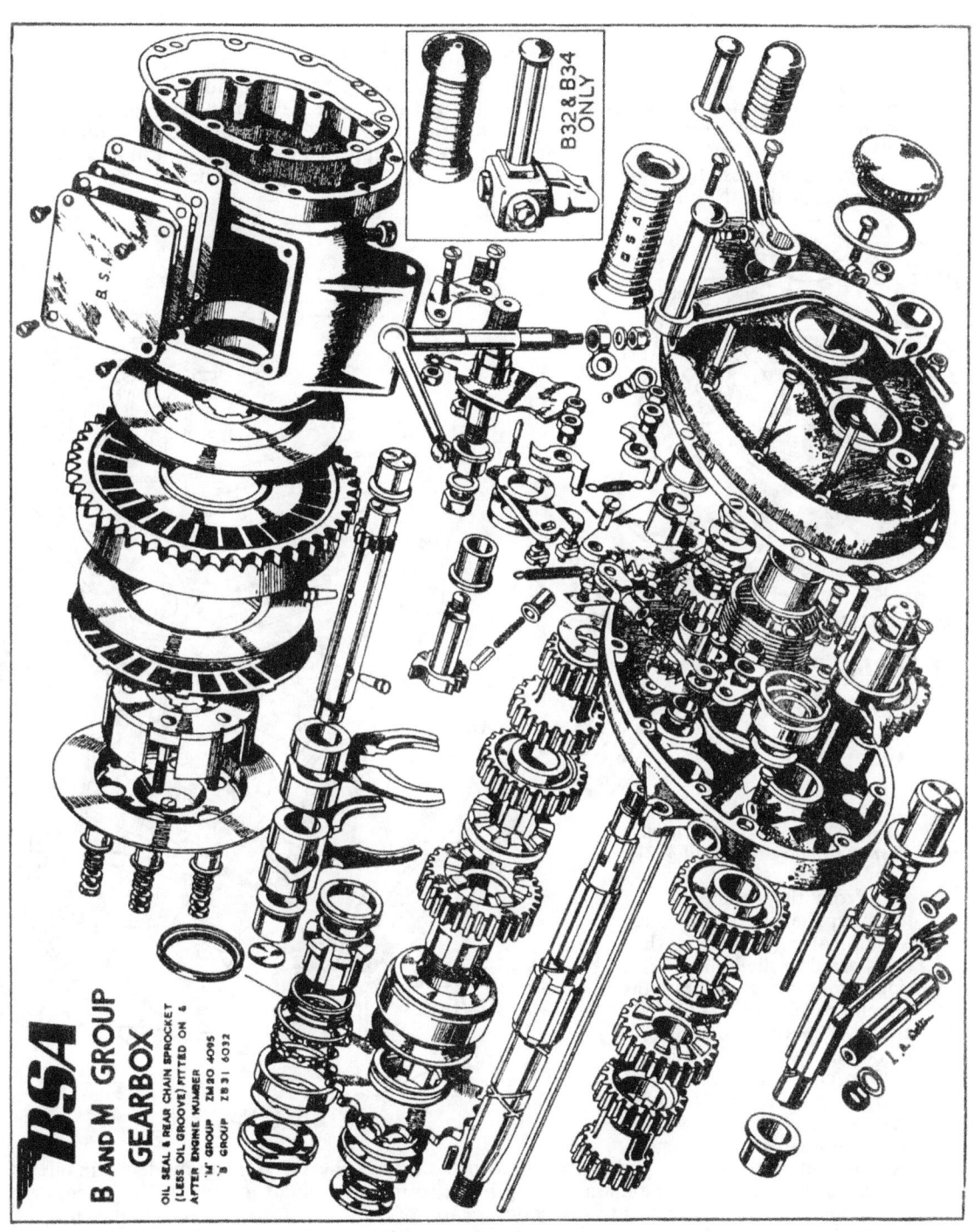

BSA SERVICE SHEET No. 603
"B" "C" and "M" Group Models

THE LUBRICATION SYSTEM

The engine lubrication system is of the dry sump type operated by a double gear pump, situated in the bottom of the crankcase on the right-hand side. The only external oilways are the supply and return pipes to the tank and the rocker feed and drainage pipes on the "B" Group. The oil drawn from the oil tank to the supply side of the pump first passes through a close mesh filter. This filter is not fitted to "M" Group machines as a felt filter is incorporated in the oil return pipe.

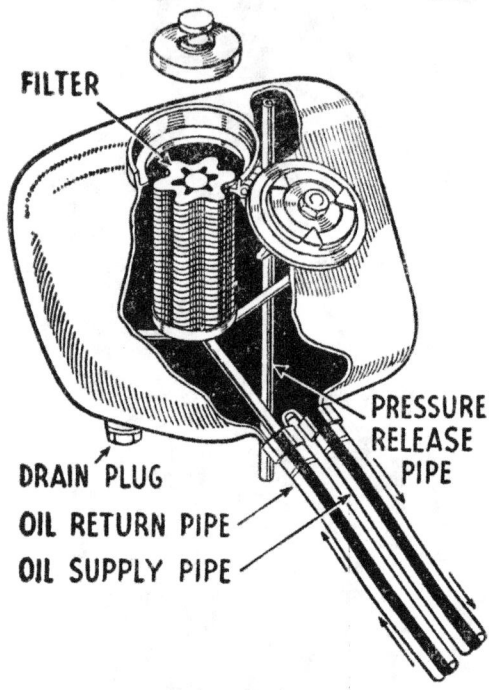

Fig. M3. *The Lubrication System* (models M20 and M21)

From the supply side of the pump the oil passes through a ball valve (A) and is then transferred to the hollow drive side mainshaft to supply the big-end roller bearing. On "B" and "M" models the transfer is made via a nozzle fitted in the timing cover which projects into the end of the drilled mainshaft and additional oilways in the timing cover provide positive lubrication to the cam pinion spindles. In the case of the "C" Group models, the oil passes through a hole in the main bearing bush, round an annular groove in the journal and thence via a radial drilling to the hollow centre of the shaft. (See Fig. M4). On C10L and C11G models a fine bleed hole from the main bearing meters a supply of oil to the camshaft and cam followers.

B.S.A. Service Sheet No. 603 (contd.)

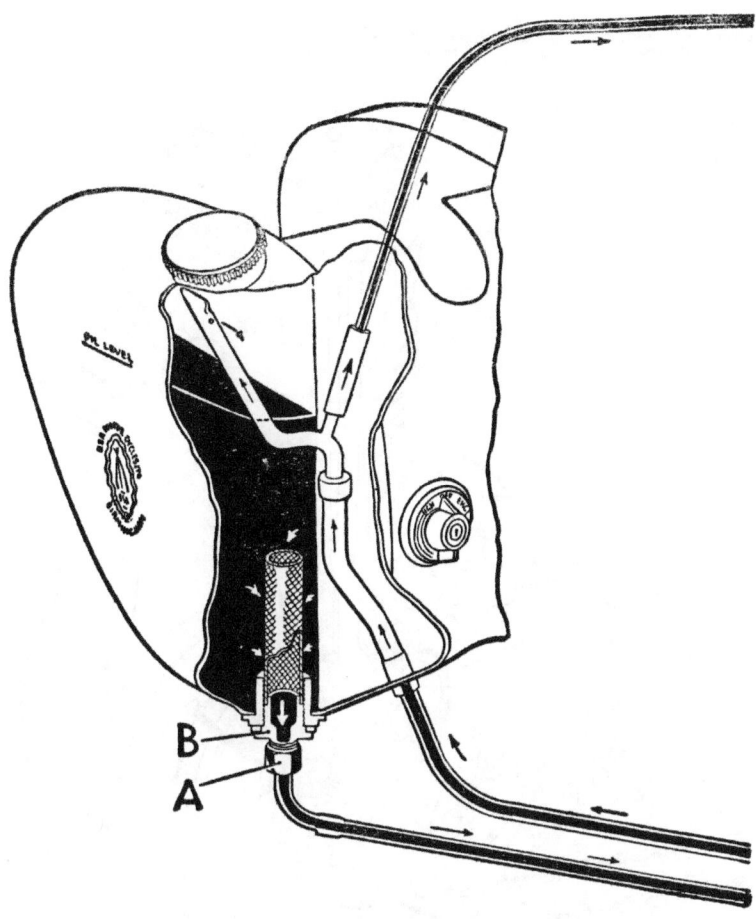

The Oil Tank C15.

MODEL C15

The lubrication system is of the dry sump type and is operated by a double gear pump situated in the bottom of the crankcase on the right-hand side. The oil tank capacity is four pints and oil is drawn from the oil tank to the supply pump (top set of gears). It is then pumped past the non-return valve (A), and along the hollow mainshaft to the big-end.

After lubricating the engine the oil flows down through a filter to the bottom of the crankcase from which it is drawn by the return pump (lower set of gears) past the non-return oil valve (C), and delivered up the return pipe to the tank. At the junction of the return pipe to the tank a by-pass pipe leads a supply of oil to the rockers, push-rods end, etc.

B.S.A. Service Sheet No. 603 (contd.)

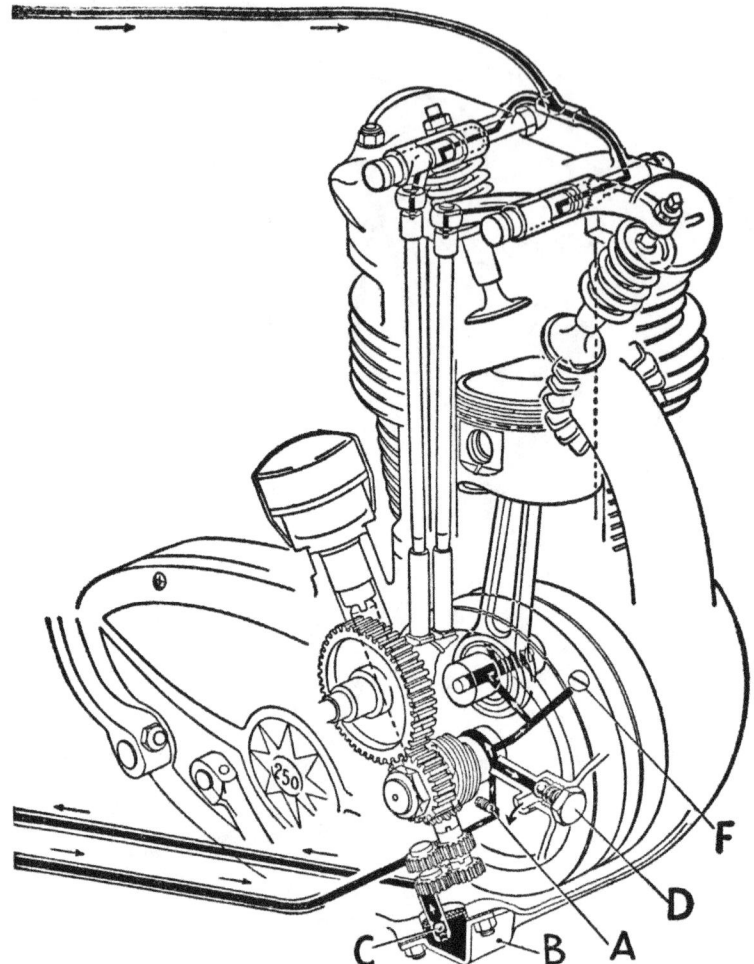

Lubrication System C15.

The valve (A) prevents oil transfer from the tank to the crankcase while the machine is standing, and together with the sludge trap (F), does not require attention until such time as the engine is completely dismantled.

A by-pass valve (D) ensures a constant pressure in the system. Surplus quantities of oil are discharged into the crankcase.

If the ball valve (C) should be stuck in its seating there will be no return of oil to the tank. In this event remove the cover plate (B) below the pump, insert a piece of wire into the valve orifice and lift the ball off its seating to free it.

B.S.A. Service Sheet No. 603 (contd.)

THE CRANKCASE BREATHER VALVE

The crankcase air release valve is of similar construction on all models although its position in the crankcase is dependant on the model and the year of manufacture.

On all "C" Group models the breather is situated on the left-hand side of the crankcase behind the primary chaincase. 1946 and 1947 "B" and "M" machines have the breather positioned at the rear of the drive-side bearing boss. Later "B" and "M" Group models have the breather positioned in the lower edge of the timing chest cover.

In each case its purpose is to allow free release of air from the crankcase as the piston descends, and to prevent air being drawn back into the crankcase as the piston ascends. A crankcase breather valve which is faulty, or partially blocked, will result in oil leakage from the engine.

Before the breather valve can be withdrawn the air release pipe must be removed by unscrewing the union nut. The complete breather valve can then be unscrewed from the crankcase. To dismantle the breather, undo the large hexagon on the outer end of the valve, the valve retaining collar can then be unscrewed with the aid of a large screwdriver thus allowing the fibre disc valve to fall free. Before reassembling, wash the components thoroughly in petrol to free them from any oil residue that may cause the valve to stick.

Before replacing the breather valve on "C" Group models the movement of the disc valve should be checked to ensure that it does not exceed .010 in. If excessive clearance is found and the disc valve is undamaged the face of the retaining collar should be ground so as to reduce the depth of the recess in which the disc valve lies. Take care not to grind too much away so that the disc valve has no clearance.

If the breather valve is fitted into the timing case cover, ensure that it is positioned so that the hole drilled in the side of the pipe inside the cover is facing towards the cover and slightly towards the rear. Failure to observe this precaution may result in excessive oil loss. Correct positioning of the hole may be effected by varying the thickness of the fibre washer fitted between the air release valve and the timing case cover.

MODELS C10L AND C11G

Instead of the pressure operated clack valve, a mechanically timed breather is employed. This takes the form of a hollow drive-side engine mainshaft with a radial drilling which, at the appropriate piston position, is brought in line with a drilled port in the crankcase thus allowing the gases to exhaust freely to the atmosphere. The engine sprocket distance sleeve, which fits over the portion of the mainshaft with the radial drilling, has six transfer ports so that it is immeterial which of the six spline-grooves locates the internal peg of the sleeve.

This type of breather is completely automatic and requires no adjustment or other maintenance whatsoever.

B.S.A. Service Sheet No. 603 (contd.)

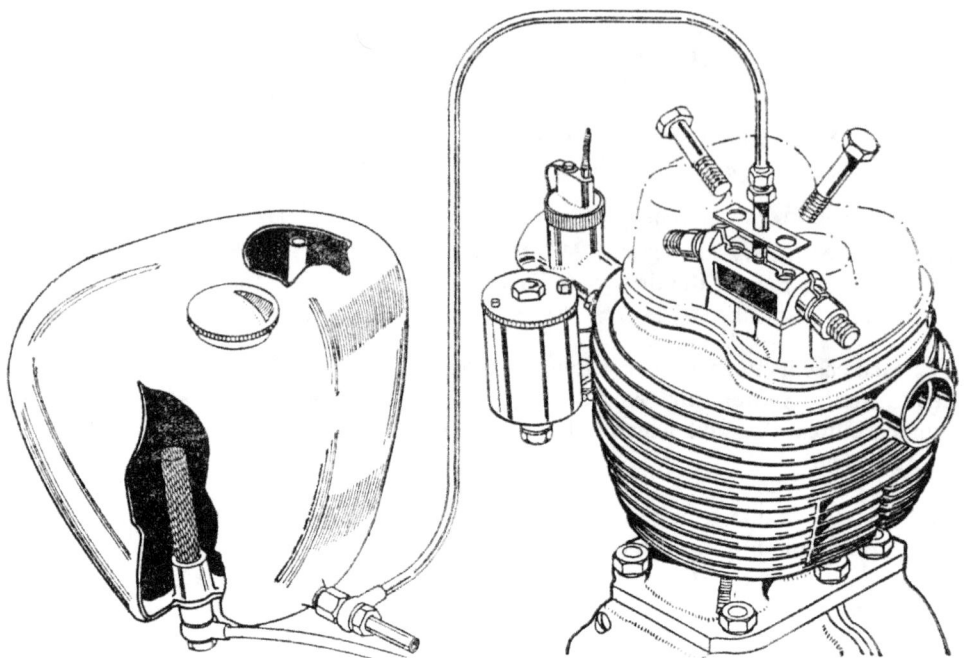

Rocker Gear Lubrication C12 (1956).

Parts required for conversion of C11 and C11G engines:—

Part No.	Description
29–2086	Rocker Oil Feed Pipe.
29–2091	Rocker Trunnion.
29–2092	Bolt.
45–2454	Locking Plate.
65–8420	Connection.
65–8421	Washer.
65–8424	Nut.

MODEL C12, 1956

The model C12 engine is identical with the C11G model. However, the lubrication system has been modified to provide positive lubrication to the valve rocker gear. The take off is from the oil tank return pipe, as on the "B" Group plunger models and the oil is fed through a rocker feed pipe to the rocker cover securing bolt which is drilled to allow the oil to pass to the trunnion. This trunnion incorporates oil grooves direct to each rocker fulcrum. After lubricating, the oil drains to the sump down the push rod tunnel, providing extra lubrication for the cams and cam followers in the process.

This modification can be adopted on the C11 and C11G engines at very low cost. The parts required are listed above, and they can be obtained through your dealer.

B.S.A. Service Sheet No. 603 (contd.)

After lubricating the big-end and circulating throughout the engine in the form of oil mist, the oil drains down, through a filter to the bottom of the crankcase from which it is drawn by the return pump past ball valve (C) and delivered up the return pipe to the tank.

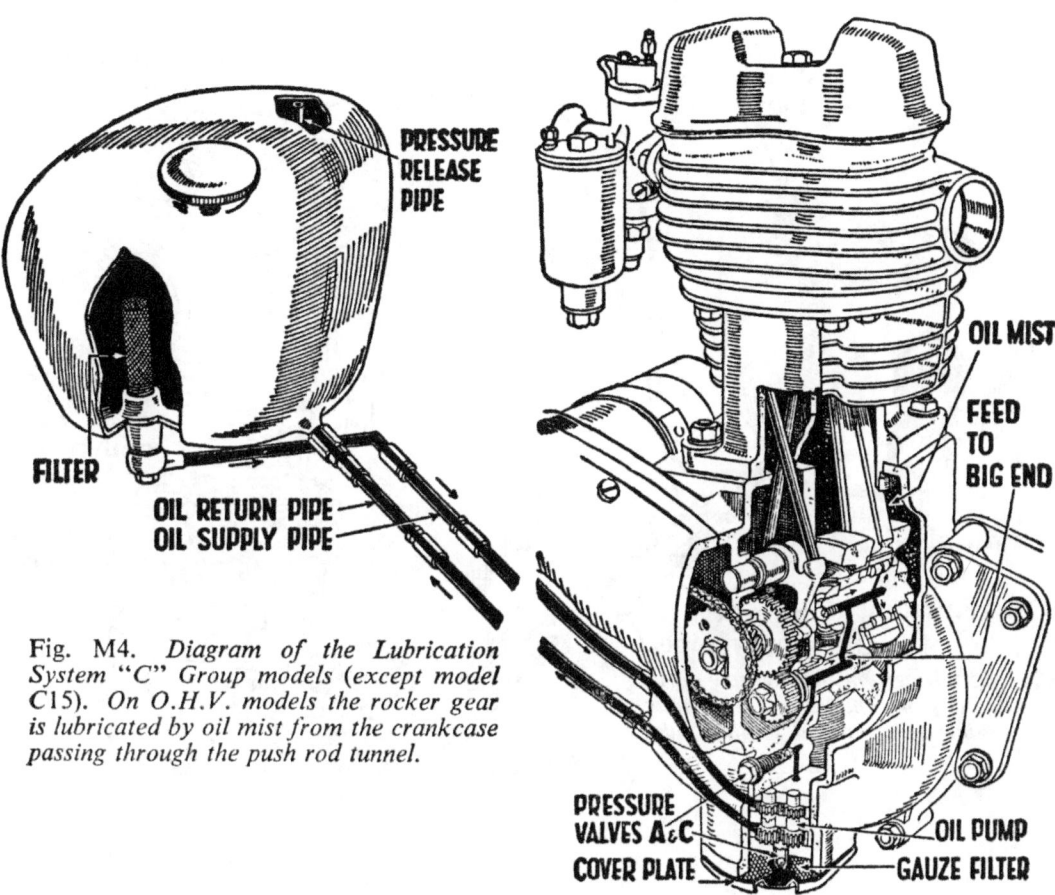

Fig. M4. *Diagram of the Lubrication System "C" Group models (except model C15). On O.H.V. models the rocker gear is lubricated by oil mist from the crankcase passing through the push rod tunnel.*

On "B" Group machines oil is fed through a union situated in the pipe between the return pump and the tank, to the rocker spindles, and after lubricating the rockers and enclosed valves, is returned to the crankcase through an external oil pipe attached to the base of the inlet valve spring housing (see Fig. M5). An internal oilway connects the two valve spring wells.

Incorrect seating of the ball valve (A) will allow oil to transfer from the tank to the engine, whilst the machine is stationary. In this event, unscrew the plug over the valve, and remove spring and ball. Clean the ball and its seating and replace. If the ball valve (C) should get stuck in its seating, there will be no return of oil to the tank. To correct, remove the cover plate below the pump and insert a piece of wire into the valve orifice, and lift the ball off its seating to free it. To check the flow of oil in the lubricating system, remove the tank filler cap whilst the engine is running. Oil should be seen issuing from the return pipe from the crankcase. The tank and crankcase should be drained periodically, and replenished with clean oil (see "Periodical Maintenance").

B.S.A. Service Sheet No. 603 (contd.)

Any restriction in the pressure release pipe in the tank will cause an increase in pressure inside the oil tank, and will result in leakage of oil at the filler cap. This can be put right by inserting a length of flexible wire into the pipe at its lower end (just in front of the rear mudguard) and pushing the wire right up the pipe, thus clearing obstruction.

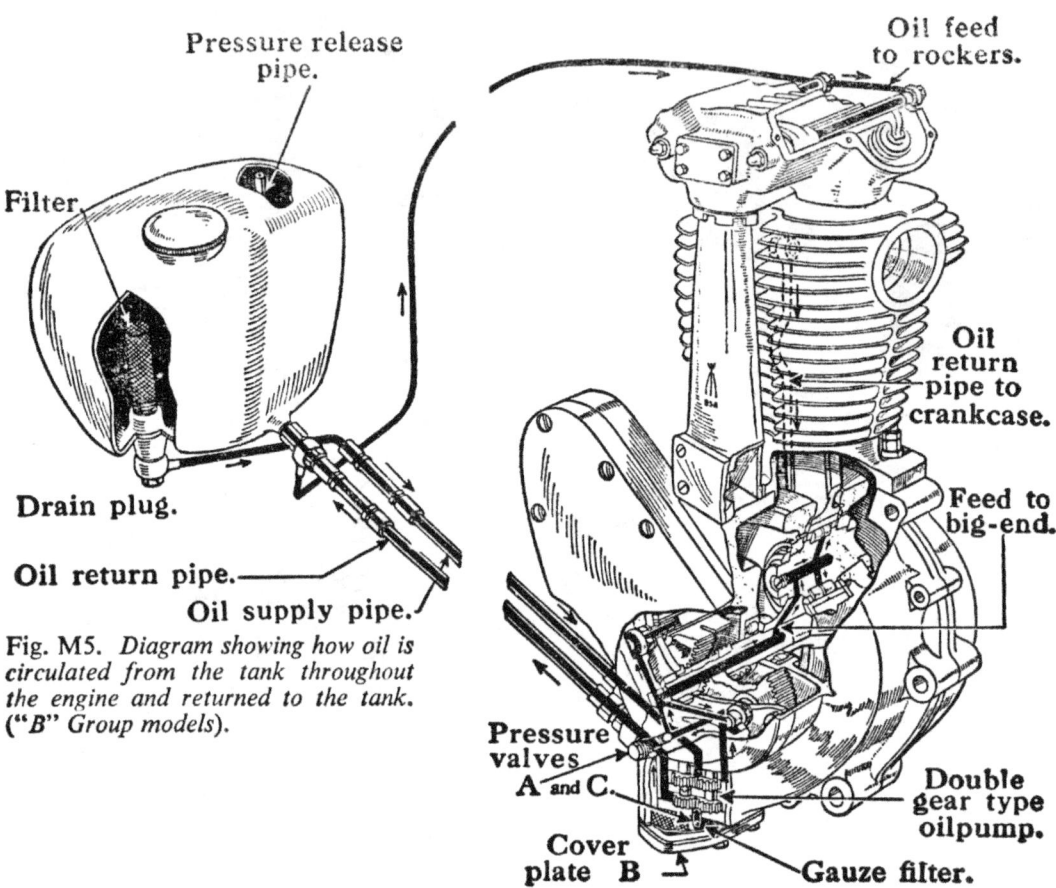

Fig. M5. *Diagram showing how oil is circulated from the tank throughout the engine and returned to the tank. ("B" Group models).*

To remove the "B" and "C" Group oil tank filter for cleaning, remove the oil pipe banjo union plug at the bottom of the tank. The filter will come out with the plug.

On models with the swinging arm type frame the oil tank is of slightly different construction but the system is the same. The oil tank filter is attached to the large hexagon nut in the outside of the tank and its removal does not entail interfering with the oil pipes.

To remove the "M" Group filter for cleaning, release the tank filler cap, release the filter cap thus exposed, and lift the filter out. In all cases the filter should be placed in a can big enough to cover it with petrol, and thoroughly washed. Before replacing make sure that it is quite dry of petrol.

The pump filter can be withdrawn after removing the cover plate (B) and should be thoroughly washed with petrol, dried and replaced.

On no account try to remove the oil pump unless it requires attention (see Service Sheet on complete "Dismantling of Engine").

B.S.A. Service Sheet No. 603 (contd.)

Crankcase Breather C15

The breather is mechanically timed as on the C10L and C11G models but takes the form of a hollow camshaft with a radial drilling which, at the appropriate piston position, is brought in line with a drilled port in the inner timing cover, this port has its outlet inside the outer timing cover. Pressure is then released through a small radial cut-away at the rear end of the outer cover joint face.

Changing the Oil C15

This should preferably be done immediately after running, so that the oil is warm and will, therefore, flow more freely. Disconnect the oil pipe union nut (A), at the base of the tank and collect the old oil in a suitable receptacle.

Filters

Remove the oil tank and crankcase filters for cleaning at regular intervals, this can be carried out in conjunction with the change of oil. After releasing the oil pipe at (A), unscrew the hexagon plug (B), which carries the filter in the tank, and wash thoroughly in petrol. Make sure that all the petrol has evaporated before replacing. Refill with the correct grade of oil.

The pump filter can be withdrawn after removing the crankcase cover plate and should be thoroughly washed with petrol, dried and replaced. The oil pump is extremely reliable and it is most unlikely that it will give trouble therefore it should not be disturbed unnecessarily. The pump is held in position by three bolts. The two other bolts hold the sections of the pump together.

B.S.A. MOTOR CYCLES LTD., Service Department, Armoury Road, Birmingham 11.
B.S.A. Press

BSA SERVICE SHEET No. 604

Reprinted October, 1966

"B" AND "M" GROUP MODELS
ENGINE ADJUSTMENTS
(which can be carried out without dismantling)

Oil Pressure Valves

There are two ball valves in the system, and both are placed between the tank and the sump to prevent the transfer of oil when the engine is not running. The spring loaded ball valve as illustrated in Fig. M6 is situated in the timing cover, and permits a supply of oil under pressure to the big-end.

In the event of dirt or foreign matter lodging between the ball and its seating oil will slowly drain from the tank and into the sump when the engine is stationary, and on starting smoke will issue from the exhaust, but will clear after the engine has been running for some time. To rectify this dismantle the pressure valve by unscrewing the hexagon-headed nut in the base of the timing cover, withdraw the spring and bolt, and carefully clean the ball and its seating. Finally replace the ball and give it a sharp tap with a hammer and copper drift to ensure a correct seating, and replace the spring, fibre washer and nut.

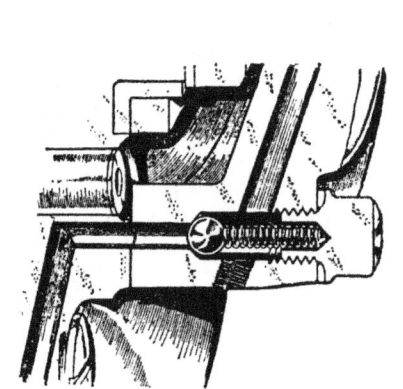

Fig. M.6. Pressure valve in timing cover.

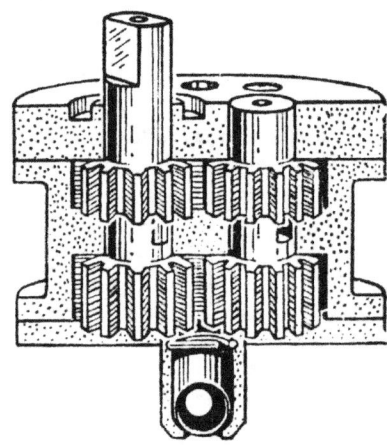

Fig. M.7. Ball valve below return pump.

The other valve is situated in the base of the oil pump (see Fig. M7) and consists of a ball bearing held on to its seat by gravity. Failure of the oil to return may be due to this ball sticking on its seat. This can be overcome by inserting a short length of wire into the valve orifice, and forcing the ball off its seating. It is not advisable to remove the pump from the crankcase unless such a procedure is absolutely essential, for unless the pump seating is oiltight, oil will transfer from the tank via the pump housing.

Exhaust Valve Lifter

At all times keep the actuating cam on the lifter clear of the rocker arm on "B" Group and M33 machines (Fig. M8) or the tappet head on M20 and M21 machines; otherwise the tappet clearances will be affected and the valve gear will be noisy. Failure to check this clearance may result in a burned exhaust valve. Adjustment is usually carried out by means of the cable adjuster, but the actuating arm can be removed and reset at any position on the serrated shaft.

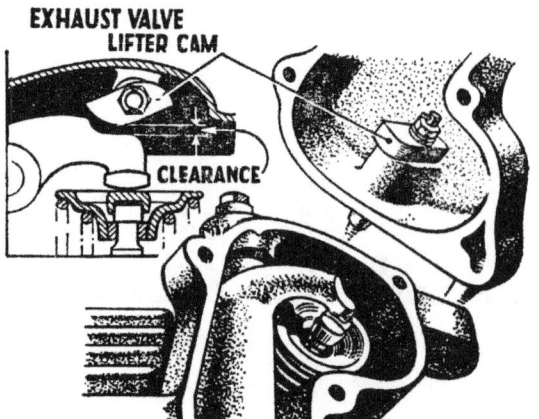

Fig. M.8. Exhaust valve lifter adjustment.

B.S.A. Service Sheet No. 604 (contd).

Tappet Adjustment
Before any attempt is made to check the tappets ensure that the exhaust lifter is adjusted in accordance with the previous instructions. Owing to the special cam design it is essential that the following directions be adhered to.

1. Rotate engine until the **inlet** valve has just closed.
2. Adjust **exhaust** tappet.
3. Turn engine until **exhaust** valve has just taken up tappet clearance, but has not started to open valve.
4. Adjust **inlet** tappet.

Obviate the possibility of an incorrect tappet clearance on O.H.V. models by lifting the push rod with the fingers before inserting feelers, or the weight of the push rod may prevent feelers being correctly inserted.

The actual adjustment is carried out by releasing the locknut (B) Fig. M9, holding the tappet with a spanner and screwing the tappet head (A) up or down. When the correct clearance is obtained tighten the locknut on to the head of the tappet and re-check clearance.

NOTE:—Correct tappet clearances are as follows:—
Models B31, B32, B33, B34, M33—
  inlet .003; exhaust .003.
Models M20, M21—
  inlet .010; exhaust .012.

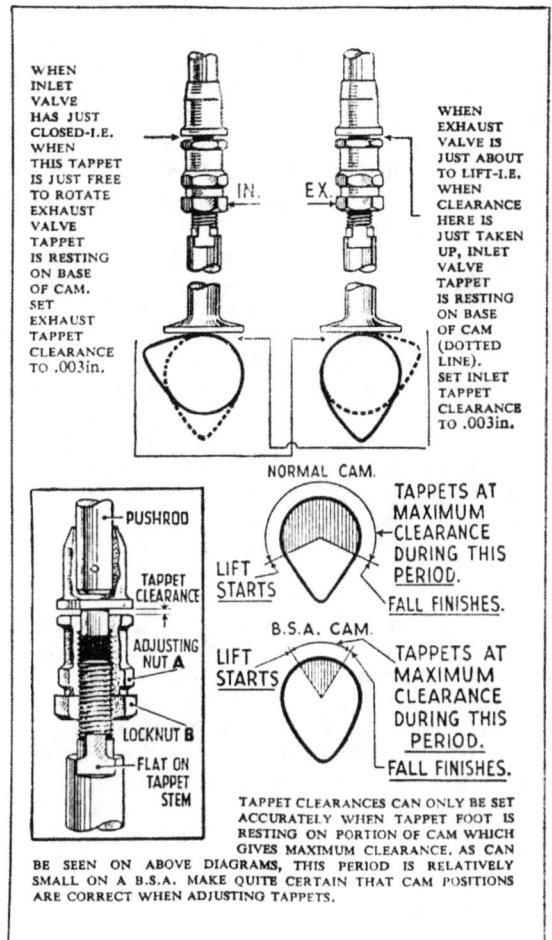

Fig. M.9.

Ignition Timing (except models with engine prefix letters G.B.)
It is a rare occurence for the magneto pinion to slacken off and upset the timing, and it is inadvisable to disturb the setting unless absolutely necessary, or unless the timing is known to be at fault.

It is advisable however, to check the timing periodically, or after carrying out any adjustment to the contact breaker points, as a slight variation tends to advance or retard the engine. If the timing requires resetting first check that the fully open gap is .010—.012 in., then remove the timing cover and in so doing take care to see that the small nozzle which feeds oil to the hollow crankshaft is not damaged; if it should be re-fitted in a bent condition, it will foul the mainshaft, and break off eventually, thus starving the big-end and piston of oil.

With the cover removed, take off the locknut which holds the magneto pinion on to its taper, and with the aid of a magneto pinion extractor, withdraw the pinion. (The pinion is fixed on its shaft by a plain taper.)

To reset the timing, turn the engine forward until the piston is at the top of the compression stroke, and then turn the engine **backwards** until the piston has descended $\frac{7}{16}$ in. Turn the contact

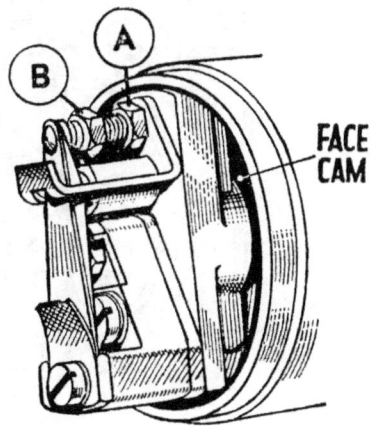

Fig. M.10.

B.S.A. Service Sheet No. 604 (contd.)

breaker in the direction of rotation until the points are just open (.002 in.) with the ignition lever fully advanced. Tap the magneto pinion lightly on to its taper, tighten up the nut carefully, and when dead tight re-check the setting.

N.B.—It is essential that the ignition setting as laid down here be adhered to or high running temperatures and the possibility of a seizure will be present.

To adjust the contact breaker gap, release the locknut (A) Fig. M10, and adjust the gap to .012 in. maximum by rotating the small bolt (B) in the desired direction.

"B" Models with Engine Prefix Letters G.B.

Ignition Timing

It is unlikely that the ignition timing will alter, but if, for any reason, it is found necessary to check or reset the ignition timing it is advisable first to check the contact breaker points and if necessary, re-adjust as described under the next heading.

To check the timing, remove the sparking plug and the contact breaker cover. Insert a slim rod through the sparking plug hole to feel the top of the piston, then rotate the engine until the piston is at top dead centre on the compression stroke (i.e. with both valves closed). Keep the rod as vertical as possible and mark top dead centre position on it. The best way of rotating the engine is to engage top gear and turn the rear wheel.

Turn the engine backwards through about 45° then bring it forward again until the contact breaker points are just on the point of opening. When the cam is moved to the fully advanced position as shown in the unit (Fig. M10A) the position of the points is best determined by inserting a piece of fine paper, (such as cigarette paper) between the points. The points are just about to open when the paper is only lightly gripped and can be withdrawn with a gentle pull.

The piston should then be $\frac{7}{16}$ in. before top dead centre for model B31, and $\frac{3}{8}$ in. for model B33, as measured by the rod through the plug hole.

If the timing is slightly out it can be set by slackening bolt (A) Fig. M10A, and rotating the contact breaker a degree or two either way as required until the points are in position as described above. Then retighten bolt (A).

To retime the ignition if this becomes necessary remove the contact breaker complete with housing by taking out the three top timing cover screws (i.e. the one at the top of the timing cover, and the one on each side of it). These are longer than the other timing cover screws, which need not be disturbed, and are provided with nuts (B) at the back. When they are taken out the contact breaker with housing can be drawn out as a complete unit together with its driving pinion still in position. Disconnect the low-tension cable (C) from its terminal.

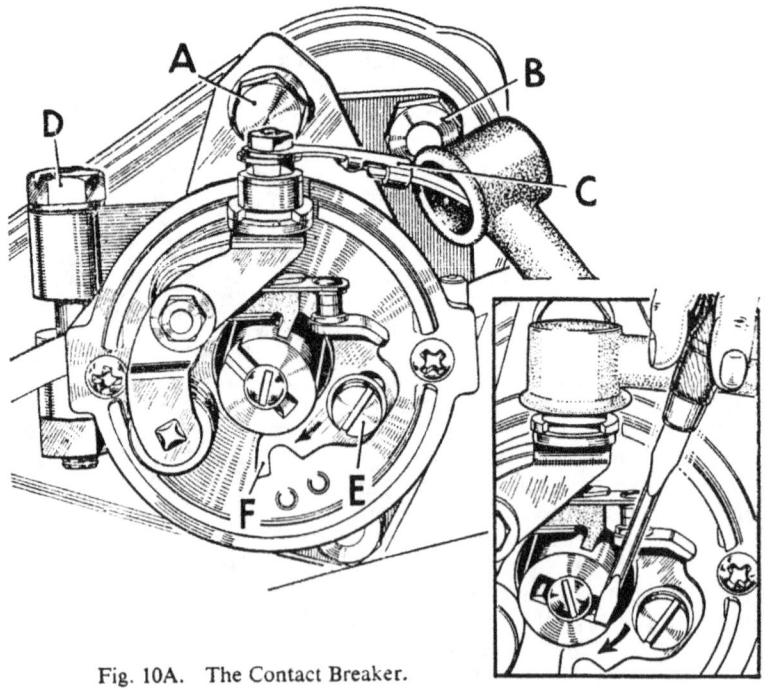

Fig. 10A. The Contact Breaker.

B.S.A. Service Sheet No. 604 (contd.)

Rotate the engine until the piston is in the correct position as described above (i.e. $\frac{7}{16}$ in. for B31 and $\frac{3}{8}$ in. for B33 before top dead centre at the end of the compression stroke). Now take the contact breaker unit, remove the cap, and turn the driving pinion until the points are just on the point of opening with the cam held in the fully advanced position as already described for checking the timing. Release the cam and hold the unit in such a position that the nut (A) and terminal (C) are vertical. (These two should be in line. If they are not, then slacken pinch bolt (D) and turn the housing until (A) comes into line with (C). Then retighten pinch bolt 'D').

Holding the unit in this position, gently insert it into its register at the back of the timing cover. If it will not go right home withdraw it and turn the pinion the least fraction of a tooth to enable it to mesh with the idler pinion which drives it and re-insert. When it is fully home refit the three screws, and check the timing, making any necessary adjustment at bolt (A).

To adjust the Contact Breaker Points

Turn the engine until the points are fully open and check with a set of feeler gauges. The correct gap is .012—.015 in. If incorrect slacken screw (E) and move plate (F) gently with a screwdriver until the correct gap is obtained. Then tighten screw (E) and re-check the gap.

Carburettor (all models)

To maintain the efficiency of the carburettor it is necessary to dismantle it periodically and wash thoroughly in clean petrol.

Renew any worn parts, particularly the needle valve if the head has a distinct ridge at the point of seating, the throttle valve if excessive side play is present, and the taper needle and clip if it is possible to rotate the needle freely in the clip.

For further attention to the carburettor and for tuning details see Service Sheet No. 708.

Sparking Plugs (all models)

The machine is supplied with Champion non-detachable type sparking plugs to suit the characteristics of the engine. If the best performance with regard to both power and economy is to be obtained then they must remain clean and properly gapped.

The sparking plugs should be removed periodically for examination. If the carburation is correct and the engine is in good condition the plugs will remain clean for considerable periods. An over-rich mixture will however cause the formation of a sooty deposit on the plug points and eventually on the plug body (see upper view of Fig. A6). Heavily leaded fuels may form a greyish

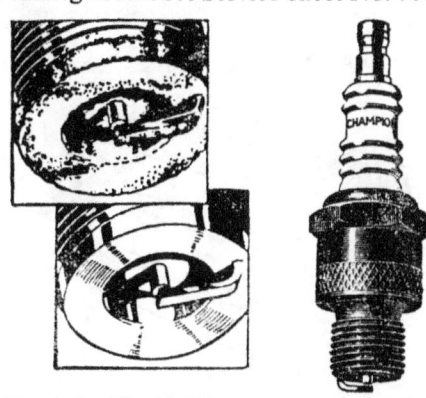

Fig. A.6. The Sparking Plug.

deposit in a similar manner. If a heavy deposit is found, the plug should be cleaned, with the aid of the sand blast type of plug cleaner found at most garages, as otherwise the performance of the machine may be affected. If a heavy deposit is allowed to build up inside the plug it may prevent the engine from firing altogether. A weak mixture will cause burning of the plug points and give the plug a whitish appearance (see Service Sheet No. 708).

Check that the gap between the sparking plug points is correct and if necessary reset to .018—.020 in. (.45—.50 mm.) by bending the side wire. In no circumstances attempt to move the central electrode as this may damage the insulation. If the points are badly burnt away or cleaning fails to restore the plug to its full efficiency then it should be replaced by a new one.

When replacing the plug make sure that the copper washer is in good condition. Use a tubular spanner to prevent damage to the plug and keep the outside of the insulation free from oil and dirt by wiping with a clean rag.

B.S.A. MOTOR CYCLES LTD., Service Department, Armoury Road, Birmingham 11.

B.S.A. PRESS

BSA SERVICE SHEET 608
"B" and "M" Group Models

October, 1948.

Reprinted August, 1965

REMOVING, DISMANTLING & REASSEMBLY OF THE GEARBOX & GEARCHANGE

The illustrations on this Service Sheet show the gearbox fitted to all "M" group models up to engine number ZM-101.

The gearbox fitted to "M" group models after this engine number and to "B" group models after engine number ZB-101 is identical except that a speedometer drive is taken from the layshaft, through a mechanism fitted to the outer cover, and the clutch operating mechanism is fully enclosed.

All instructions given for removal, dismantling and re-assembly will apply, but the speedometer drive must be removed before the inner cover is dismantled and replaced after it is assembled. Detailed instructions for removal and re-assembly are given below.

Removal.

Instructions as to the procedure to be adopted for removal of the chaincase and clutch are contained in Service Sheet No. 610 in the case of "M" group machines or Service Sheet No. 304 in the case of "B" group machines. In this case, however, there

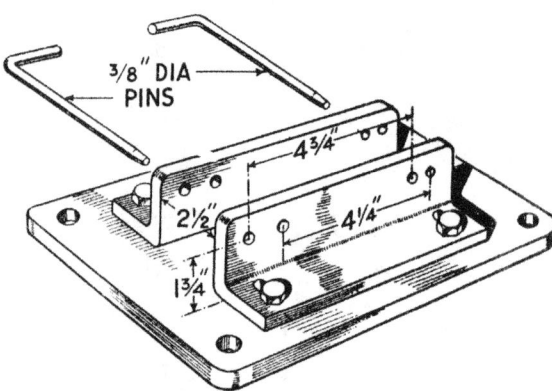

Fig. M26. Gearbox fixture.

is no need to dismantle the clutch entirely; it is only necessary to take off the cover plate (if fitted) and thrust plate when the clutch may be withdrawn from its shaft as a complete unit. Before that is done, i.e., with chain and clutch still in position, it is advisable to engage a gear, and get an assistant to apply the rear brake, so that the engine shaft cush drive ring nut may be unscrewed, thus releasing the cush drive assembly. Uncouple the primary chain and remove the clutch using the extractor shown in Fig. M36.

The inner half of the chaincase can now be taken off. Note that in addition to the three bolts holding it to the crankcase, there is a nut attaching the rear chainguard to the chaincase and this must also be removed. Access to the nut will be made much easier if the three crankcase bolts are unscrewed first and the chaincase pulled off the crankcase register.

The oil tank breather pipe is next to be removed and this is only a matter of releasing the clip bolts.

Turning now to the right-hand side of the machine, first take off the footrest, then uncouple the clutch cable from its operating arm and unscrew the cable adjuster from the gearbox.

In order that the bolts which hold the gearbox to the yoke plates may be removed it is necessary to take off the exhaust pipe and silencer.

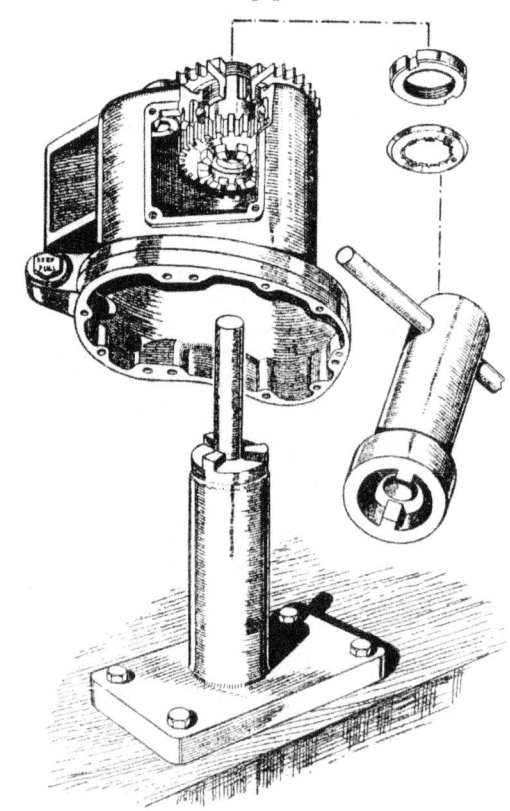

Fig. M27. Pinion sleeve removal tool 61-3064.

B.S.A. Service Sheet No. 608 (contd.)

The box itself can be prised upwards out of the yoke plates. If the latter grip the gearbox lugs too tightly for this to be carried out easily, slacken the bolts and studs which clamp the yoke plates to the crankcase. No difficulty should then be experienced in removing the gearbox.

Dismantling the Gearbox.

It will greatly help work on the gearbox if it is held in a simple fixture such as that illustrated in Fig. M26. The device can be made from suitable pieces of angle iron, spaced to suit the gearbox lugs. If it is not possible to make the fixture, gearbox can be held in a vice.

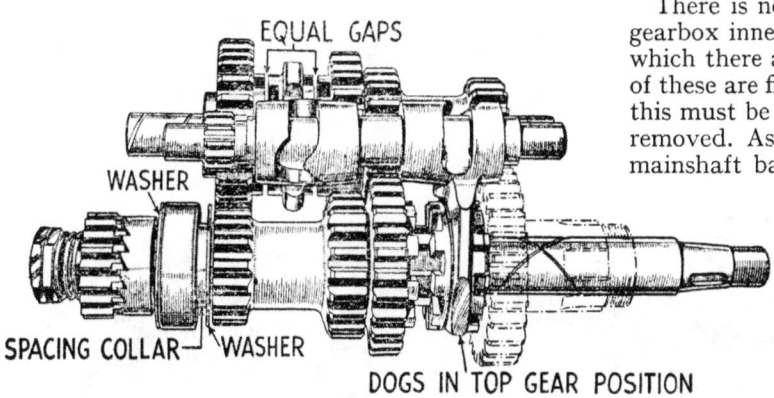

Fig. M28. Gear train.

Commence dismantling by taking off the rectangular inspection cover and follow this with kickstarter crank. The latter is fixed by means of a cycle type cotter. The foot change pedal is held in position by means of a pinch bolt which must be slackened off before the pedal can be removed.

On models before engine number ZM-101, there are two circlips behind this pedal. The larger circlip retains the gear indicator disc in position, and the circlip and disc should be removed. No indicator disc is fitted to later models. Leave the small circlip in position for the time being.

The gearbox outer cover is now ready for removal. On earlier models it is held on by seven cheese-head screws, and, on the face behind the gear change mechanism, by three bolts and one nut. On later models seven cheese-head screws and four nuts, all on the outer cover hold it in position. When the outer cover is taken off it will contain the kickstarter quadrant and spring, but these need not be disturbed unless obviously requiring attention.

Next, remove the pin from the link rod between the selector quadrant and the gearchange mechanism at the latter end and unscrew the nut off the rear of the gearchange spindle. The gearchange mechanism can now be taken out as a complete unit, and dismantled later. Take care not to lose the small plunger and spring exposed by the removal of the previous parts.

The ratchet mechanism on the mainshaft must be dismantled next. First unscrew the locknut, straighten the tag washer, and remove it. By unscrewing the next nut, all the remaining parts of the ratchet mechanism will be free and can be taken off.

Removing the Speedometer Drive.

Slack off the large nut on the drive and give the end of the drive a tap with a hide mallet. Remove the locating screw.

The large nut can now be used to withdraw the drive, distance pieces being built up behind the nut until the drive is fully withdrawn.

When replacing, after fitting the locating screw, fully tighten the large nut. Do not omit the fibre washer behind the nut or oil leaks may result.

There is now no obstacle to the removal of the gearbox inner cover except for its fixing screws of which there are four (three on later models). Two of these are fixed by a locking strip and the ends of this must be straightened before the screws can be removed. As the cover comes off, it will contain the mainshaft ballrace, and leave exposed loosely on the mainshaft an oil flinger (thin) and spacing collar (thick). Also assembled on the inner cover is the gear selector quadrant, but here again this need not be disturbed unless attention is obviously required. If it has to be removed, take care not to lose the plunger and spring and make sure they are refitted when assembling.

If, when the inner cover is withdrawn, the three shafts (main, lay and selector) also come out still assembled in the cover, they may be quite easily detached, as they are a running fit in their bushes. In the same way if the shafts are still in the box, after removing the gearbox cover, they can be withdrawn with similar ease by removing all the shafts together. The layshaft bushes are, of course, a press fit in the gearbox and, if necessary, must be driven out with the aid of a soft punch (15/16 in. diameter).

Fig. M29. Selector quadrant.

The top gear pinion sleeve is now the only part still left in the gearbox, and if the sprocket locknut is unscrewed, after suitable attention to the tag washer, the sprocket may be removed and the pinion tapped into the gearbox with the aid of a wooden mallet. If difficulty is experienced in holding the pinion whilst the sprocket is unscrewed, a fixture similar to that in Fig. M27 will solve the problem.

B.S.A. Service Sheet No. 608 (contd.)

Do not disturb the ballrace unless it is suspected of being faulty. Wash it thoroughly in paraffin, to remove all traces of oil, when any play will be immediately detected.

Examine the various parts for wear and if the forks which actuate the sliding dogs show signs of seizure it is advisable to replace them. Attempts to erase the seizure marks will result in excessive side play. Replacement sliding dogs may be found to have convex faces on the dogs but this will not affect interchangeability, if the originals had flat faces.

Loose pinions on the lay and mainshafts may be rebushed if required, and of course, pinions with damaged teeth should also be replaced.

Fixed pinions on the layshaft and mainshaft are pressed on and new components must be a tight fit.

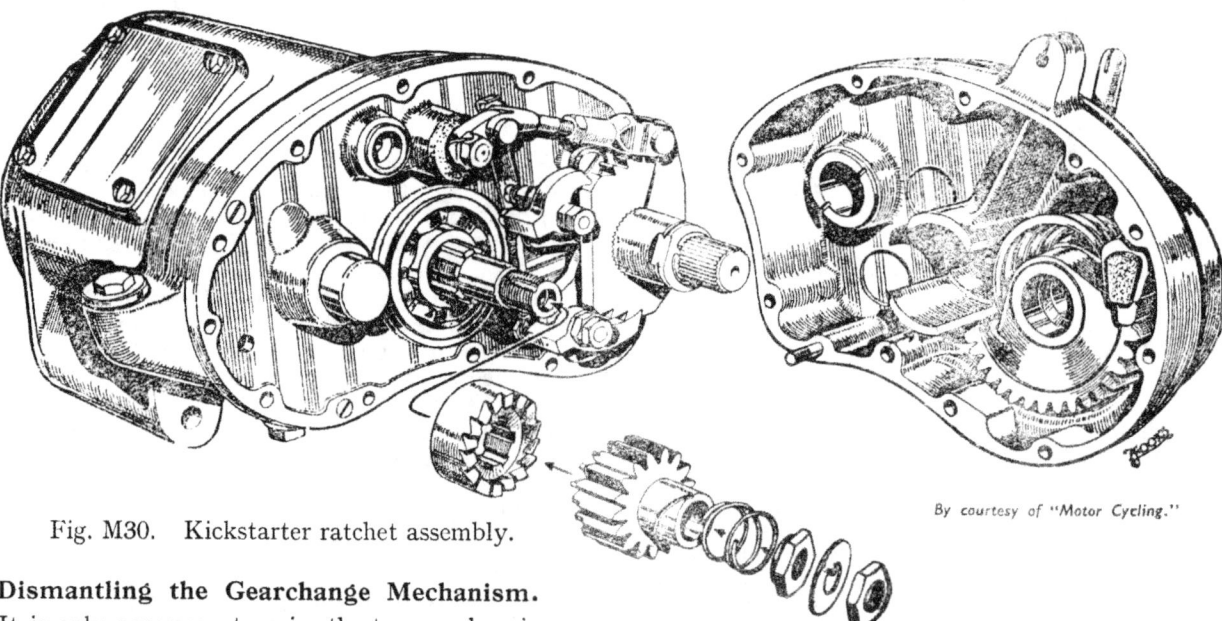

Fig. M30. Kickstarter ratchet assembly.

Dismantling the Gearchange Mechanism.

It is only necessary to prise the two pawl springs off their pegs, and to remove the circlip, when the whole unit can be stripped into separate components. The only parts which are likely to show signs of excessive wear are the pawls and the ratchet plate, and new components should be fitted if required. If the pawl springs show signs of stretching, they too, should be replaced.

Reassembly of the Gearbox and Gearchange Mechanism.

If it has been decided to fit a new ballrace to the top gear pinion, make sure that the oil flinger washers are correctly positioned. In order to remove the ballrace easily, warm the gearbox in boiling water. The flat washer should be placed between the pinion teeth and the bearing while the remaining washer fits on the opposite side of the bearing with its depressed face against the bearing. If the sprocket teeth are worn hook-shaped a new one must be fitted, otherwise rapid chain wear will result.

Do not forget to set the lockwasher into the grooves machined in the locknut after the latter has been tightened up. The tabs in the centre of the locknut washer must fit properly into the sprocket splines.

It is only possible to refit the shafts and their pinions in the box provided that the shafts are first assembled (with pinions in top gear position) outside the gearbox and then all fitted together.

Commencing with the layshaft, take off the low gear pinion only (this is the largest on the shaft) and hold the shaft in the left hand with the drilled end towards the wrist. Take up the selector shaft and fit the fork nearest to the small pinion into the dog clutch on the layshaft. Pick up the mainshaft, which should be complete with its dog clutch, and put it in position so that the second selector fork engages with the mainshaft dog clutch. The whole assembly can now be fitted into the gearbox, the mainshaft being the first to enter its bearing. Verify again through the inspection cover that the pinions are set in the top gear position (see Fig. M28). In this position the dog clutch on the mainshaft is in mesh with the pinion sleeve.

Replace the low gear pinion on the layshaft and if all has been assembled correctly, the face of this pinion should be just flush with its mating pinion on the mainshaft. The oil flinger washer and spacing collar can now be refitted to the mainshaft (see Fig. M28).

The inner cover is next to be assembled. Set the selector quadrant in the top gear position (see Fig. M29) and replace the cover. The paper washer between the inner cover and the gearbox shell should be smeared with jointing compound before final assembly. If the cover will not fit properly at the

B.S.A. Service Sheet No. 608 (contd.)

first attempt, a **slight** movement of the selector, by means of a spanner, will cause the selector teeth to mesh properly with the selector shaft pinion and then the cover may be pressed home. Replace the four screws and locking strip, bending the corners of the latter to suit. All shafts should have the minimum of end play, and engagement of dogs should be checked in each gear.

The ratchet mechanism may now be refitted to the mainshaft, the parts assembling in the following order: ratchet, bush, ratchet pinion, spring and shouldered nut. The latter should be tightened by finger pressure only. Replace the lockwasher and note that the tongue in this washer engages with the groove machined in the mainshaft. Screw up the locknut very tightly, and tap the edge of the washer over the nut.

Reassembly of the Gearchange.

The ratchet sleeve plate (i.e., the plate in which there are a series of teeth) should be held in the left hand with the shortest diameter of the sleeve uppermost (see Fig. M31). One of the pawl carrier plates will be seen to have thin washers welded on to both faces, and this plate should now be super-imposed upon the ratchet plate so that the pawl fits into one of the teeth adjacent to the link pin hole. Place the remaining pawl carrier on top of the original one so that its pawl engages with the second set of teeth on the ratchet plate.

Still holding the gearchange assembly in the left hand, take up the gearchange spindle in the right hand, holding it by the threaded end and fit it into the ratchet sleeve so that the plate fixed to the spindle lies between the spring anchor pegs. With the aid of a pair of pliers, replace the two springs and then fit the circlip in position. The whole process of reassembly of the gearchange mechanism will be made much easier by a study of the illustration (Fig. M31).

The unit is now ready for reassembly into the gearbox. Make sure that the spring loaded plunger is in position behind the unit before it is replaced. Couple the link arm to the ratchet plate and take care to replace the split pin. It should not be necessary to make any adjustment to the length of the link itself; this has been set when the gearbox was originally built, but if the gears will not engage properly a slight adjustment to the length of the link will be sufficient.

Before the reassembly is carried a stage further, loosely replace the gearchange pedal **and check the operation of all gears by inspection through the cover.** It will, of course, be necessary to move the gearbox sprocket by hand when endeavouring to engage the gears.

When all is found to be correct, set gears in top gear position again, and remove the gearchange pedal. The clutch push rod is next to be replaced, and with this in position the small felt washer must be added. This washer is important since its function is to prevent any possibility of oil passing along the hollow mainshaft, to the clutch plates.

Finally, put back the gearbox cover, carefully tighten all screws, and replace the kickstarter crank and gearchange pedal. As the gearbox is still set in the top gear position when the indicator disc (if fitted) is replaced this also should be set to top gear.

Replacement of the Gearbox.

The replacement of the gearbox should not present any difficulties. When the box is in position and the fixing bolts are about to be tightened up, make sure that the flats just below the bolt heads register properly in the slots machined in the yoke plates.

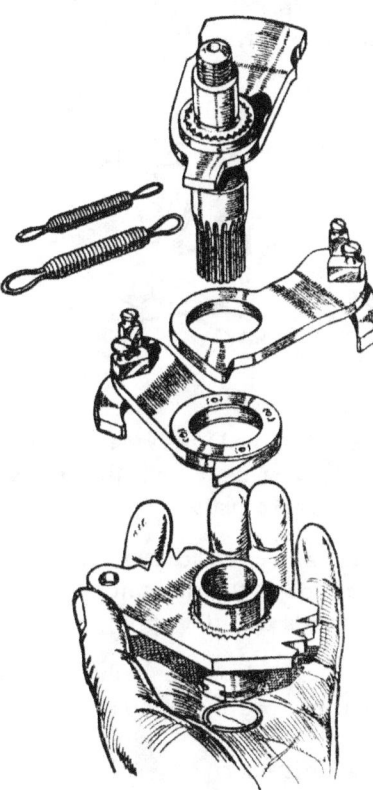

Fig. M31. Gearchange mechanism.

Also, on the rear bolt, an adjuster is provided for tensioning the primary chain; this must be in position and the chain tension adjusted before the gearbox bolts are finally tightened. The latter must be really tight after the adjustment is made. There should be about ½-in. total play in chain (see "Front Chain," Service Sheet No. 609).*

Replace the oil tank pressure release pipe together with the clutch cable and its adjuster.

The inner half of the primary chaincase may now be fitted, followed by the cush drive, chain and clutch, together with its pressure plate and cover. Finally refit the outer half of the chaincase and then the footrest.

The refitting of the clutch and primary chaincase is described in "Reassembly of the Clutch" in Service Sheet No. 610.* The clutch adjustment may require setting and this should be carried out in accordance with the instructions given in Service Sheet No. 609.* It is also possible that the rear chain will require re-tensioning and this may be done by movement of the rear wheel (Service Sheet No. 609).*

B.S.A. MOTOR CYCLES LTD., Service Dept., Armoury Road, Birmingham 11.

Printed in England.

* NOTE REGARDING 'B' GROUP MODELS:
Service Sheets No's 609 and 610 referenced in the above text are appropriate for "M" group machines. For "B" group models Service Sheets No's 310, 314 and/or 308, 315 should be substituted (as appropriate).

BSA SERVICE SHEET No. 612

Reprinted Sept. 1960

All Models

BRAKE RELINING

Brake Shoe Removal and Replacement

After the brake plate has been removed from the wheel, the brake cam lever A (Fig. M40) should be detached and the cam spindle B pushed in slightly to allow the shoes to clear the brake plate. Insert a screwdriver between the brake shoes at the fulcrum pin C and twist the screwdriver.

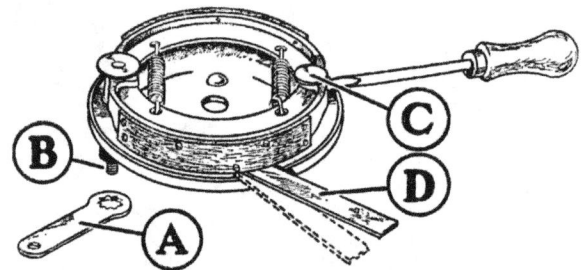

Fig. M40. Removing the Brake Shoes

Place a small lever D between one of the shoes and the cover plate and lever the shoe away from the cover plate until the spring pressure is released. Both shoes can then be lifted from the brake plate.

The shoes can be replaced by the reverse procedure. Hook the springs on to the shoes and place the ends of the shoes in position on the fulcrum pin and cam lever. Then push the shoes outwards until the springs pull them into their correct position.

NOTE: The brake shoe springs are quite strong and care should be taken that the fingers are not trapped by the brake shoes during these operations.

Brake Shoe Relining

With the shoes removed the linings can best be removed by drilling away the heads of the rivets and punching the shanks out to the inside of the shoe with a suitable drift.

New linings are die pressed to suit the curvature of the shoes, but will require drilling and counter-boring for the rivets. Position the lining and hold it in place at one end by means of clamps. Using the holes in the shoes as guides, drill holes of the correct size for the rivets adjacent to the clamp. Turn the shoe over, and counterbore the holes just drilled sufficiently deep so that the rivet heads will stand below the lining surface; this is important, since the rivets will otherwise score the brake drum.

B.S.A. Service Sheet No. 612 (continued)

Insert the rivets into the holes and rivet them over on the inside of the shoe. This is easily accomplished by holding in a vice a short length of rod, whose diameter is equal to that of the rivet head, and using it as an anvil upon which to rest the rivet head while hammering the shank over. (See Fig. M41.) This will also make sure that the rivets do not stand proud of the lining.

Move the clamps to the next pair of holes, taking care that the lining is kept in firm contact with the shoe the whole time, and repeat the above procedure. When the lining is finally riveted down, bevel off the ends of the linings and file off any local high spots.

Precautions to be observed when fitting the relined shoes to the hubs are given in the Service Sheet on Hubs and Brakes.

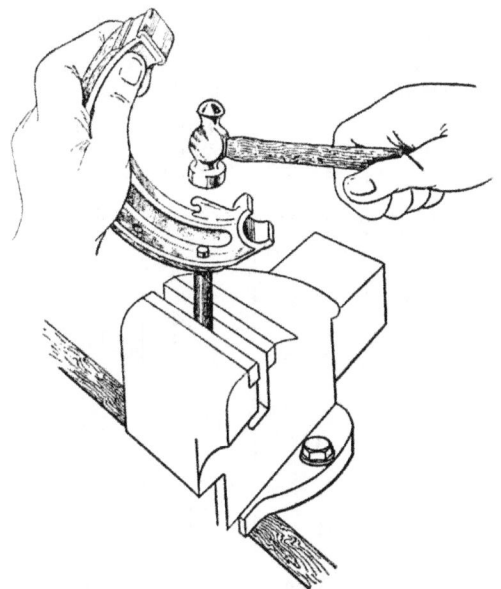

Fig. M41. Riveting the Linings

Works reconditioned brake shoes can be obtained through the medium of your Dealer from the B.S.A. Exchange Replacement Service.

B.S.A. MOTOR CYCLES LTD.
Service Dept., Waverley Works, Birmingham 10
Printed in England.

U/B5305

BSA SERVICE SHEET No. 701

ALL MODELS — USEFUL DATA

MODEL	C10	C11	C12	C15 Std.	B31	B32	B33	B34	M20
Engine bore (mm.)	63	63	63	67	71	71	85	85	82
Engine stroke (mm.)	80	80	80	70	88	88	88	88	94
Engine capacity (c.c.)	249	249	249	249	348	348	499	499	496
Petrol tank capacity (galls.)	2½	2½	2¾	2½	3	3	3	3	3
Oil tank capacity (pints)	4	4	4	4	4	4	4	4	5
Gearbox capacity (pint)	*½	*½	½	½	1	1	1	1	1
Tappet clearance cold:									
inlet (in.)	.004	.003	.010	.008	.003	.003	.003	.003	.010
exhaust (in.)	.006	.003	.012	.010	.003	.003	.003	.003	.012
Tyres—front	3.00×19	3.00×20†	3.00×19	3.25×17	3.25×19	2.75×21	3.25×19	2.75×21	3.25×19
Tyres—rear	3.00×19	3.00×20†	3.00×19	3.25×17	3.25×19	4.00×19	3.25×19	4.00×19	3.25×19
Piston ring gap:									
plain (in.)	.010	.010	.010	.010	.010	.010	.010	.010	.010
oil control (in.)	.010	.010	.010	.010	.010	.010	.010	.010	.010
Piston ring side clearance (in.)	.002–.004	.002–.004	.002–.004	.002–.004	.002–.004	.002–.004	.002–.004	.002–.004	.002–.004
Piston clearance:									
bottom of skirt	.0045–.0065	.0035–.0055	.0035–.0055	.0025–.004	.0040–.0055	.0040–.0055	.0045–.0065	.0045–.0065	.0040–.0060
Gear ratios:									
Top	6.6	6.6	6.26	5.98	5.6	7.1	5.0	5.6	5.3
third	—	—	7.64	7.65	7.3	9.2	6.5	7.4	7.0
second	9.8	9.8	11.1	10.54	11.1	14.2	10.0	11.5	10.9
first	14.5	14.5	16.15	15.96	15.9	20.2	14.2	16.8	15.8
Ignition setting (in. before T.D.C.):									
fully advanced	—	—	—	11/32	7/16	7/16	7/16	7/16	7/16
fully retarded	1/32	1/32	T.D.C.	—	—	—	—	—	—
Carburetter:									
jet	90	80	140	—	150	150	200	200	170
with air cleaner	90	80	100	140	150	150	170	170	—
Sparking plug:									
C.I. cylinder head	L.10	L.10S	L.10S	—	L.10S	L.10S	L.10S	L.10S	—
Al. alloy cylinder head	N.8	—	—	N.5	—	NA.8	—	NA.8	N.8
Compression ratio	5.1 : 1	6.5 : 1	6.5 : 1	7.25 : 1	6.5 : 1	6.5 : 1	6.8 : 1	6.8 : 1	4.9 : 1
Valve timing—inlet (deg.):									
opens before T.D.C.	25	25	34	26	25	25	25	25	25
closes after B.D.C.	70	70	78	70	65	65	65	65	65
Valve timing—exhaust (deg.):									
opens before B.D.C.	70	70	74	61½	65	65	65	65	65
closes after T.D.C.	25	25	38	34½	25	25	25	25	25
Distributor points gap (in.)	.012	.012	.015	.012	—	—	—	—	—
Magneto points gap (in.)	—	—	—	—	.012	.012	.012	.012	.012
Plug points gap (in.)	.015–.018	.015–.018	.018–.020	.020–.025	.015–.018	.015–.018	.015–.018	.015–.018	.015–.018
Tyre pressures:									
front (lb. per sq. in.)	20	20	18	16	16	—	16	—	17
rear (lb. per sq. in.)	28	28	26	22	20	—	17	—	22

For Swinging Arm and other models not listed see appropriate series.

*Four-speed gearbox, 1 pint.   †3.00 × 19 on later models.

B.S.A. SERVICE SHEET No. 701 (contd.)

MODEL	M21	M33	A7 (up to Eng. No. ZA7-11192)	A7 ST 2 carburetters	A7 (on and after Eng. No. AA7-101)	A7 S/T & S/S (on & Eng. No. AA7S-101)	A10	R/R & S/R
Engine bore (mm.)	82	85	62	62	66	66	70	70
Engine stroke (mm.)	112	88	82	82	72.6	72.6	84	84
Engine capacity (c.c.)	591	499	495	495	497	497	646	646
Petrol tank capacity (galls.)	3	3	3	3½	3½	3½	4¼	2 or 4
Oil tank capacity (pints)	5	5	4	4	4	4	4	5½
Gearbox capacity (pint)	1	1	1	1	1	1	1	14 fl. oz.
Tappet clearance—cold:								
inlet (in.)	.010	.003	.015	.015	.010	.008	.010	.008
exhaust (in.)	.012	.003	.015	.015	.016	.012	.016	.008
Tyres—front	3.50 × 19	3.25 × 19	3.25 × 19	3.25 × 19	3.25 × 19	3.25 × 19	3.25 × 19	—
Tyres—rear	3.50 × 19	3.50 × 19	3.50 × 19	3.50 × 19	3.50 × 19	3.50 × 19	3.50 × 19	—
Piston ring gap:								
plain (in.)	.010	.010	.013	.013	.013	.013	.013	—
oil control (in.)	.010	.010	.011	.011	.011	.011	.011	—
Piston ring side clearance	.002–.004	.002–.004	.002–.004	.002–.004	.002–.004	.002–.004	.002–.004	.002–.004
Piston clearance:								
bottom of skirt (in.)	.0040–.0060	.0045–.0065	.0030–.0050	.0030–.0050	.0030–.0050	.0030–.0050	.0030–.0050	.0030–.0050
Gear ratios:						s/T s/s		
Top	5.9	4.8	5.1	5.1	5.1	5.0 5.28	4.42	4.53
third	7.8	6.3	6.2	6.2	6.2	6.05 6.38	5.36	5.48
second	12.2	9.9	9.0	9.0	9.0	8.8 9.28	7.77	7.96
first	17.8	14.3	13.2	13.2	13.2	12.9 13.62	11.41	11.68
Ignition setting (in. before T.D.C. fully advanced)	7/16	7/16	3/8	3/8	5/16	3/8	11/32	3/8
Carburetter:								
jet	170	200	—	110	—	—	—	250
with air cleaner	—	170	140	—	140	160	170	240
Sparking plug:								
C.I. cylinder head	L.10	L.10S	L.10S	L.10S	L.10S	L.10S	L.10S	NA.10
Al. alloy cylinder head	N.8	—	—	—	—	—	—	—
Compression ratio	5 : 1	6.8 : 1	6.6 : 1	7 : 1	6.6 : 1	7.25 : 1	6.5 : 1	R/R 8 : 1 S/R 8.26:1
Valve timing—inlet (deg.):								
opens before T.D.C.	25	25	24	24	30	42	30	42
closes after B.D.C.	65	65	65	65	70	62	70	62
*Valve timing—exhaust (deg.):								
opens before B.D.C.	65	65	60	60	65	67	65	67
closes after T.D.C.	25	25	21½	21½	25	37	25	37
Distributor points gap	—	—	—	—	—	—	—	—
Magneto points gap (in.)	.012	.012	.012	.012	.012	.012	.012	.012
Plug points gap (in.)	.015–.018	.015–.018	.015–.018	.015–.018	.015–.018	.015–.018	.015–.018	.018–.020
Tyre pressures:								
front (lb. per square inch)	16	17	17	17	17	17	17	17
rear (lb. per square inch)	18	18	18	18	18	18	18	19

*NOTE.—Standard A7's after engine number CA7-5232 and Standard A10's after engine number DA10-1647 have the same camshaft as the S/S and R/R machines and valve timing is therefore the same.

B.S.A. MOTOR CYCLES LTD., Service Department, Armoury Road, Birmingham 11.

PRINTED IN ENGLAND—B.S.A. PRESS

BSA SERVICE SHEET No. 702

Reprinted June, 1959.

ALL MODELS

WORKSHOP DATA

ENGINE, BUSH AND SHAFT DIAMETERS

(All Dimensions in Inches, after Reaming or Grinding).

	D1	C10, C11	B31, B32	M33 B33, B34	M20, M21	A7 Up to Engine No. ZA7 11192	A7 On and After Engine No. AA7 101	A10
Overhead Rocker Arm	—	.569 .567 C10 only	.562 .563	.562 .563	—	.4995 .5005	.4995 .5005	.4995 .5005
Inlet Valve Guide	—	.313 .314	.313 .314	.3525 .3515	.3525 .3515	.313 .314	.313 .314	.313 .314
Exhaust Valve Guide	—	.313 .314	.352 .353	.3785 .3795	.3525 .3535	.313 .314	.313 .314	.313 .314
Inlet Tappet Guide	—	.3125 .3135 C10 only	.3745 .3755	.3745 .3755	.3745 .3755	.3125 .3135	—	—
Exhaust Tappet Guide	—	.3125 .3135 C10 only	.3745 .3755	.3745 .3755	.3745 .3755	.3125 .3135	—	—
Cam Pinion Bush	—	—	.6255 .6245	.6255 .6245	.6255 .6245	—	—	—
Cam Shaft Bush	—	.687 .688	—	—	—	.7485 .7495	.7485 .7495	.7485 .7495
Idler Pinion Shaft Bush	—	—	—	—	—	.7485 .7495	.7485 .7495	.7485 .7495
Idler Pinion Bush	—	—	.7505 .7495	.7505 .7495	.7505 .7495	.7485 .7495	.7485 .7495	.7485 .7495
Cam Shaft Bush T/Cover	—	1.0005 .9995	—	—	—	—	—	—
Crankshaft Bush G/S	—	.983 .982	—	—	—	1.375 1.3745	1.375 1.3745	1.375 1.3745
Conrod Big End	—	—	1.7704 1.7702	1.7704 1.7702	1.7704 1.7702	1.4495 1.4500	1.4495 1.4500	1.4495 1.4500
Gudgeon Pin Bush	.4697 .4692	.6255 .625	.7506 .7503	.7506 .7503	.7506 .7503	.6881 .6878	.6881 .6878	.7506 .7503

B.S.A. Service Sheet No. 702 (Contd.).

GEARBOX—BUSH DIAMETERS

(All Dimensions in Inches, after Reaming or Grinding)

	D Group	C Group	B Group 1945/48	M Group 1945/48	A Group	B & M 1949 on
Pinion Sleeve Bush	.4975 .4965	—	.7505 .7495	.8755 .8745	.812 .813	.8755 .8745
Layshaft Bush (Shell)	.501 .500	—	.687 .688	.687 .688	.687 .688	.687 .688
Mainshaft Bush (I/Cover)	—	.751 .752	.687 .688	—	—	—
Layshaft Bush (K/S Quadrant)	—	—	—	.687 .688	.7495 .7505	.687 .688
Layshaft 1st Gear Bush	—	—	.8125 .8135	.8765 .8755	.7495 .7505	.8765 .8755
Layshaft Pinion/s Bush	—	.562 .563	—	—	—	—
M/Shaft 3rd L/Shaft 2nd Gear Bush	—	—	.9375 .9385	1.0005 1.0015	—	1.0005 1.0015
K/S Quadrant Bush I/Cover	—	.9995 1.0005	1.1245 1.1255	—	.561 .563	—
K/S Quadrant Bush O/Cover	—	.812 .813	.812 .813	1.187 1.188	.7495 .7505	1.187 1.188
Control Shaft Bush (Shell)	—	—	.562 .563	.562 .563	—	.562 .563
Control Shaft Bush (I/Cover)	—	.689 .688	—	.562 .563	—	.562 .563
Control Quadrant Bush (I/Cover)	—	—	—	.562 .563	—	.562 .563
Pedal Spindle Bush (I/Cover)	—	.7495 .7505	.6245 .6255	.6245 .6255	.467 .468	.6245 .6255
Pedal Spindle Bush (O/Cover)	—	.7495 .7505	.8745 .8755	.8745 .8755	.6245 .6255	.8745 .8755
Speedo Spindle Small Bush	—	—	.218 .219	—	.218 .219	.218 .219
Speedo Spindle Long Bush	—	—	.281 .282	—	.281 .282	.281 .282
Clutch Push Rod Bush	—	.257 .258	—	—	—	—

B.S.A. MOTOR CYCLES LTD., Service Dept., Waverley Works, Birmingham, 10.   *Printed in England.*

BSA SERVICE SHEET No. 703

Revised Dec. 1958.

All Models
WORKSHOP DATA (BEARINGS) 1956

B.S.A. Part No.	Hoffman No.	Skefko No.	Ransome & Marles No.	British Timkin No.	Fischer No.
24–722	RM.9L	CFM7/C2	MRJA.$\frac{7}{8}$	—	RFM.9
24–724	R.325L	402454.B	MRJA.25	—	MFM.25
24–732	325	6305	MJ.25	—	6305
24–4065	135	6207	LJ.35	—	6207
24–4217	L.S.8	RLS.6	LJ.$\frac{3}{4}$	—	LS.8
24–6860	—	2K.1178X 2K.1130N1	—	1178X 1130.N1	—
27–261	MS.9	RM.S7	MJ.$\frac{7}{8}$	—	MS.9
27–4027	LS.11	RL.S9	LJ.$1\frac{1}{8}$	—	—
29–3857	130	6206	LJ.30	—	6206
29–6211	MS.7	RM.S5	MJ.$\frac{5}{8}$	—	MS.7
42–5819	120	—	—	—	—
65–1388	RMS.11	CRM.9	MRJ.$1\frac{1}{8}$	—	RMS.11
65–2045	125	6205	LJ.25	—	6205
65–5883	LS.9	RLS.7	LJ.$\frac{7}{8}$	—	LS.9
67–670	R.130L	NFL.30	LRJA.30	—	NFL.30
89–3022	LS.10	RLS.8	LJ.1	—	LS.10
89–3023	LS.8	RLS.6	LJ.$\frac{3}{4}$	—	LS.8
90–10	117	6203	LJ.17	—	6203
90–11	LS.7	RLS.5	LJ.$\frac{5}{8}$	—	LS.7
90–12	S.9	EE.8J	KLNJ.$\frac{7}{8}$	—	EE.8
90–5525	112	6201	LJ.12	—	6201
90–5559	—	—	—	A.2126	—
90–6063	115	6202	LJ.15	—	6202

B.S.A. SERVICE SHEET No. 703 (continued)

LOCATION OF BEARINGS

Model	Crankcase Roller Bearing Driveside	Crankcase Ball Bearing Driveside	Crankcase Roller Bearing Gearside	Crankcase Ball Bearing Gearside	Crankcase Ball Bearing (Small)	Crankcase Ball Bearing (Large)	Gearbox Pinion Sleeve Ball Bearing	Gearbox Mainshaft Ball Bearing	Front Hub Ball Bearing	Rear Hub Ball Bearing	Rear Hub Brake Drum and C/Wheel Ball Bearing
Dandy	—	—	—	—	90–6063	24–4217	90–6063 (Output shaft)	90–6063 (Input shaft)	—	—	—
D1, D3 & D5	—	—	—	—	90–10	24–4217	90–12	90–11	90–5525	90–6063	—
D1, D3 (Comp.)	—	—	—	—	—	—	—	—	90–5559	—	—
C10L	—	24–732	—	—	—	—	29–3857	90–11	—	90–6063	—
C12	—	24–732	—	—	—	—	29–3857	90–11	65–5383	90–11 O/S 29–6211 N/S	—
C15	—	24–782	—	—	—	—	29–3857	—	90–10	90–10 O/S 42–5819 N/S	—
B31 S/A	24–724	65–2045	24–722	—	—	—	24–4065	24–4217	89–3022	89–3022	89–3022
B31 S/A (1958)	—	—	—	—	—	—	—	—	42–5819	42–5819	89–3022
B32 Comp. Rigid	24–724	65–2045	24–722	—	—	—	24–4065	24–4217	65–5883	65–5883	65–5883
B32/34 Gold Star	65–1338	65–2045	24–722	—	—	—	24–4065	24–4217	65–5883	65–5883	65–5883
B33 S/A	24–724	65–2045	24–722	—	—	—	24–4065	24–4217	89–3022	89–3022	89–3022
B33 S/A (1958)	—	—	—	—	—	—	—	—	42–5819	42–5819	89–3022
B34 Comp. Rigid	24–724	65–2045	24–722	—	—	—	24–4065	24–4217	65–5883	65–5883	65–5883
M21 Rigid	24–724	65–2045	24–722	27–261	—	—	24–4065	24–4217	65–5883	24–6860 (Tapered Roller)	—
M21 Plunger	24–724	65–2045	24–722	27–261	—	—	24–4065	24–4217	65–5883	65–5883	89–3022
M33	24–724	65–2045	24–722	—	—	—	24–4065	24–4217	65–5883	65–5883	89–3022
A7 and Shooting Star	67–670	—	—	—	—	—	24–4065	24–4217	89–3022	89–3022	89–3022
A7 & S/S (1958)	—	—	—	—	—	—	—	—	42–5819	42–5819	89–3022
A10 S/A	67–670	—	—	—	—	—	24–4065	24–4217	89–3022	89–3022	89–3022
A10 S/A (1958)	—	—	—	—	—	—	—	—	42–5819	42–5819	89–3022
A10 Plunger	67–670	—	—	—	—	—	24–4065	24–4217	65–5883	65–5883	89–3022
A10 Road Rocket	67–670	—	—	—	—	—	24–4065	24–4217	65–5883	89–3022	89–3022
A10 Super Rocket	67–670	—	—	—	—	—	24–4065	24–4217	42–5819	42–5819	89–3022

Printed in England B.S.A. MOTOR CYCLES LTD., Service Dept., Birmingham 11.

BSA SERVICE SHEET No. 704

ALL MODELS
PISTON CLEARANCES

To avoid the possibility of seizure or piston tap, pistons must be fitted with adequate but not excessive clearance.

The following are the recommended total clearances between the bottom of the piston and the cylinder wall.

MODEL			Tolerances
Dandy 70		7.25 : 1	.003—.004"
D1			.0027—.0045"
D3, C15			.0025—.004"
D5, D7			.003—.005"
C10, C10L			.0045—.0065"
C11, C11G, C12			.0035—.0055"
C15	(Star Group)	6.4 : 1 to 10 : 1	.0017—.0033"
B31			.004—.0055"
B31	(Split skirt)		.0005—.0016"
B32A			.002—.004"
BB32	Gold Star	8 : 1	.003—.0045"
		6.5 : 1	.004—.0055"
		7.5 : 1	.002—.004"
		9 : 1	.003—.0045"
CB32	Gold Star	6.5 : 1	.002—.004"
		8 : 1	.003—.0045"
		8.5 : 1	.003—.0045"
		9 : 1	.003—.0045"
		12.25 : 1	.004—.0055"
		13 : 1	.004—.0055"
DB32	Gold Star	7.25 : 1	.0025—.004"
		8 : 1	.003—.0045"
		9 : 1	.003—.0045"
B40	(Star Group)	7.0 : 1 to 8.7 : 1	.0015—.003"
B33			.0045—.0065"
B33	(Split skirt)		.0006—.00275"
B34A			.0045—.0065"
BB34	Gold Star	7.5 : 1 Standard	.0045—.0065"
		8 : 1	.0025—.0045"
		9 : 1	.0025—.0045"
		6.8 : 1	.0045—.0065"
		11.1	.0025—.0045"
CB34	Gold Star	7.25 : 1	.003—.0045"
		8 : 1	.003—.0045"
		9 : 1	.003—.0045"
DB34	Gold Star ⎱	8 : 1	.003—.0045"
DBD34	Gold Star ⎰	8.75 : 1	.003—.0045"

B.S.A. Service Sheet No. 704 (contd.)

MODEL			Tolerances
M20			.004—.006"
M21			.004—.006"
M33			.0045—.0065"
M33	(Split skirt)		.0006—.00275"
A7		6.7 : 1	.002—.004"
	(Split skirt)	6.7 : 1	.0011—.0031"
		7.25 : 1	.002—.004"
	(Split skirt)		.0011—.0031"
A7	(Star Twin)		.002—.004"
A7	(Split skirt)	(Star Twin and Shooting Star)	.001—.0031"
A7	(Shooting Star)	8 : 1 (after Engine No. CA7SS-4501)	.0035—.005"
A50	(Star Twin)	8.0 : 1 to 9.0 : 1	.0011—.0025"
A10	(Golden Flash)	6.5 : 1	.003—.0045"
	(Split skirt)	6.5 : 1	.0025—.0045"
	(Split skirt)	7.25 : 1	.0025—.0045"
A10	(Super Flash and Road Rocket)	8 : 1	.003—.0045"
A10	(Golden Flash)	7.5 : 1 (after Engine No. DA10-651)	.0035—.005"
A10	(Super Rocket)	8.5 : 1 (after Engine No. CA10R-6001)	.004—.0055"
A10	(Rocket Gold Star)	8.75 : 1	.001—.0025"
A65	(Star Twin)	7.5 : 1 to 9.0 : 1	.0012—.0027"

B.S.A. MOTOR CYCLES LTD., Service Department, Armoury Road, Birmingham 11

B.S.A. PRESS

BSA SERVICE SHEET No. 705

All Models
October, 1948
Reprinted April, 1960

PERIODICAL ATTENTIONS.

HUBS.   **Every 1,000 miles.**

Inject grease through the nipples located in the centres of the hubs. Do not overdo this, otherwise grease will penetrate to the brake linings and cause ineffective brakes. Three or four strokes of the gun should be ample. Where no grease nipple is provided the bearings should be removed and packed with grease when the machine is in need of complete overhaul.

BRAKE CAM SPINDLES.

Grease sparingly. Two or three strokes of the gun only, or if no grease nipple is provided, apply a few drops of engine oil between the brake arm and the spindle.

SPEEDOMETER DRIVE.

Grease well. Three or four strokes of the gun regularly.

ENGINE OIL.   **Every 2,000 miles (except 2-stroke models).**

The oil tank and sump should be drained (preferably when the engine is warm after a longish run), and the tank refilled with fresh oil.

In case of new or re-conditioned engines, the oil should be drained and renewed after the first 250 miles, and again after 1,000 miles.

REAR CHAIN.

Remove the rear chain, clean thoroughly in paraffin, and soak in engine oil or molten grease and graphite.

CONTACT BREAKER (except A and C Group Models).

A very small quantity of thin oil should be injected into the lubrication wick, and the face cam smeared with oil. The wick is accessible after removing the spring contact arm (held by the round-headed screw at the opposite end to the contact point) and is located in the hollow end of the round-headed screw which is revealed when the spring arm is removed.

When replacing the arm, it is important that the small curved backing spring is refitted correctly, i.e., with the bent portion facing outwards.

DYNAMO ARMATURE BUSH (A and C Group Models fitted with lubricator).

A few drops of oil injected through the lubricator are sufficient.

Every 5,000 miles.

Drain the gearbox and refill with new oil up to the level of the filler plug.

Drain the telescopic forks and refill each leg with correct amount of new oil.

In the case of new or re-conditioned gearboxes, change the oil after the first 1,000 miles.

New Machines.

CYLINDER HEAD BOLTS (except B and M O.H.V. engines).

Examine the cylinder head joint daily, and if leakage becomes apparent, tighten the bolts, working diagonally so as to pull the head down evenly. Do not over-tighten otherwise there is a possibility of distortion or bolt stretch.

CYLINDER BASE NUTS (except B and M O.H.V. engines).

There are five of these—one at each of the four corners outside, and one inside the tappet chest on the single cylinder models. A Group Models have eight cylinder base nuts and Model C11 six nuts. Tighten after the first 100 miles.

CYLINDER BARREL AND HEAD FIXING (B and M O.H.V. engines).

The barrel and head are both secured to the crankcase by four long bolts coupled to bushes screwed into the latter. Apply a spanner to the upper hexagon for tightening. These bolts have right-hand threads, and, being inverted, are tightened by turning the spanner to the right.

B.S.A. MOTOR CYCLES LTD.,
Service Dept., Waverley Works, Birmingham, 10

(PRINTED IN ENGLAND)

BSA SERVICE SHEET No. 706

TELESCOPIC FORKS

'A', 'B' AND 'M' GROUP, C10, C11G AND C12 MODELS

Of robust design B.S.A. telescopic forks require the minimum of maintenance it being necessary only to replenish the oil occasionally between major overhauls.

For normal use each fork leg should contain a quarter pint of oil (142 c.c.) or three-eighths of a pint (213 c.c.) according to model as detailed below.

Quarter-pint Capacity
Models C10, C10L (1956 onwards), C11, C11G, C12, B31-33 (up to 1956), B32-34 and Gold Stars (up to 1952), M20, M21, M33, 'A' Group (up to 1952).

Three-eighth Pint Capacity
Models B31-33 (1956 onwards), B32-34 and Gold Stars (1952 onwards), 'A' Group (1952 onwards).

Oil Changes
To replenish the oil remove the drain plugs at the base of the fork tubes and remove the fork top nuts. Allow the oil to drain off. Replace the plugs and pour either a quarter or three-eighths pint of oil into the hollow tubes revealed when the top plugs are removed.

Dismantling
Before beginning to overhaul the forks have the following tools and replacement parts available in case they are required:—

61-3001	Fork top nut spanner.
61-3003	Fork plug spanner.
61-3005	Oil Seal holder assembly tool.
61-3006	Oil seal extractor.
61-3007	Oil seal assembly tool.
61-3350	Fork leg assembly and removal tool.
29-5334	Packing shim (.005 in.).
29-5335	Packing shim (.010 in.).
29-5336	Packing shim (.020 in.).
29-5337	Packing shim (.030 in.).
65-5424 (2)	Fork top bush ('A' and 'B' Group).
29-5347 (2)	Fork bottom bush ('A', 'B', C11G and C12).
29-5346 (2)	Fork top bush (C10L, C11G and C12).
29-5313 (2)	Fork oil seal (all models).
	Number 5 twine (approx 18 in.).

B.S.A. Service Sheet No. 706 (contd.)

Remove the front wheel and front mudguard. Take out the fork top cap (A) Fig. X1, screw service tool part number 61-3350 into the thread at the top of the fork shaft using the larger of the fine threads.

Slacken off the pinch bolt (B) Fig. X1.

Take a firm grasp of the lower fork sliding tube and strike the top of the tool smartly with a hammer. This will release the shaft from its taper and the complete fork leg can be drawn down and removed from the machine.

Repeat the operation on the other leg.

To dismantle the lower section of the fork hold the fork sliding tube by gripping the wheel spindle lug in a soft-jawed vice and lift off the spring (see Fig. X2).

Enter service tool part number 61-3005 until the dogs on the tool engage in the slots at the bottom of the oil seal holder (D) Fig. X2. Pressing the tool down and turning at the same time unscrew the oil seal holder. Slide the holder up the shaft until it becomes tight on the tapered section of the shaft. Do not use excessive force or the oil seal may be damaged.

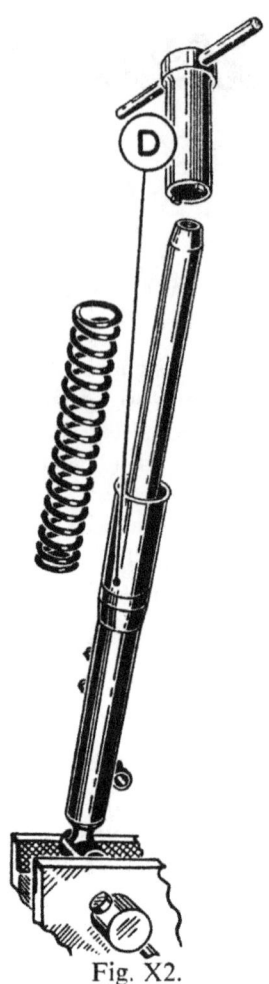
Fig. X2.

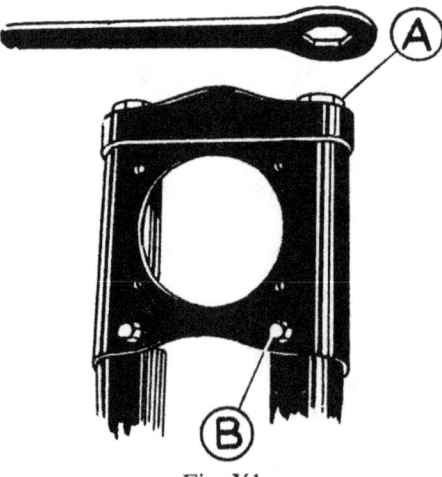
Fig. X1.

The top fork bearing is retained in the fork leg by a circlip (E) Fig. X3, which can be prised out with a sharp tool such as the tang end of a file. There may be a number of shims fitted between the circlip and the top bearing. These must be replaced if the bushes are not renewed when assembling.

Grip the shaft in a vice using soft-jaw clamps on the unground portion of the shaft and unscrew the gland nut (F) Fig. X4. Service tool part number 61-3003 is designed for this purpose. Remove the gland nut which secures the lower bearing and both bearings, shims, circlip and oil seal holder will then slide off the shaft.

B.S.A. Service Sheet No. 706 (contd.)

If it is necessary to remove the oil seal place the lower edge of the holder on a soft wooden block and enter service tool part number 61-3006 into the top of the holder. Give this tool a sharp tap with a hammer and the oil seal will be driven out.

Reassembly

Reassembly is carried out in the reverse order. Cleanliness is essential and before attempting to reassemble clean all parts thoroughly and clean down the bench on which the forks have been dismantled.

If the oil seal is to be replaced care must be taken that the feather edge of the seal is not damaged. Enter the oil seal (*I*) Fig. X6 into the holder, metal part first, and drive home using B.S.A. service tool part number 61-3007 (*H*) Fig. X6. Place the oil seal holder over the shaft and pass it up the shaft until it is firmly held on the tapered section. Do not use excessive force or the oil seal may be damaged. Place the circlip over the shaft followed by the shims and top bearing and then the bottom bearing. Place the steel washer over the thread of the gland nut, screw up the gland nut and holding the shaft firmly in a soft-jawed vice as described in dismantling procedure firmly tighten the gland nut.

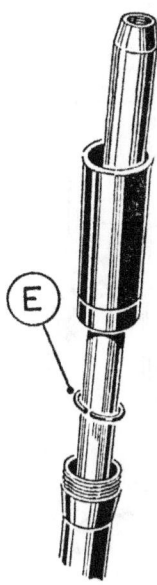

Fig. X3.

Place the lower sliding tube in a vice and enter the fork shaft with parts assembled into the lower sliding tube. Fit the circlip and check for up and down movement on the

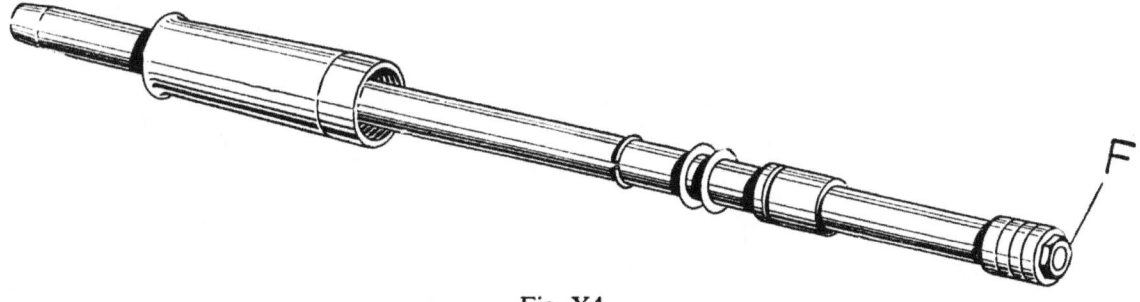

Fig. X4.

top bush. If a new bush has been fitted it may be necessary to add to, or take from, some of the existing shims. Packing shims are available in the following sizes:—

.005 in.   Part Number 29-5334
.010 in.   Part Number 29-5335
.020 in.   Part Number 29-5336
.030 in.   Part Number 29-5337

B.S.A. Service Sheet No. 706 (contd.)

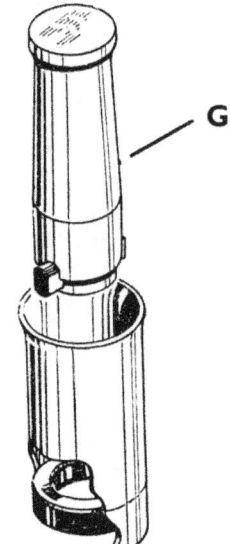

Fig. X5.

If the bush is not properly shimmed a tapping noise may be heard when the machine is ridden.

Having shimmed up the bush correctly and fitted the circlip firmly in position, screw down the oil seal holder and take one turn of number five twine around the base of the thread to provide an additional seal. Screw down the oil seal firmly using B.S.A. service tool part number 61–3005.

To fit the main tubes to the fork yokes screw B.S.A. service tool part number 61–3350 into the top of the tube and pass it up through the two yokes, then fit the collar and nut and draw the tube firmly home into the yokes. When the tube is fully home the pinch bolts on the lower yoke should be tightened. The tool may then be removed and after filling the legs with the correct amount of oil the top plugs can be replaced and fully tightened. Finally slacken the pinch bolt. position the top outer shroud centrally over the lower leg Check that the top nuts are completely tight and retighten the pinch bolts.

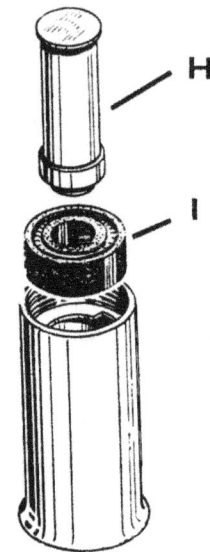

Fig. X6.

B.S.A. MOTOR CYCLES LTD., Service Department, Armoury Road, Birmingham 11.
PRINTED IN ENGLAND — B.S.A. PRESS

BSA SERVICE SHEET No. 707

Reprinted March, 1966

Gold Star and Competition Models
USEFUL DATA

Engine Stroke	88mm.
Engine Bore	B32 71mm. B34 85mm.
Engine Capacity	B32 348c.c. B34 499c.c.
Oil Tank Capacity	5 pints.
Gearbox Capacity	1 pint.
Front Fork Capacity (each leg)	⅜ pint (212c.c.)

Tappet Clearances (cold engine):
- Cam. 65-2420 — .003in. Inlet and Exhaust.
- Cams. 65-2434 to 65-2440 — .001in. Inlet and Exhaust.
- Cams. 65-2442 to 65-2452 — .008in. Inlet. .010in. Exhaust.
- 1954 onwards (Clubmans Models) — .006in. Inlet and Exhaust.

Piston Ring Gap	Top .012in. 2nd and Scraper .010in.
Piston Ring Side Clearance	.0015in.
Piston Clearance (bottom of skirt)	.0025in. – .0045in.
Contact Breaker Gap	.012in.

Ignition Setting B.T.D.C. (fully advanced):
350c.c. Touring, Trials and Scrambles, 7/16 in.
500c.c. Touring and Trials, ½ in.   Scrambles, 7/16 in.

Racing (Clubmans)	15/32 in.
Racing (Alcohol)	350c.c., ¾ in. 500c.c., 7/8 in.
Racing (Petrol Benzol)	350c.c., 13/32 in. 500c.c., ½ in.

Sparking Plug		
Touring and Trials		Champion NA8.
Scrambles		Champion NA10 or NA12.
Racing		Champion NA14.

Carburetter		
Trials – Standard		Touring – Standard or T.T.10.
Scrambles – T.T.10		Racing – T.T.10; T.T.10 R.N. or G.P.

Engine Sprockets available	16, 17, 18, 19, 20 Teeth.
Gearbox Sprockets available	16, 19 Teeth.
Clutch Sprocket	43 Teeth (44 Teeth to Special Order).
Chainwheel Sprocket	42 Teeth.

Internal Gear Ratios:

	Marked.	Top.	3rd.	2nd.	Bottom
Plunger Frame Models, Extra Close	(Ex. Close)	1.0	1.1	1.31	1.78
Close	(Close)	1.0	1.32	1.72	2.48
Standard		1.0	1.32	2.05	2.98
Swinging Arm Frame, Extra Close	(R.R.)	1.0	1.099	1.326	1.929
Close	(Day)	1.0	1.101	1.460	2.124
Scrambles	(Sc)	1.0	1.325	1.754	2.343
Standard	(Std)	1.0	1.210	1.758	2.580
Wide Ratio	(Tri)	1.0	1.549	2.339	3.167

Chain Sizes (Front)	½ in. x .305in.
(Rear)	⅝ in. x .250in.

Tyre Sizes (Front): Touring and Scrambles, 3.00 x 21; Trials, 2.75 x 21
Racing, 3.00 x 19 or 21
(Rear): Touring and Racing, 3.25 x 19 (350c.c.); 3.50 x 19 (500c.c.)
Trials and Scrambles, 4.00 x 19.

B.S.A. MOTOR CYCLES LTD. Service Department, Armoury Road, Birmingham 11.

B.S.A. PRESS

BSA SERVICE SHEET No. 708

ALL MODELS

CARBURATION. Monobloc and Seperate Float Chamber Type

How the Carburetter Works

The function of the carburetter is to atomise the petrol and proportion it correctly with the air drawn in through the intake on the induction stroke. The action of the float and needle in the float chamber maintains the level of fuel at the needle jet, and when the engine is stopped and no further fuel is being used the needle valve cuts off the supply.

The twist-grip controls, by means of a cable, the position of the throttle slide and the throttle needle and so governs the volume of mixture supplied to the engine.

The mixture is correct at all throttle openings, if the carburetter is correctly tuned.

The opening of the throttle brings first into action the mixture supply from the pilot jet, then as it progressively opens, via the pilot by-pass the mixture is augmented from the needle jet. Up to three-quarter throttle this action is controlled by the tapered needle in the needle jet, and from three-quarters onwards the mixture is controlled by the main jet.

The pilot jet (J), which in the older type of carburetter is embodied in the jet block, has been replaced in the Monobloc carburetter by a detachable jet (9) Fig. X5, assembled in the carburetter body and sealed by a cover nut.

The main jet does not spray directly into the mixing chamber, but discharges through the needle jet into the primary air chamber and goes from there as a rich petrol/air mixture through the primary air choke into the main air choke.

Although the maintenance and tuning instruction contained in this Service Sheet apply equally well to the Monobloc and separate float chamber types of carburetter, the new instrument has been designed with a view to giving improved performance, and certain constructional changes have been made.

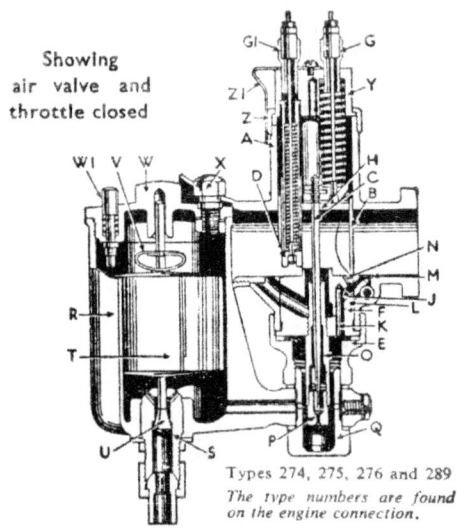

Showing air valve and throttle closed

Types 274, 275, 276 and 289
The type numbers are found on the engine connection.

A. Mixing Chamber.
B. Throttle Valve.
C. Jet Needle and Clip above.
D. Air Valve.
E. Mixing Chamber Union Nut.
F. Jet Block.
G/G1. Cable Adjusters.
H. Jet Block Barrel.
J. Pilot Jet.
K. Passage to Pilot.
L. Pilot Air Passage.
M. Pilot Mixture Outlet.
N. Pilot by-pass.
O. Needle Jet.
P. Main Jet.
Q. Float Chamber Holding Bolt.
R. Float Chamber.
S. Needle Valve Seating.
T. Float.
U. Float Needle Valve.
V. Float Needle Clip.
W. Float Chamber Cover.
W1. Tickler.
X. Float Chamber Lock Screw.
Y. Mixing Chamber Top Cap.
Z. Mixing Chamber Lock Ring.
Z1. Mixing Chamber Security Spring.

Fig. X4. *A sectioned illustration of Needle Jet Carburetter.*

B.S.A. Service Sheet No. 708 (contd.)

The float chamber is a drum-shaped reservoir, die cast in one piece with the mixing chamber. The material used being zinc-alloy. The float is designed to pivot instead of rising and falling, as in the separate float chamber type, and as it does so, it impinges on a nylon needle controlling the inflow of fuel.

Variations of up to 20° in the angle of the carburetter when fitted, do not affect the working of the float, therefore it lends itself to use for down draught carburation and is not so greatly effected by the degree of lean when cornering. Access to the float (Fig. X6) is gained by removing a plate held in place by three screws.

Compensation for over-rich mixture which results from snap throttle openings, is provided by bleed holes in the needle jet (Fig. X5). A compensatory air bleed is provided, this is the larger of the two holes at the mouth of the air intake, which leads to the space around the needle jet (Fig. X5).

The pilot intake is the smaller of the two holes, and operates in conjunction with the detachable pilot jet (Fig. X5). This pilot mixture is adjusted as before, by an adjusting screw (Fig. 8a).

Hints and Tips—Starting from Cold
Flood the carburetter by depressing the tickler and close the air control, set the ignition say, half-retarded. Then open the throttle about ⅛ in., then kick-start. If the throttle is too far open, starting will be difficult.

Starting—Engine Hot
Do not flood the carburetter, but it may be found necessary with some engines to close the air lever, set the ignition to half-retarded, the throttle to ⅛ in. open and kick-start. If the carburetter has been flooded and won't start because the mixture is too rich—open the throttle wide and give the engine several turns to clear the richness, then start again with the throttle ⅛ in. open, and air valve wide open. Generally speaking it is not advisable to flood at all when an engine is hot.

Starting—General
By experiment, find out if and when it is necessary to flood, also note the best position for the air lever and the throttle for the easiest starting. Excessive flooding, particularly when the engine is hot, will make starting more difficult. It is necessary only to raise the level of petrol in the float chamber, by depressing the tickler.

Starting—Single Lever Carburetters
Open the throttle very slightly from the idling position and flood the carburetter more or less according to the engine being cold or hot respectively.

B.S.A. Service Sheet No. 708 (contd.)

SECTIONAL ILLUSTRATIONS OF CARBURETTERS. Types 375, 376 and 389

(FOR KEY TO DIAGRAM NUMBERS SEE BELOW)

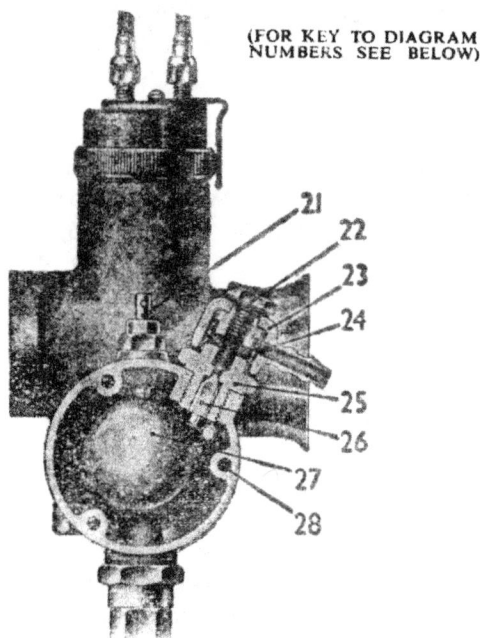

(MONOBLOC)
Fig. X6. *Section through Float Chamber.*

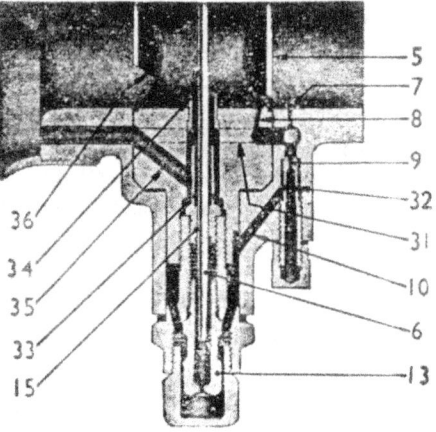

Diagrammatic section of Carburetter showing only the lower half of the throttle chamber with the throttle a little open—and the internal primary air passages to the main jet and pilot system.

FOR KEY TO DIAGRAM NUMBERS SEE BELOW
Fig. X5.

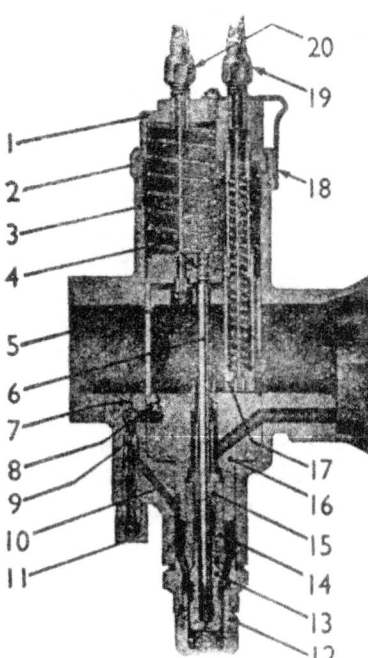

Fig. 7. *Secttion through Mixing Chamber, showing Air Valve and Thaottle closed.*

1. Mixing Chamber Top.
2. Mixing Chamber Cap.
3. Carburetter Body.
4. Jet Needle Clip.
5. Throttle Valve.
6. Jet Needle.
7. Pilot outlet.
8. Pilot by-pass.
9. Pilot Jet.
10. Petrol Feed to Pilot Jet.
11. Pilot Jet Cover Nut.
12. Main Jet Cover.
13. Main Jet.
14. Jet Holder.
15. Needle Jet.
16. Jet Block.
17. Air Valve
18. Mixing Chamber Cap Spring.
19. Cable Adjuster (air).
20. Cable Adjuster (throttle).
21. Tickler.
22. Banjo Bolt.
23. Banjo.
24. Filter Gauze.
25. Needle Seating.
26. Needle.
27. Float.
28. Side Cover Screws.
31. Air to Pilot Jet.
32. Feed Holes in Pilot Jet.
33. Bleed Holes in Needle Jet.
34. Primary Air Choke.
35. Primary Air Passage.
36. Throttle Valve Cut-away

29. PILOT AIR ADJUSTING SCREW
This screw regulates the strength of the mixture for "idling" and for the initial opening of the throttle. The screw controls the depression on the pilot jet by metering the amount of air that mixes with the petrol.

30. THROTTLE ADJUSTING SCREW
Set this screw to hold the throttle open sufficiently to keep the engine running when the twist-grip is shut off.

B.S.A. Service Sheet No. 708 (contd.)

Cable Controls

See that there is a minimum of backlash when the controls are set back and that any movement of the handlebar does not cause the throttle to open; this is done by the adjusters on the top of the carburetter. See that the throttle shuts down freely.

Petrol Feed

Verification. Detach petrol pipe union at the float chamber end; turn on petrol tap momentarily and see that fuel gushes out. Avoid petrol pipes with vertical loops as they cause air-locks. Flooding may be due to a worn or bent needle or a leaky float, but nearly all flooding with new machines is due to impurities (grit, fluff, etc.) in the tank—so clean out the float chamber periodically till the trouble ceases. If the trouble persists the tank might be drained, swilled out, etc. Note that if the carburetter, either vertical or horizontal, is flooding with the engine stopped, the overflow from the main jet will not run into the engine but out of the carburetter through a hole at the base of the mixing chamber.

Fixing Carburetter and Air Leaks

Erratic slow running is often caused by air leaks, so verify there are none at the point of attachment to the cylinder or inlet pipe—check by means of oil placed around the joint, if there are leaks the oil will be sucked in, and eliminate by new washers and the equal tightening up of the flange nuts. Also in old machines look out for air leaks caused by a worn throttle or worn inlet valve guides.

Explosions in Exhaust

May be caused by too weak a pilot mixture when the throttle is closed or nearly closed—also, it may be caused by too rich a pilot mixture and an air leak in the exhaust system; the reason in either case is that the mixture has not fired in the cylinder and has fired in the hot silencer. If the explosion occurs when the throttle is fairly wide open the trouble will be ignition—not carburation.

Excessive Petrol Consumption

On a new machine may be due to flooding, caused by impurities from the petrol tank lodging on the float needle seat and so preventing its valve from closing. If the machine has had several years use, flooding may be caused by a worn float needle valve. Also excessive petrol consumption will be apparent if the throttle needle jet (o) Fig. X4. or (15) Fig. X5, has worn; it may be remedied or improved by lowering the needle in the throttle, but if it cannot be, then the only remedy is to get a new needle jet.

Air Filters

These may affect the jet setting, so if one is fitted afterwards to the carburetter the main jet may have to be smaller. If a carburetter is set with an air filter and the engine is run without it, take care not to overheat the engine due to too weak a mixture; testing with the air control will indicate if a larger main jet and higher needle position are required.

B.S.A. Service Sheet No. 708 (contd.)

Faults
The trouble may not be carburation; if the trouble cannot be remedied by making mixtures richer or weaker with the air control, and you know the petrol feed is good and the carburetter is not flooding, the trouble is elsewhere.

Fault Finding
There are only *two* possible faults in carburation, either *richness* of mixture or *weakness* of mixture, so in case of trouble decide which is the cause, by:—

1. Examining the petrol feed ...
   - Verify jets and passages are clear.
   - Verify ample flow.
   - Verify there is no flooding.

2. Looking for air leaks ...
   - At the connection to the engine.
   - Or due to leaky inlet valve stems.

3. Defective or worn parts ...
   - As a slack throttle-worn needle jet.
   - The mixing chamber union nut not tightened up, or loose jets.

4. *Testing with the air control* to see if by richening the mixture the results are better or worse.

Indications of

Richness:

Black smoke in exhaust.
Petrol spraying out of carburetter.
Four strokes, eight-stroking
Two strokes, four-stroking.
Heavy, lumpy running.
Heavy petrol consumption.
? If the jet block (F) is not tightened up by washer and nut (E) richness will be caused through leakage of petrol.
? Air cleaner choked up.
? Needle jet worn large.
Sparking plug sooty.

Weakness:

Spitting in carburetter.
Erratic slow running.
Overheating.
Acceleration poor.
Engine goes better if:—
Throttle not wide open, or air control is partially closed.
? Has air cleaner been removed.
? Jets partially choked up
Removing the silencer or running with a racing silencer requires a richer setting and large main jet.

Note
Verify correctness of fuel feed, stop air leaks, check over ignition and valve operation and timing. *Decide by test whether richness or weakness is the trouble and at what throttle position.* See throttle opening diagrams, Fig. X6.

B.S.A. Service Sheet No. 708 (contd.)

Procedure
If at a particular throttle opening you partially close the air control, and the engine goes better, weakness is indicated; or on the other hand the running is worse, richness is indicated. *Then you proceed to adjust the appropriate part as indicated for that position.*

Fault at Throttle Positions indicated on Fig. X9

To Cure Richness:		To Cure Weakness:
Fit smaller main jet.	1st	Fit larger main jet.
Screw out pilot air screw.	2nd	Screw pilot air screw in.
Fit a throttle with larger cut-away.	3rd	Fit a throttle with smaller cut-away.
Lower needle one or two grooves.	4th	Raise needle one or two grooves.

Notes
It is not correct to cure a rich mixture at half-throttle by fitting a smaller main jet because the main jet may be correct for power at full throttle: the proper thing to do is to lower the needle.

Information on throttle slides and needle position is given in paragraphs (*f*) and (*e*) respectively in the next section entitled "Tuning".

Changing from Standard Petrols to Special Fuels.
Such as alcohol mixtures will, with the same setting in the carburetter, certainly cause weakness of mixture and possible damage from overheating.

TUNING
(*a*) Figs. X8 and 8a are two diagrammatic sections of the carburetter to show:
1. The throttle stop screw.
2. The pilot air screw.

(*b*) **Throttle Stop Screw**
Set this screw to prop the throttle open sufficiently to keep the engine running when the twist-grip is shut off.

(*c*) **Pilot Air Screw**
This screw regulates the strength of the mixture for "idling" and for the initial opening of the throttle. The screw controls the suction on the pilot petrol jet by metering the amount of air that mixes with the petrol.

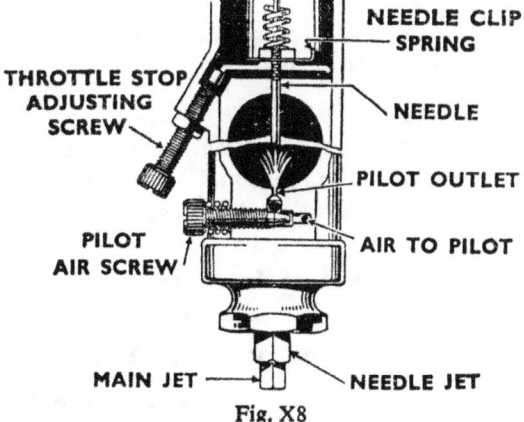

Fig. X8

NOTE:—The air for the pilot jet may be admitted internally or externally according to one or other of the designs, but there is no difference in tuning.

(*d*) **Main Jet**
The main jet controls the petrol supply when the throttle is more than three-quarters open, but at smaller throttle openings although the supply of fuel goes through the main jet, the amount is diminished by the metering effect of the needle in the needle jet.

Each jet is calibrated and numbered so that its exact discharge is known and two jets of the same number are alike.

B.S.A. Service Sheet No. 708 (contd.)

Never reamer a Jet out, get another of the right size

The bigger the number the bigger the jet. Spare jets *are sealed*.

To get at the main jet, undo the float chamber holding bolt (Q) Fig. X4, or main jet cover number 12 (Fig. X7). The jet is screwed into the needle jet so if the jet is tight, hold the needle jet also carefully with a spanner whilst unscrewing the main jet.

(e) Needle and Needle Jet

The needle is attached to the throttle and being tapered either allows more or less petrol to pass through the needle jets as the throttle is opened or closed throughout the range, except when idling or nearly full throttle. The needle jet is of a defined size and is only altered from standard when using alcohol fuels.

The taper needle position in relation to the throttle opening can be set according to the mixture required by fixing it to the throttle with the needle clip spring in a certain groove (see illustration above), thus either raising or lowering it. Raising the needle richens the mixture and lowering it weakens the mixture at throttle openings from quarter to three-quarter open (see illustration, Fig. X9).

(f) Throttle Valve Cut-away

The atmospheric side of the throttle is cut away to influence the depression on the main fuel supply and thus gives a means of tuning between the pilot and needle jet range of throttle opening. The amount of cut-away is recorded by a number marked on the throttle, viz.: 6/3 means throttle type 6 with number 3 cut-away; larger cut-aways, say 4 and 5, give weaker mixtures, and 2 and 1 richer mixtures.

(g) Air Valve

Is used only for starting and running when cold, and for experimenting with, otherwise run with it wide open.

(h) Tickler

A small plunger located in the float chamber lid. When pressed down on the float, the needle valve is pushed off its seat and so "flooding" is achieved. Flooding temporarily enriches the mixture until the level of the petrol subsides to normal.

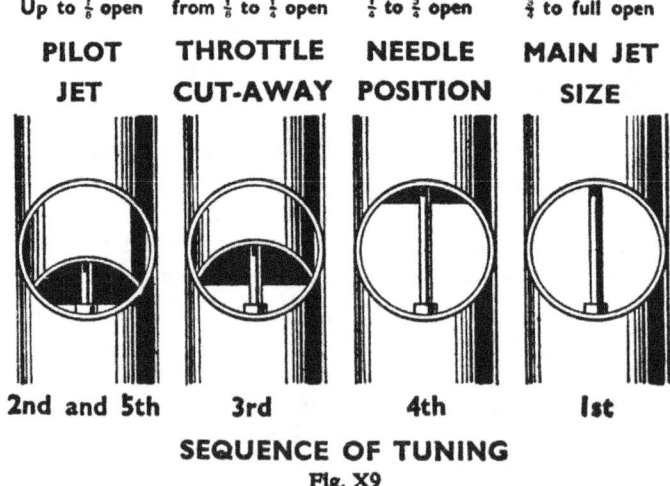

Phases of Amal Needle Jet Carburettor Throttle Openings

SEQUENCE OF TUNING

Fig. X9

B.S.A. Service Sheet No. 708 (contd.)

Sequence of Tuning

Tune up. In the following order only, by so doing you will not upset good results obtained.

NOTE.—The carburetter is automatic throughout the throttle range—the air control should always be wide open except when used for starting or until the engine has warmed up. We assume normal petrols are used.

Read remarks on "Fault Finding" and "Tuning" for each tuning device and get the motor going perfectly on a quiet road with a slight up gradient so that on test the engine is pulling.

1st Main Jet with Throttle in position

Test the engine for full throttle; if when at full throttle, the power seems better with the throttle less than wide open or with the air valve closed slightly the main jet is too small. If the engine runs "heavily" the main jet is too large. If testing for speed work note the jet size is rich enough to keep engine cool, and to verify this, examine the sparking plug by taking a fast run, declutching and stopping engine quickly. If the plug body at the end has a bright black appearance, the mixture is correct; if sooty, the mixture is rich; or if a dry grey colour, the mixture is too weak and a larger jet is necessary.

2nd Pilot Jet with Throttle in positions 2 and 5

With engine idling too fast with the twist-grip shut off and the throttle shut down on to the throttle stop screw, and ignition set for best slow running: (1) Loosen stop screw nut and screw down until engine runs slower and begins to falter, then screw the pilot air screw in or out to make engine run regularly and faster. (2) Now gently lower the throttle stop screw until the engine runs slower and just begins to falter, then lock the nut lightly and begin again to adjust the pilot air screw to get best slow running; if this second adjustment makes engine run too fast, go over the job again a third time. Finally, lock up tight the throttle stop screw nut without disturbing the screw's position.

3rd Throttle Cut-away with Throttle in position

If, as you take off from the idling position, there is objectionable spitting from the carburetter, slightly richen the pilot mixture by screwing the air screw in about half a turn, but if this is not effective, screw it back again and fit a throttle with a smaller cut-away. If the engine jerks under load at this throttle position and there is no spitting, either the throttle needle is much too high or a larger throttle cut-away is required to cure richness.

4th Needle with Throttle in position 4

The needle controls a wide range of throttle opening and also the acceleration. Try the needle in as low a position as possible, viz., with the clip in a groove as near the end as possible; if acceleration is poor and with air valve partially closed the results are better, raise the needle by two grooves; if very much better try lowering needle by one groove and leave it where it is best.

NOTE:—If mixture is still too rich with clip in groove number 1 nearest the end—the needle jet probably wants replacement because of wear. The needle itself never wears out.

5th Finally go over the idling again for final touches.

B.S.A. MOTOR CYCLES LTD., Service Department, Armoury Road, Birmingham 11.
Printed in England
B.S.A. Press.

BSA SERVICE SHEET No. 708B

ALL MODELS
CARBURATION AT HIGH ALTITUDES

The carburetter settings of all B.S.A. motor cycles are designed to give the best all round performance at altitudes of a few thousand feet.

At greater altitudes the air becomes rarefied with the result that the mixture is incorrect.

To overcome this difficulty it is necessary to reduce the size of the main jet, the reduction depending on the altitude at which the machine is mainly used.

The table below shows the percentage of reduction at given altitudes, but it must be emphasised that while the alteration to jet size will correct the mixture, it will not replace the lost power. This can only be corrected by "blowing" or super-charging.

It may also be advisable to re-tune the carburetter for smaller throttle openings this should be done in accordance with Service Sheet 708.

Altitude.	Percentage of reduction in jet size.
3,000 feet	5%
6,000 feet	9%
9,000 feet	13%
12,000 feet	17%

B.S.A. MOTOR CYCLES LTD., Service Dept., Armoury Road, Birmingham 11.

B.S.A. Press.

BSA SERVICE SHEET No. 709

ALL MODELS
FAULT FINDING

No adjustments should be made, or any part tampered with, until the cause of the trouble is known. Otherwise adjustments which are correct may be deranged.

Engine Stops Suddenly:
Petrol shortage in tank, or choked petrol supply pipe or tap.
Choked main jet, or water in float chamber.
Oiled up or fouled sparking plug.
Water on high-tension pick-up or on sparking plug.

Engine Fails to Start, or is difficult to start:
Lack of fuel, or insufficient flooding if cold.
Excessive flooding, allowing neat petrol to enter the cylinder.
Oil sparking plug, or stuck-up valve or valve stem sticky.
Weak valve spring, or valve not seating properly.
Throttle opening too large, or pilot jet choked.
Contact points dirty, or gap incorrect.
Flat battery, if coil ignition, or faulty electrical connections in ignition circuit.

Loss of Power:
Valve, or valves, not seating properly.
Weak valve spring or springs, or sticking valve.
No tappet clearance, or excessive clearance.
Lack of oil in tank.
Brakes adjusted too closely.
Badly fitting or broken piston rings.
Punctured carburettor float.
Incorrect ignition timing.

Engine Overheats:
Lack of proper lubrication.
Weak valve springs, or pitted valve seats.
Worn piston rings, or late ignition setting.
Carburettor setting too weak, or partly choked petrol pipe.

Engine Misses Fire:
Weak valve spring.
Defective or oiled sparking plug, or oil on contact points.
Incorrectly adjusted contact points or tappets.
Faulty condenser.
Defective sparking plug or high-tension cable.
Loose sparking plug terminal.
Carburettor flooding, due to stuck or defective float.
Partly choked main jet.
Choked vent hole in petrol tank filler cap.

Excessive Oil Consumption:
Stoppage, or partial stoppage, in pipe returning oil from engine to tank.
Clogged, or partially clogged, filter in sump, or oil tank.
Badly worn or stuck-up piston rings, causing high pressure in engine crankcase.
High crankcase pressure, caused by release valve (breather) action.
Air leak in dry sump oiling system.
Non-return valve in system not seating.
Ball valve in oil pump stuck on its seat.

B.S.A. MOTOR CYCLES LTD., Service Department, Armoury Road, Birmingham 11

B.S.A. PRESS

BSA SERVICE SHEET No. 710

ALL MODELS
CHAIN ALTERATIONS AND REPAIRS

A chain rarely breaks if it is kept properly lubricated and adjusted. Usually it is worn out long before it reaches breaking point. The rear chain is the most heavily stressed and is therefore the one most likely to give trouble. Spare parts should be carried to enable the rider to carry out a repair on the road with the aid of a chain rivet extractor (see Fig. X7). The front chain will probably be worn out before it requires shortening.

How to use the Chain Rivet Extractor
First press down lever (A) Fig. X7 to open the two jaws (B). Insert the link to be removed so that the jaws grip the roller and support the uppermost inner side plate. The punch (C) is then screwed on to the rivet head until the rivet is forced through the outer plate.

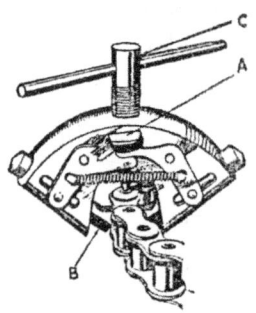

Fig. X7.

To shorten a worn Rear Chain
After a big mileage, the rear chain may have stretched so that no further adjustment is possible by the usual method. In this case it is possible to shorten the chain by one link or pitch, so increasing its useful life. First remove the single connecting spring link (A) securing the two ends of the chain, Fig. X8. If the chain terminates in two ordinary links as in Fig. X8 (in which case the chain will be an even number of pitches) extract the third and fourth rivets (B) from the end and replace the detached three pitches by a single connecting link (C). The connection is made with an additional spring link (D). If one end of the chain has a double cranked link, Fig. X9—in which case the chain will have an odd

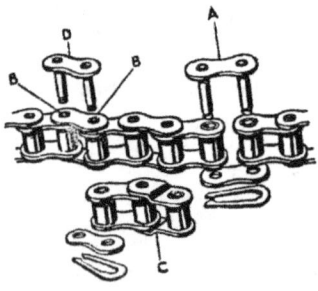

Fig. X8.

Printed in England

B.S.A. Service Sheet No. 710 (contd.)

number of pitches—extract the second and third rivets (A), releasing the cranked link unit complete, which can be retained for further use. Replace with one inner link (B) and again connect up with an additional single connecting link (C).

To repair a damaged Chain

If a roller or link has been damaged (X) Fig. X9, remove rivets (D), take out the damaged link and replace with one inner link, secured by two single connecting links.

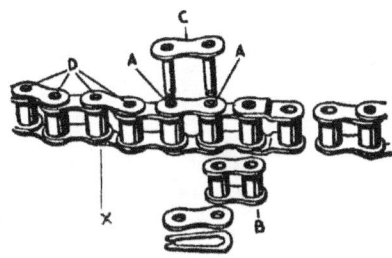

Fig. X9.

It is important that the spring clip fastener should always be put on so that the *closed* end faces the direction of travel of the chain—i.e. when clip is on top run of chain, closed end is toward front of machine—when clip is on bottom run, closed end is towards rear of machine.

It should be noted that once a rivet has been extracted it must not be used again, so that it is important to check that the correct rivet is being removed before actually removing it. In the case of double cranked links, the complete unit comprises an inner link and the cranked outer link—three rollers in all—and these must never be separated.

Fitting Rear Chain

To fit a new rear chain, turn wheel until the spring link of the old chain is located on rear sprocket. Disconnect, and allow the lower run to drop down. Join the top run of the old chain to the new chain by means of the connecting link, and then by pulling on the bottom run of the old chain the new one will be carried round the gearbox sprocket. Then the old chain can be disconnected and the ends of the new one joined together.

When the rear chain breaks and falls from its sprockets, the new or repaired chain can be replaced without taking off the chainguards. One end of the chain must be fed (from the rear) under the front end of the rear top chainguard on to the gearbox sprocket A long bladed screwdriver or a piece of stiff wire may assist this operation When the chain has located on the sprocket teeth, engage a gear and gently turn gearbox over with the kickstarter This will feed chain round gearbox sprocket When sufficient length of chain is hanging below sprocket, disengage gear and chain can then be pulled round until both runs can be fed inside rear chainguard and engaged on rear wheel sprocket.

B.S.A. MOTOR CYCLES LTD., Service Department, Armoury Road, Birmingham 11.

SERVICE SHEET No. 710x

MARCH, 1969

FRAME REPAIRS

ALL MODELS

Frame repairs must not be attempted unless adequate workshop facilities are available.

The information given in this sheet is intended for the use of Dealers who are unable to take advantage of the B.S.A. repair service and who have frame repair facilities.

Spotting points to enable frame trueing to be carried out can be determined by making use of the dimensions given.

B.S.A. Motor Cycles Ltd., Armoury Road Birmingham 11.
PRINTED IN ENGLAND

IT IS DIFFICULT TO UNDERSTAND WHY B.S.A. ISSUED THE FOLLOWING FRAME DRAWINGS IN VARYING SCALES AND AT SUCH SMALL SIZES - MAKING SOME OF THE DIMENSIONS ALMOST IMPOSSIBLE TO READ. HOWEVER, THEY ARE INCLUDED FOR THE SAKE OF COMPLETENESS

A7-10 RIGID FRAME

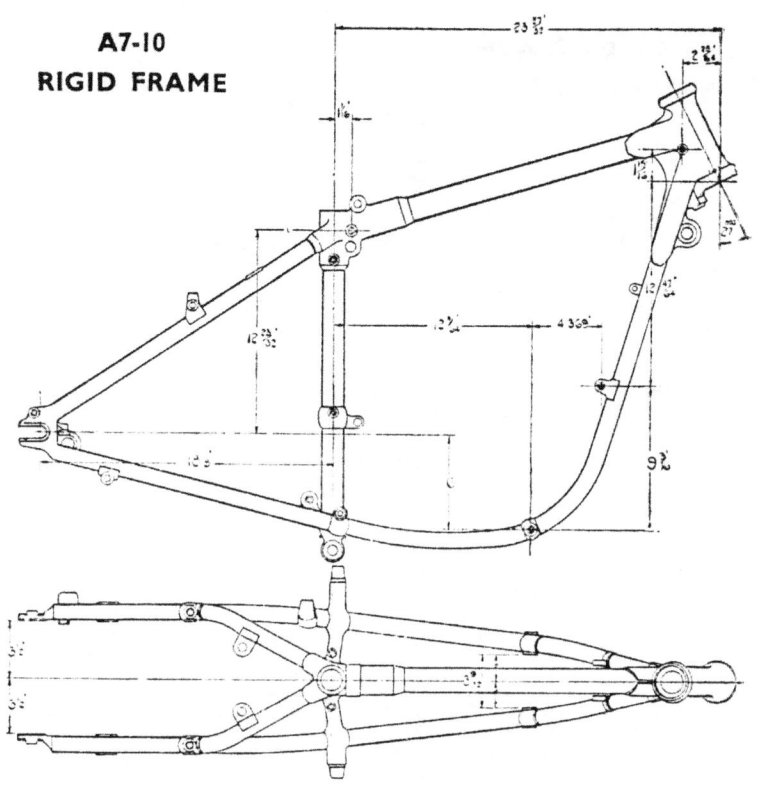

A7-10 SPRING FRAME

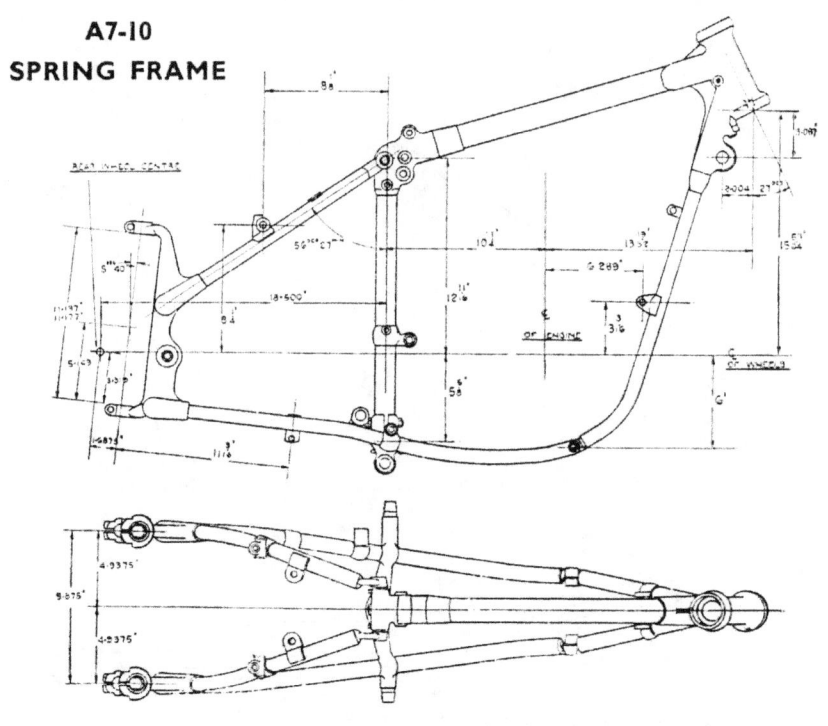

1953 SUPER FLASH SPRING FRAME

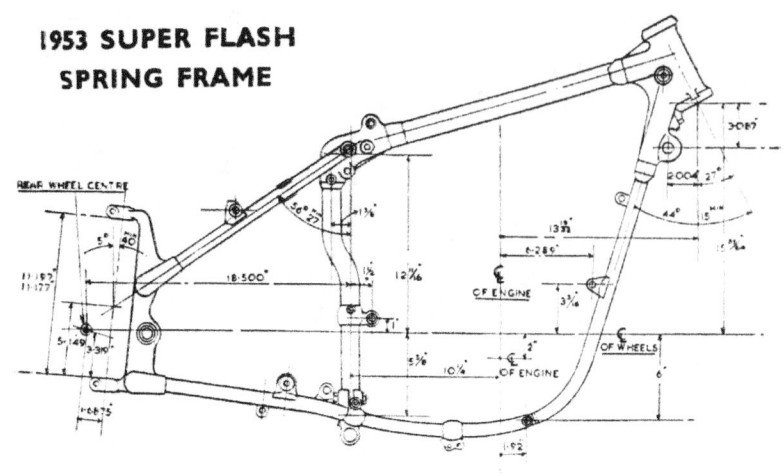

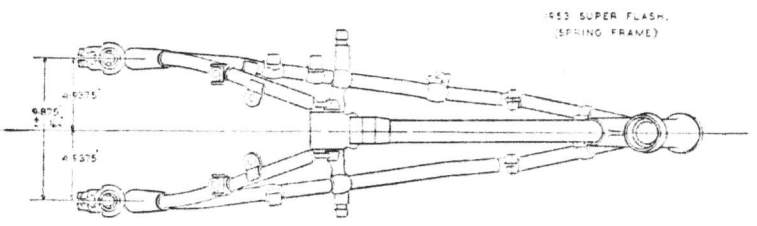

M20, M21 and M33 RIGID FRAME
1945 - 1948

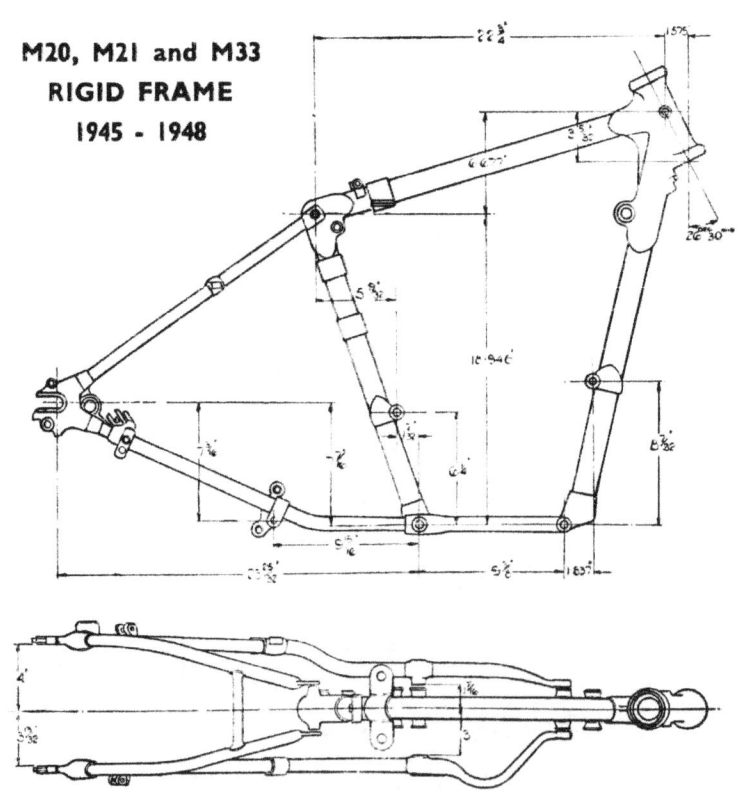

M20, M21 and M33 RIGID FRAME
1949 onwards

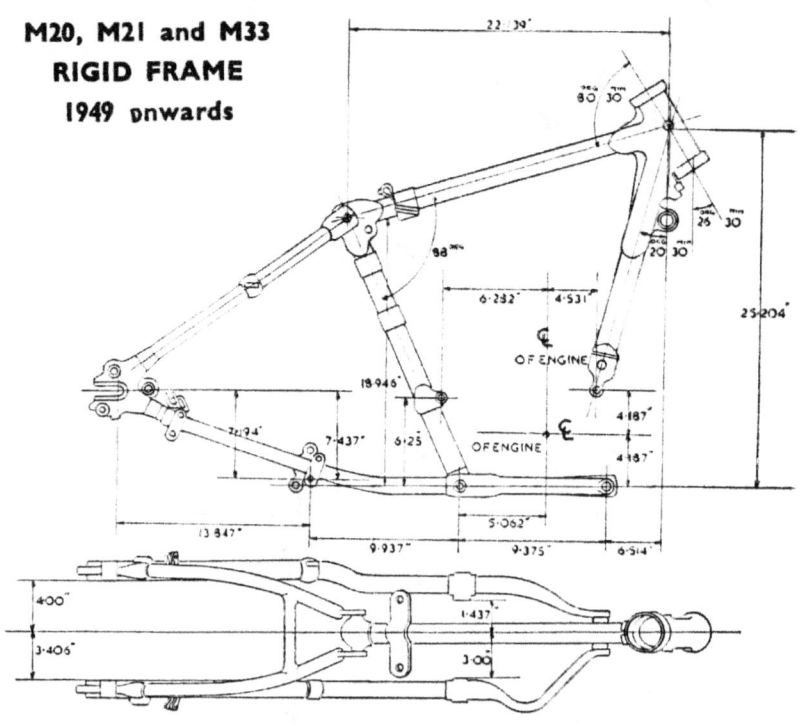

M20, M21 and M33 SPRING FRAME

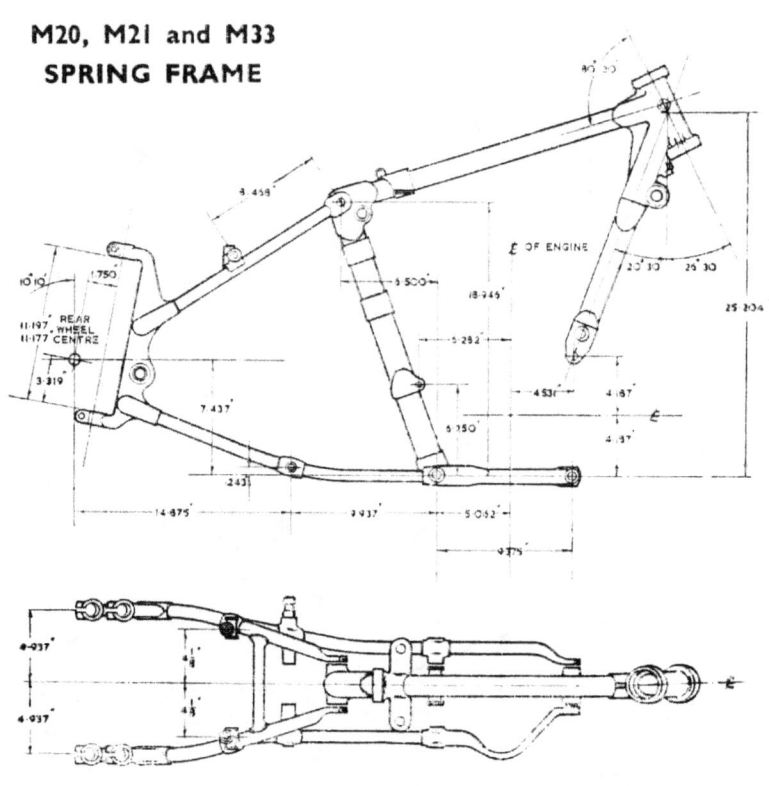

B31-32-33-34 RIGID FRAME

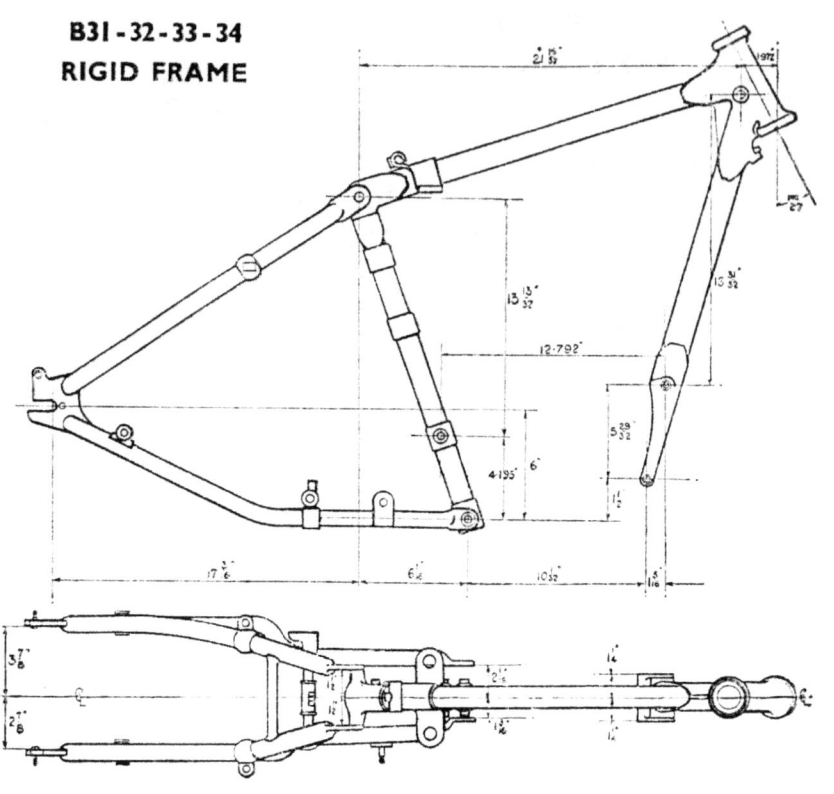

B31-32-33-34 SPRING FRAME

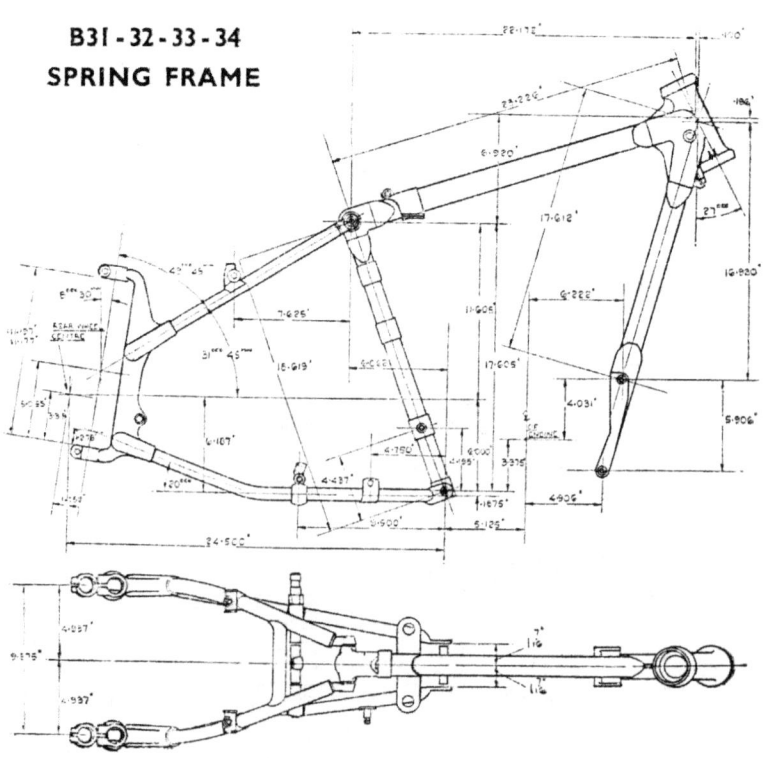

D1 and D3 RIGID FRAME

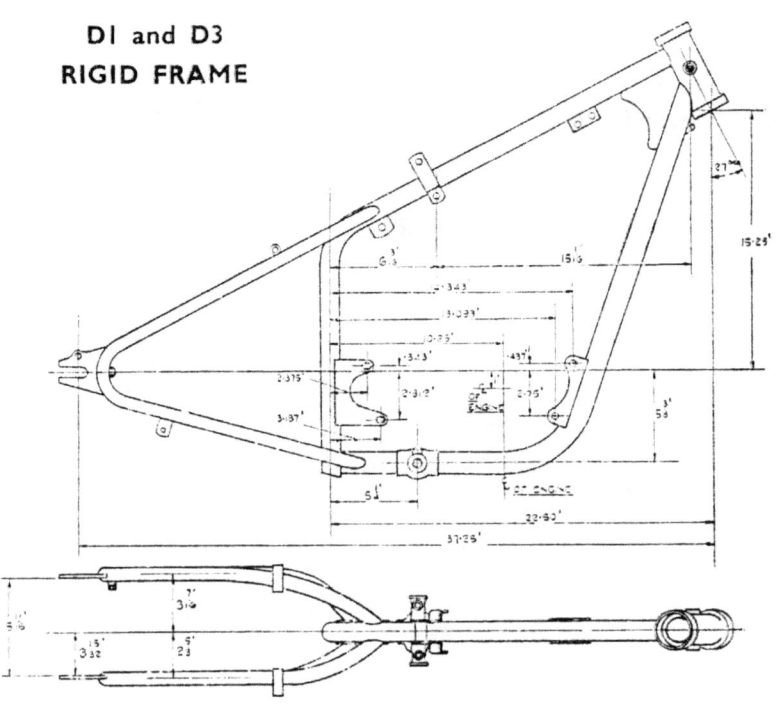

D1 and D3 SPRING FRAME

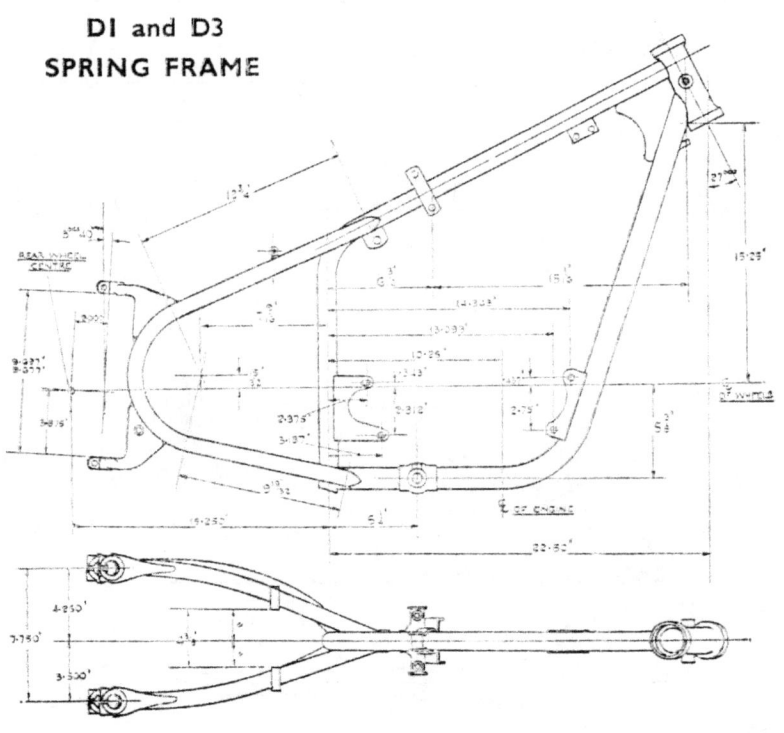

C10L SPRING FRAME

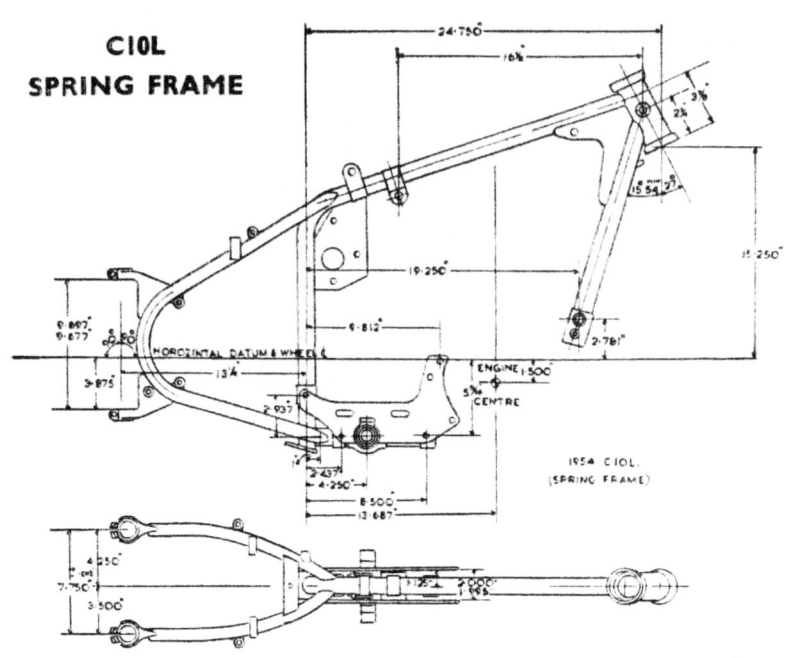

C10, C11, C11G RIGID FRAME

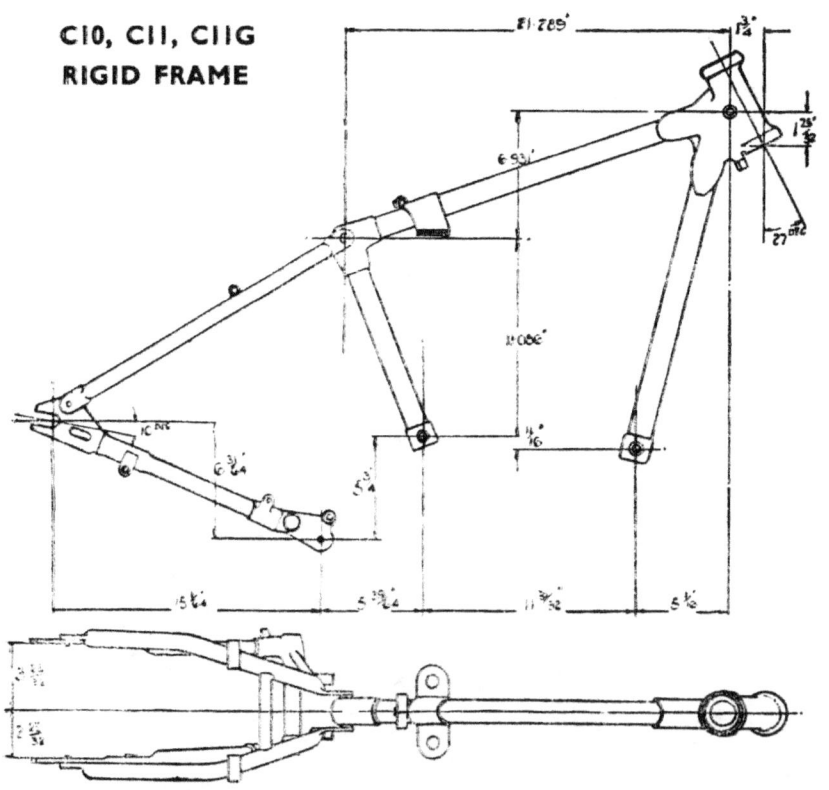

C10, C11, C11G SPRING FRAME 3 SPEED GEARBOX

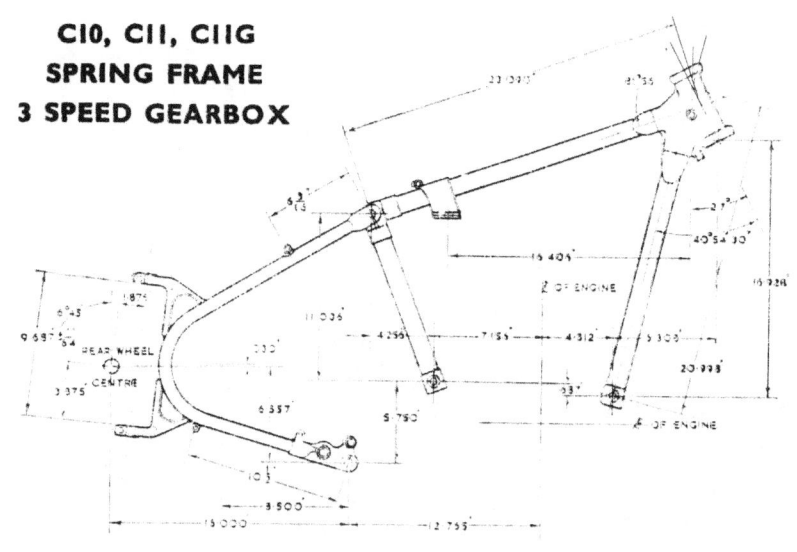

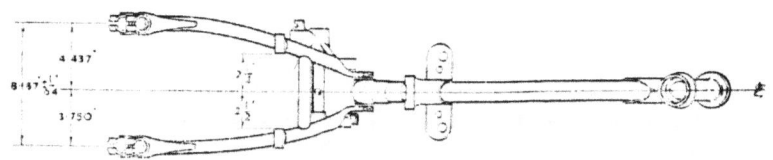

C10, C11, C11G SPRING FRAME 4 SPEED GEARBOX

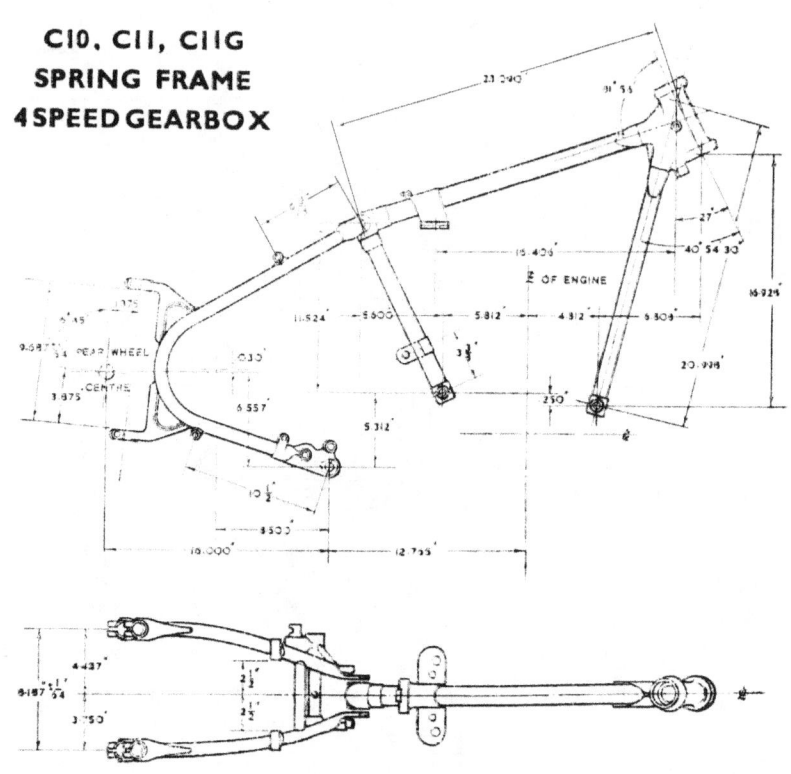

1953 GOLD STAR SWINGING ARM

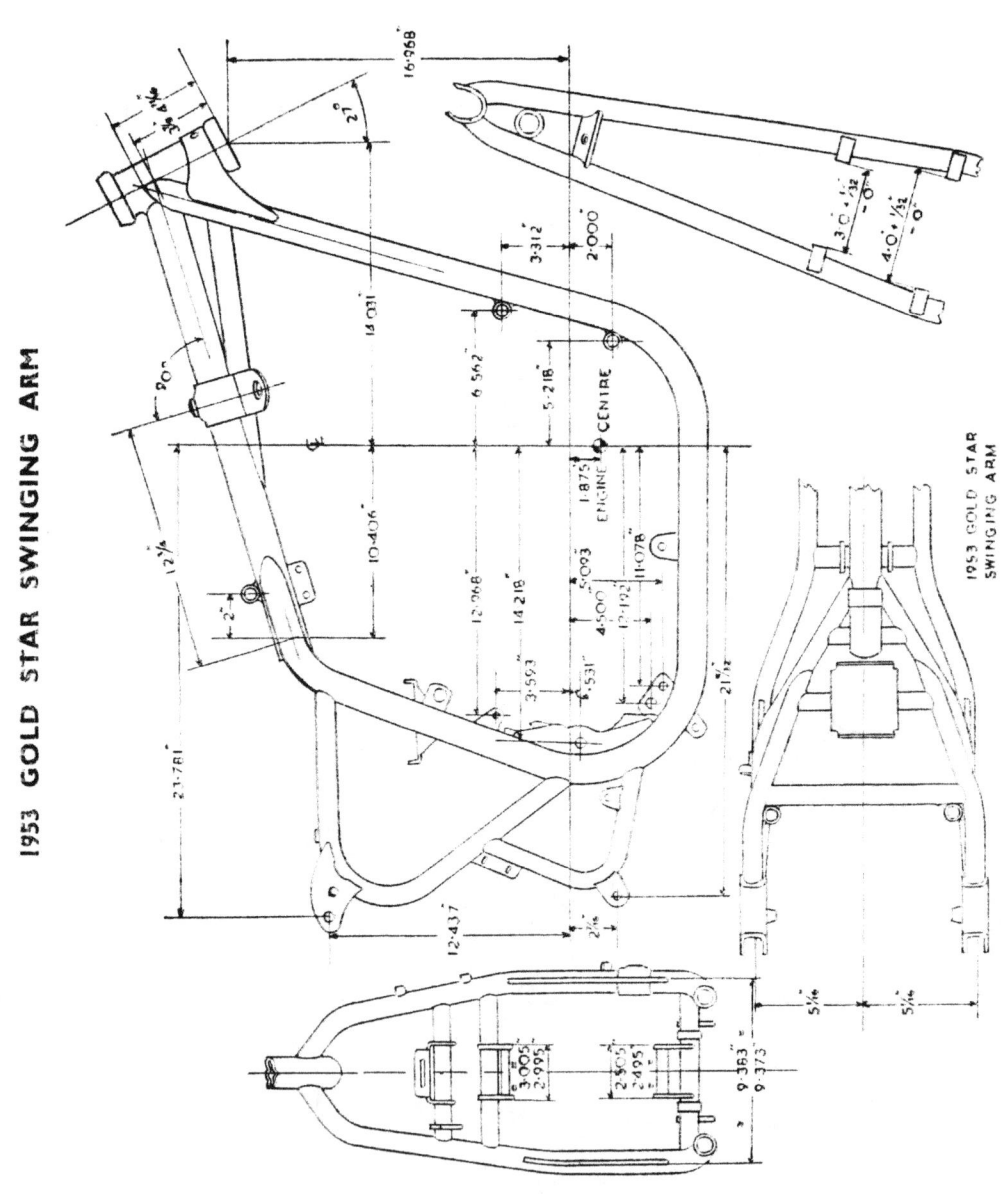

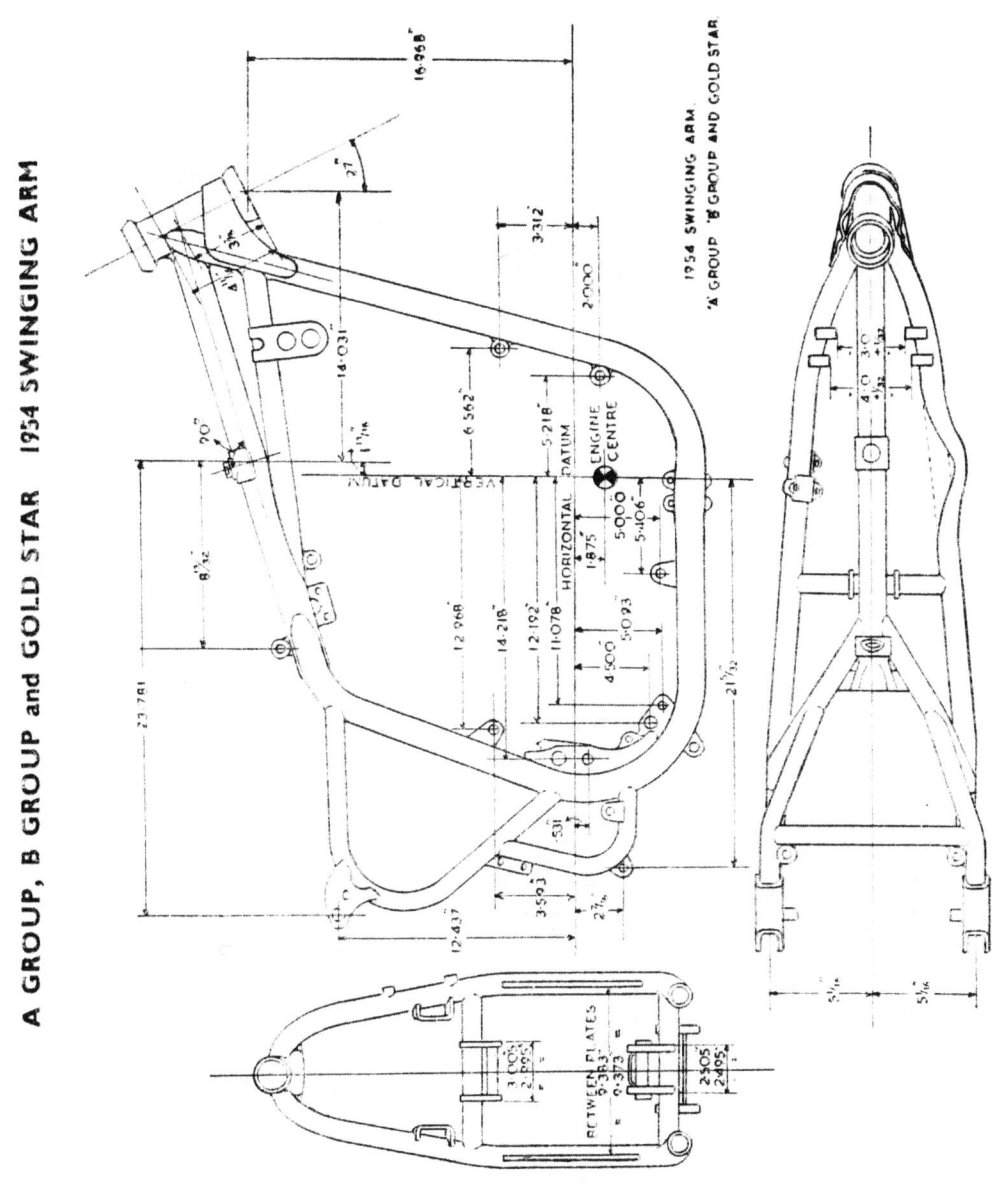

B32 and B34
1954 RIGID FRAME

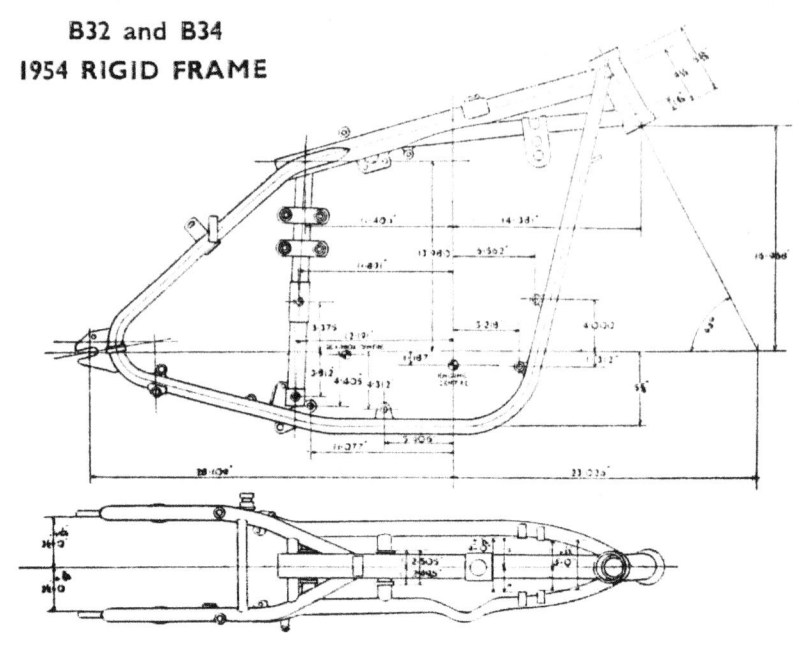

D3 SWINGING ARM

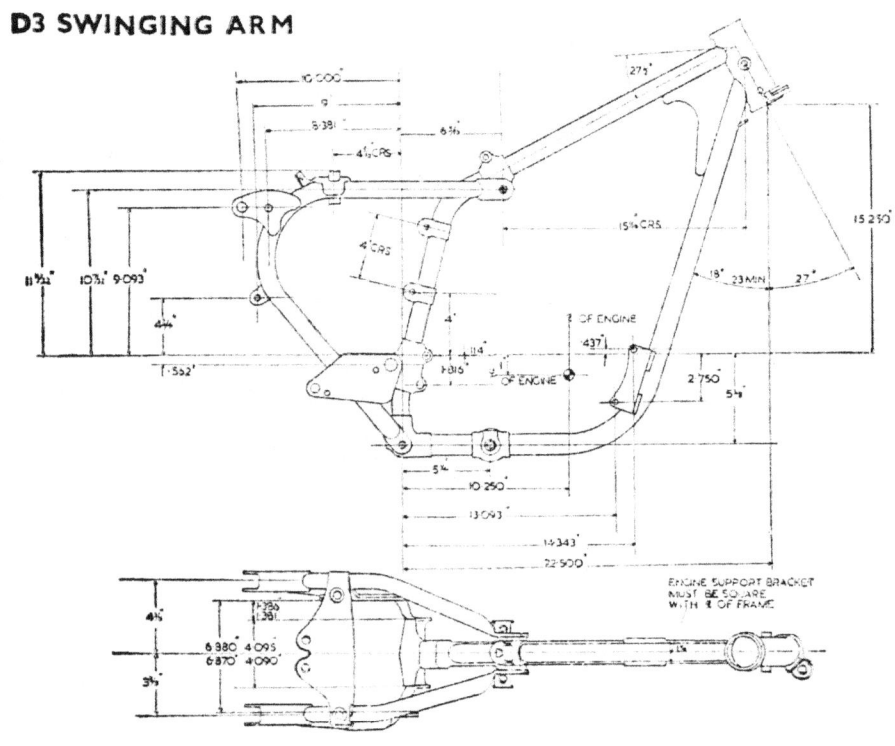

C12 SWINGING ARM

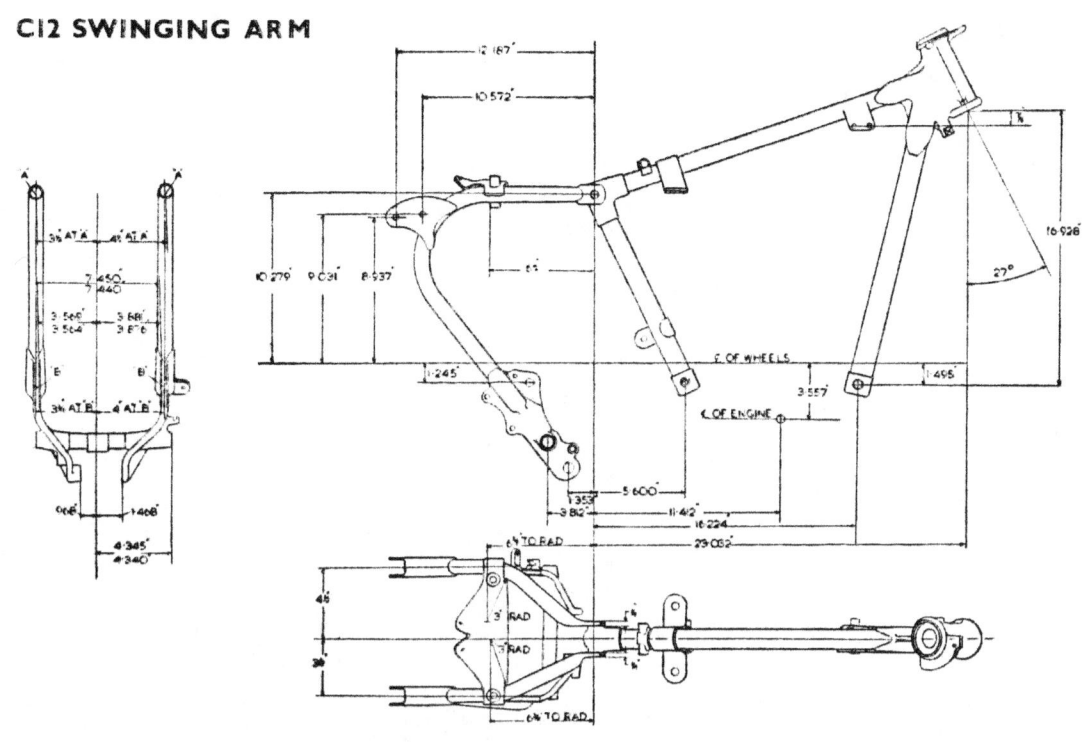

D5 SWINGING ARM

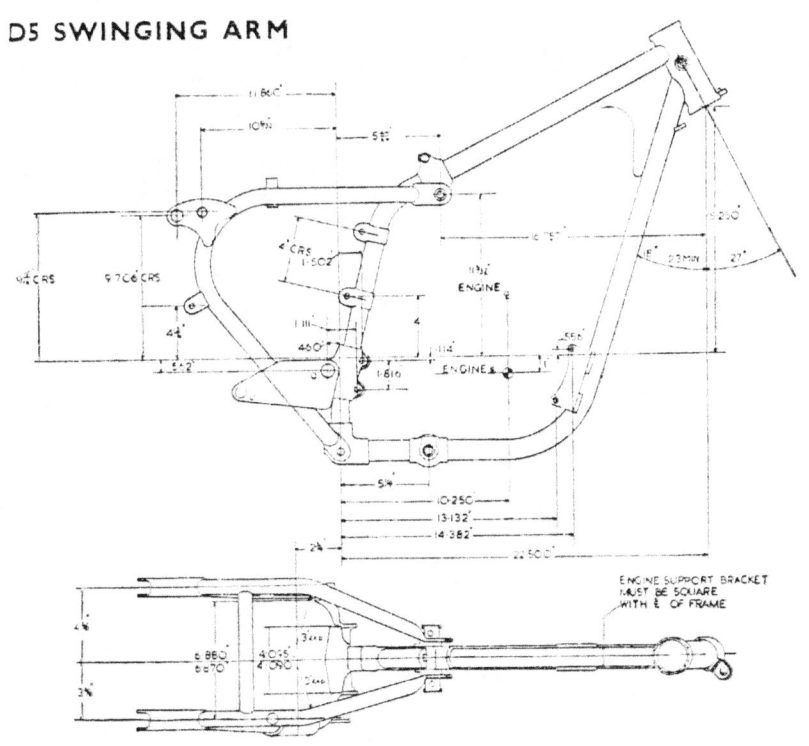

D7 SWINGING ARM

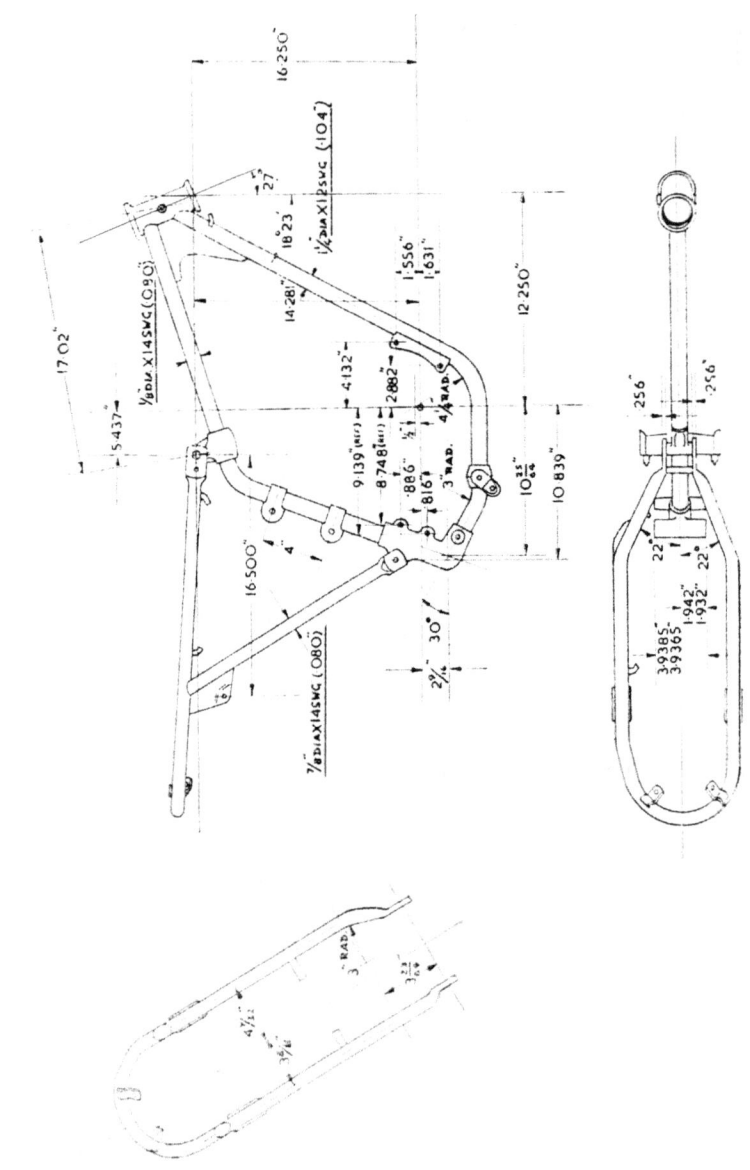

C15 STAR AND C15 SPORTS STAR

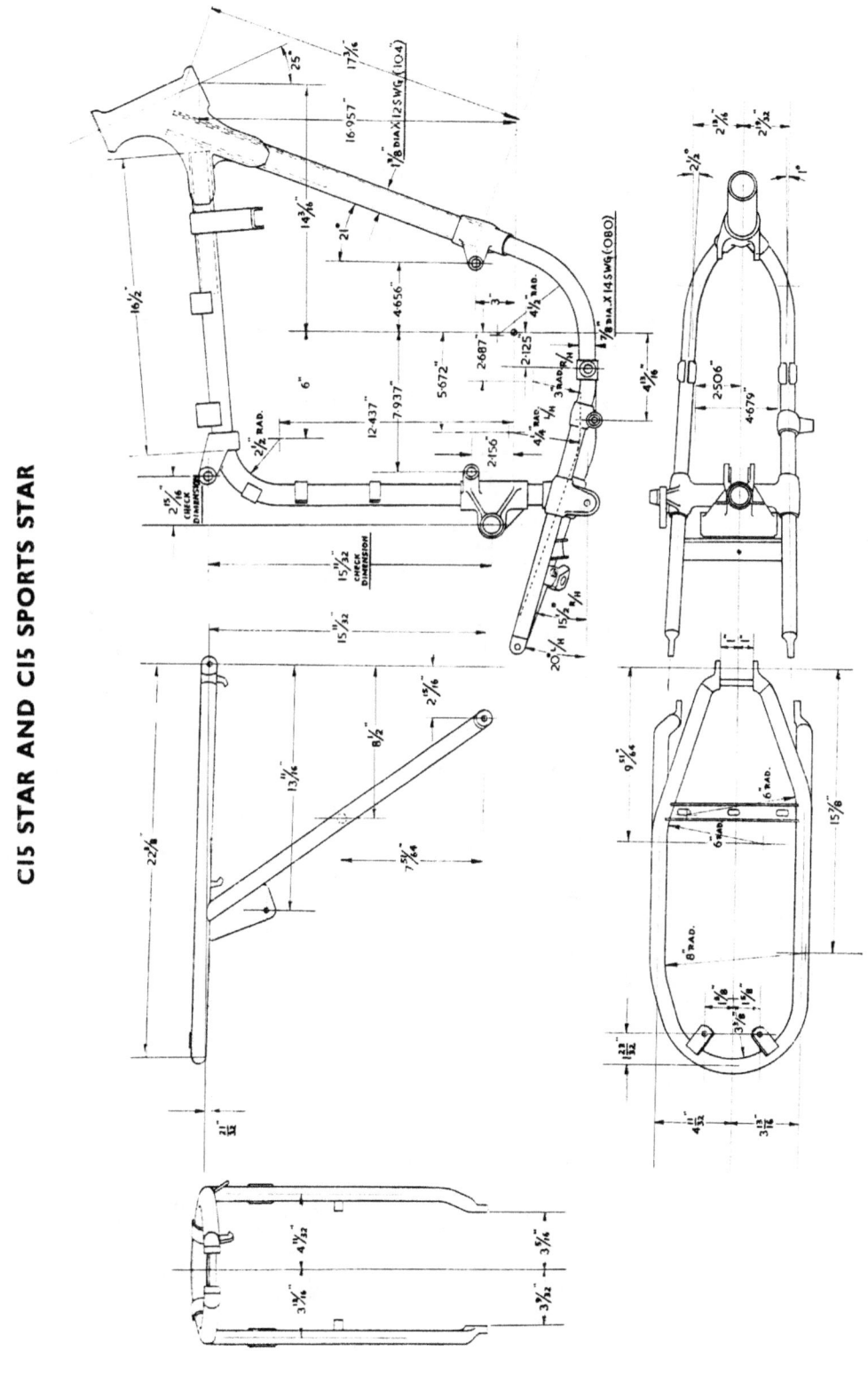

C15 TRIALS AND C15 SCRAMBLES

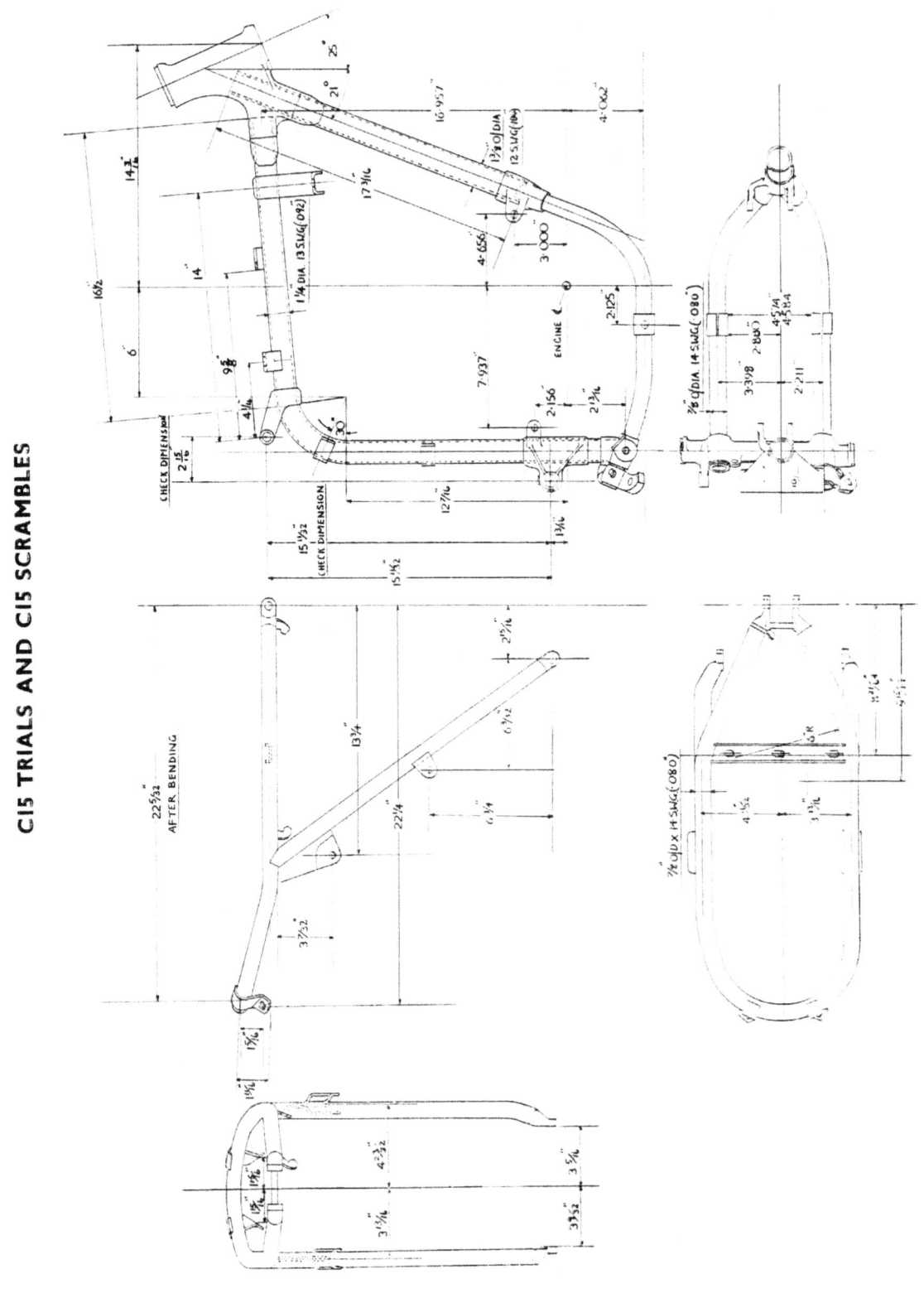

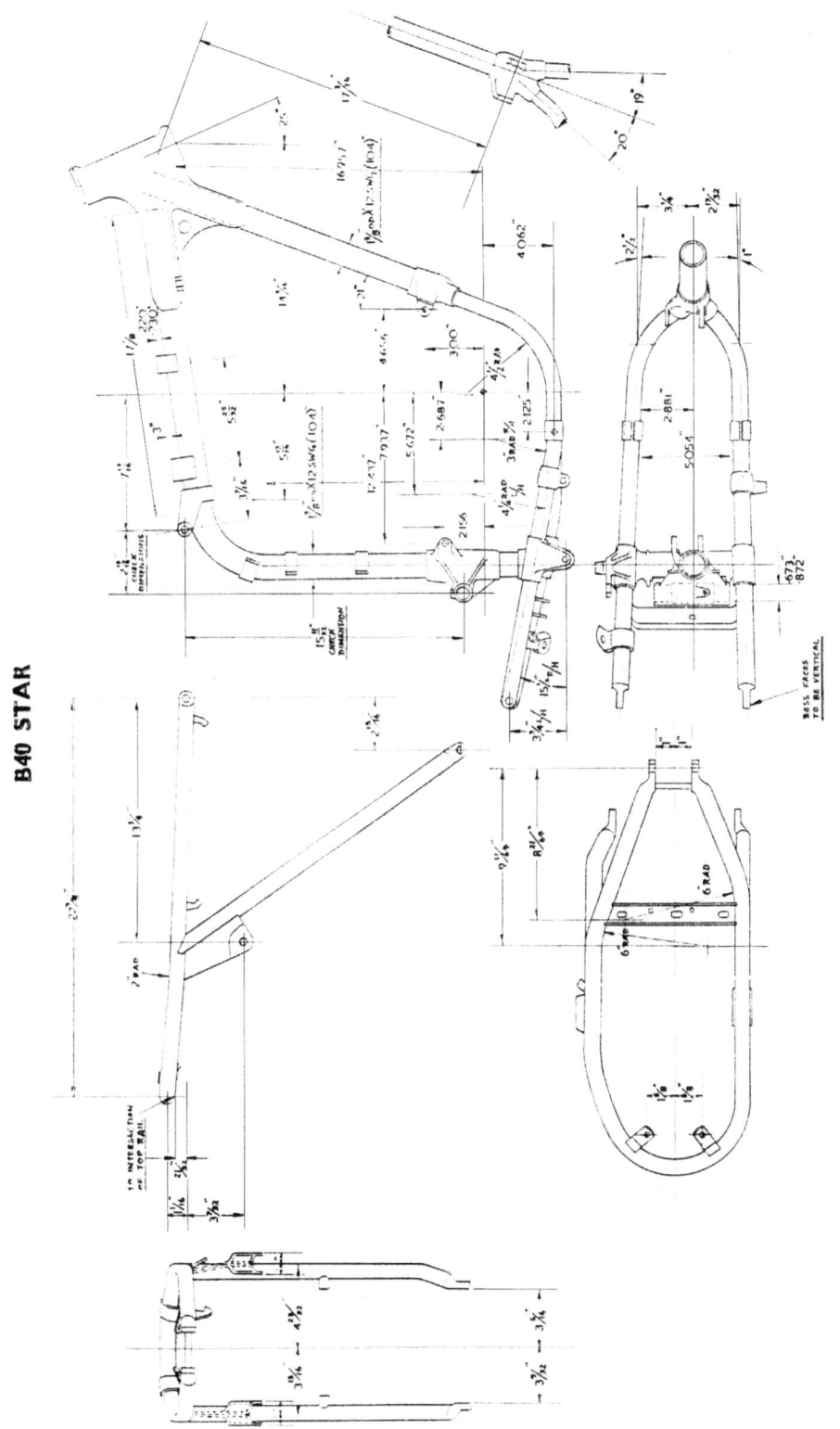

500 c.c. STAR AND 650 c.c. STAR MODELS A50 AND A65

B.S.A. Service Sheet No. 711
Revised Sept. 1958.

SERVICE TOOLS

for all

MOTOR CYCLES
1946 to 1958 Inclusive

Use in conjunction with
Service Sheet No. 711A
For Details of Models and Prices.

BSA SERVICE SHEET No. 711

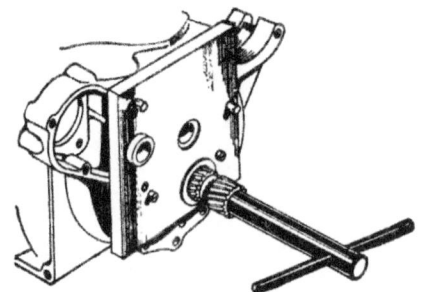

61-3281 Reaming Jig (mainshaft and camshaft gear bushes)
61-3275 Reaming Jig (mainshaft and camshaft gear bushes)

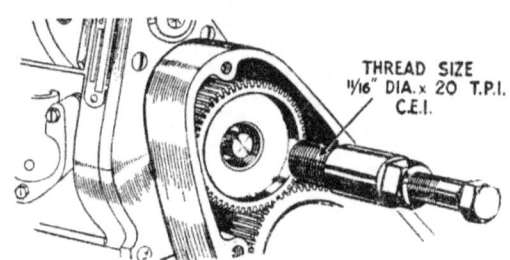

61-1903 Magdyno Driving Pinion Extractor Tool complete.
For Models fitted with Magdyno Lighting Equipment.

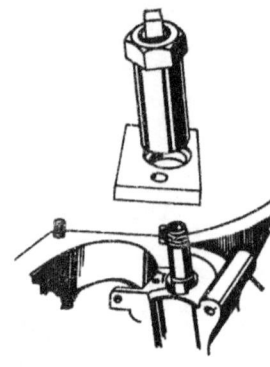

61-3069 Inlet Tappet Guide Extractor

61-3284 Mainshaft Bush Reamer
61-3285 Pilot for Jigs 61-3275
61-3286 Pilot for Jigs 61-3281
61-3287 Shell Reamer Holder
61-3288 Tommy Bar for 61-3287

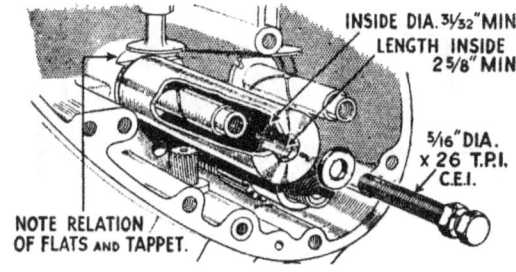

61-691 Cam Pinion Post Extractor

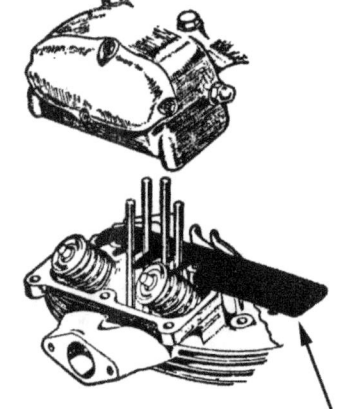

67-9114 Push Rod Assembly Tool

61-3167 Reamer for use with 61-3162 61-3281 and 61-3275

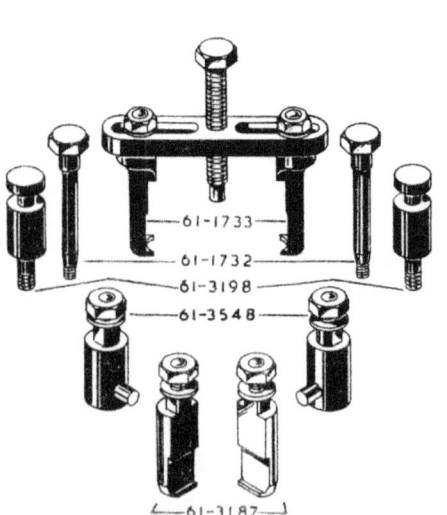

61-3256 Extractor Set Complete

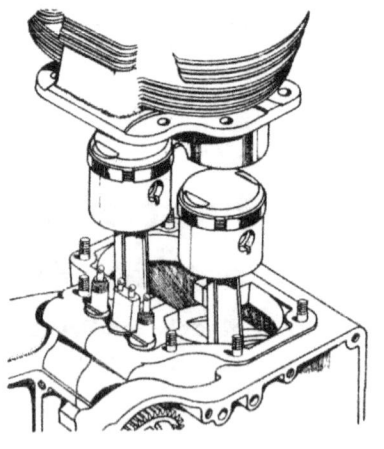

61-3061 Piston Ring Slipper
61-3334 Piston Ring Slipper,
61-3262 Piston Ring Slipper, (2 per set)

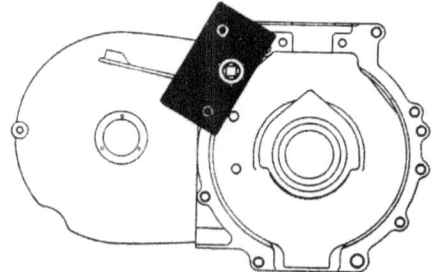

61-3159 Camshaft Bush Extractor

B.S.A. SERVICE SHEET No. 711—*continued*

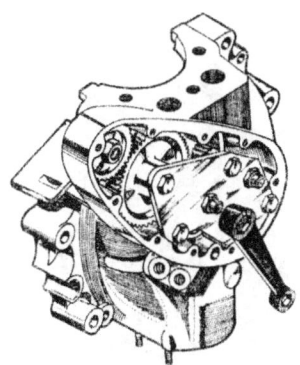

15-832 Mainshaft Nut Spanner

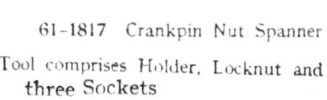

61-1817 Crankpin Nut Spanner

Tool comprises Holder, Locknut and three Sockets

Sockets for 61-1817
61-1754
61-1755
61-3228

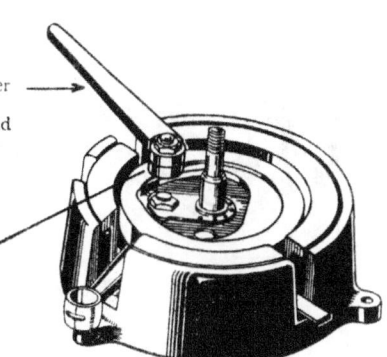

61-1751 Flywheel Bolster
61-1750 "   "   Gauge Rod
61-1747 "   "   Ring
61-1749 "   "   "

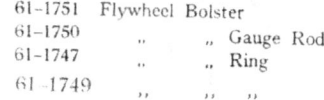

61-658 Gudgeon Pin Bush Extractor comprising Spindle with various size bushes.

65-9243 C Spanner and Fork Top Nut Spanner

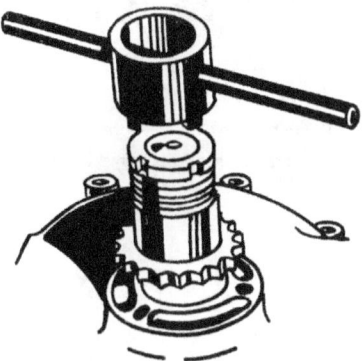

61-3220 Cush Drive Nut Tube Spanner

61-3305 Valve Seating Tool complete

Comprising Tommy Bar 61-3291
Holder 61-3290

Cutters
61-3298 .. 1 7/8" × 45° × 20°
61-3299 .. 1 1/2" × 45° × 20°
61-3300 .. 1 5/8" × 45° × 20°
61-3301 .. 1 3/4" × 45° × 20°
61-3302 .. 1 7/8" × 45° × 20°

Pilots
61-3293 .. 5/16"
61-3294 .. .350"
61-3295 .. 3/8"

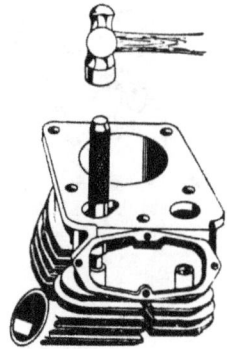

61-3263 61-3264 61-3265 61-3267 61-3268
Valve Guide fitting and extracting punches

65-9240 Valve Grinding Tool

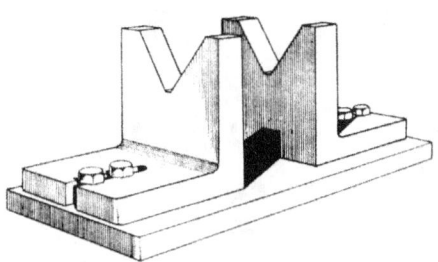

61-692 Vee Block and Base Plate

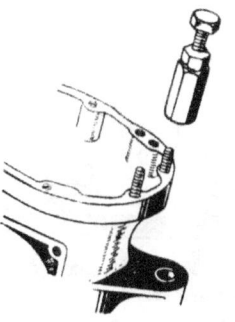

61-699 1/4" C.E.I. Stud Boxes
61-317 5/16"   "   "   "
61-545 3/8"   "   "   "

121

B.S.A. SERVICE SHEET No. 711—continued

61-3049 Cylinder Head Spanner

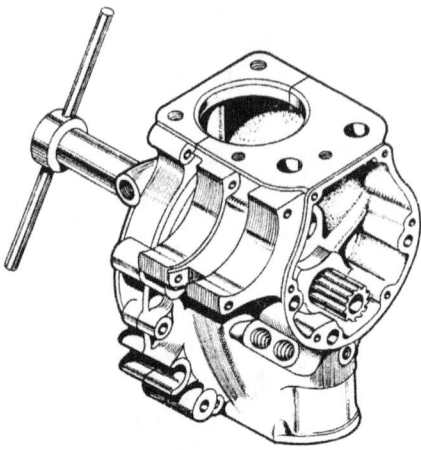

61-1932 Reamer and Holder complete (mainshaft bush)
61-1922 Reamer for 61-1932

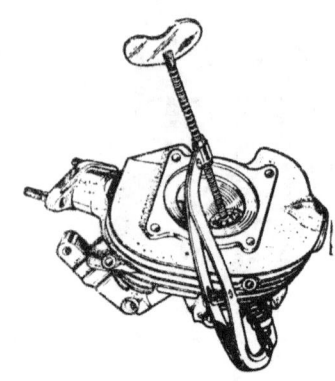

61-3340 Valve Spring Compressor with Adaptor
Models M33
"B" Group, "A" Group, and Sunbeam

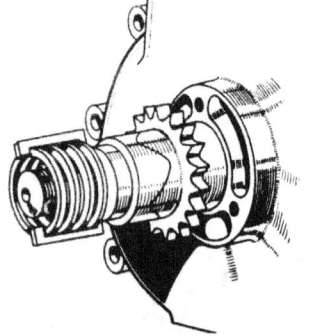

61-1822 Cush Drive Spring Assembly Tool
For holding Spring compressed whilst fitting Lockring.
(2 per set)

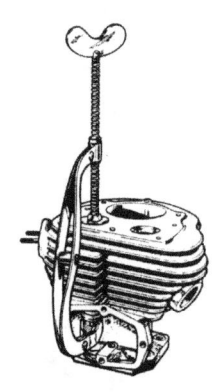

61-3340 Valve Spring Compressor
Models C10, C11, M20, M21
(Use without adaptor)

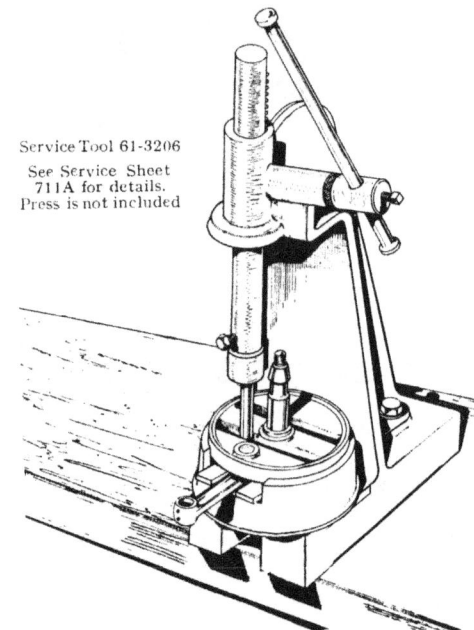

Service Tool 61-3206
See Service Sheet 711A for details.
Press is not included

61-3052 Cylinder Base Nut Spanner

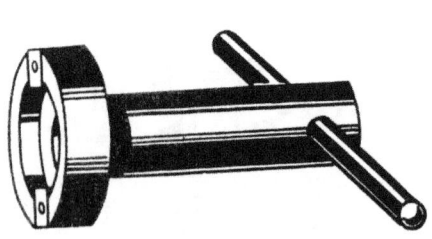

61-3257 Gearbox Sprocket Locknut Spanner,
61-3258 Gearbox Sprocket Locknut Spanner,

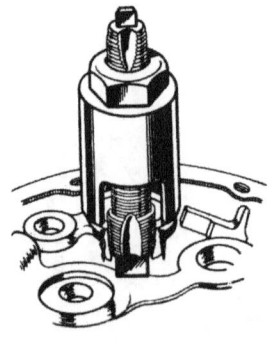

61-3185 Bush Extractor

61-3246 Gudgeon Pin Bush Reamer (.4687")
61-3367 Gudgeon Pin Bush Reamer (.625")
61-3556 Gudgeon Pin Bush Reamer (.6875")
61-3366 Gudgeon Pin Bush Reamer (.750")
61-3580 Gudgeon Pin Bush Reamer (.4375")
61-3581 Gudgeon Pin Bush Reamer (.5625")

B.S.A. SERVICE SHEET No. 711—continued

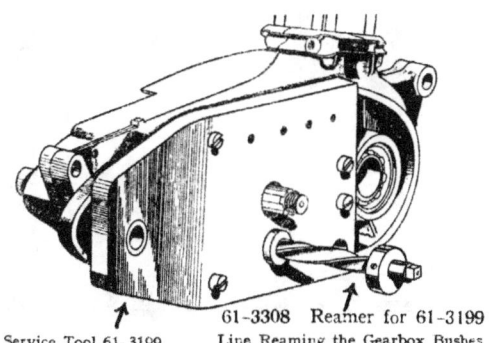

Service Tool 61-3199.
61-3308 Reamer for 61-3199
Line Reaming the Gearbox Bushes

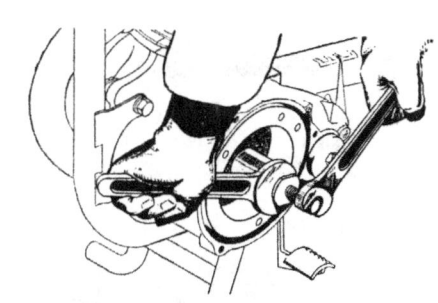

61-3188 Generator Flywheel Removal Tool (Wico Pacy)
90-297 Generator Flywheel Removal Tool (Lucas)

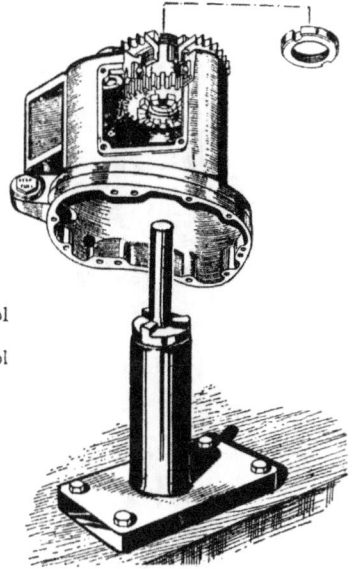

61-3064 Pinion Sleeve Extractor

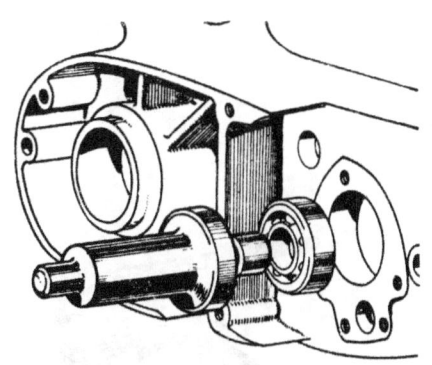

61-3214 Ballrace Pilot (gearbox pinion bearing)
61-3215 Ballrace Pilot (gearbox mainshaft bearing)

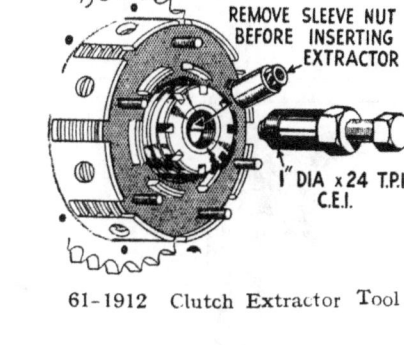

61-1912 Clutch Extractor Tool

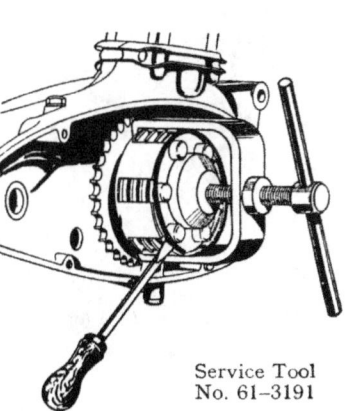

Service Tool No. 61-3191
Removing the Clutch Plate Circlip

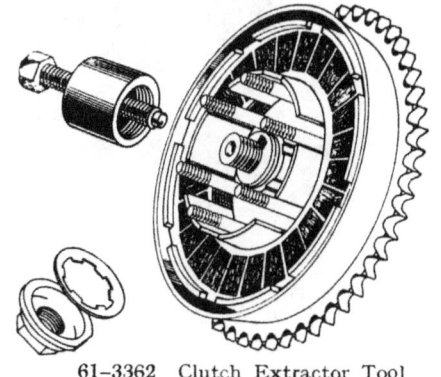

61-3362 Clutch Extractor Tool

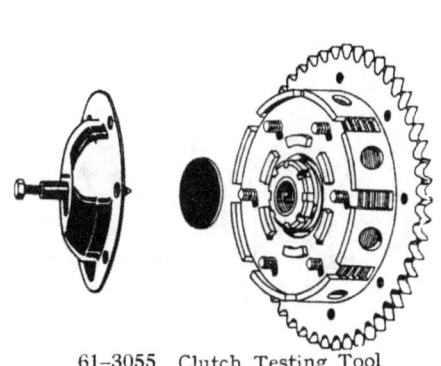

61-3055 Clutch Testing Tool

61-3212 Ballrace Pilot for large engine bearing
61-3213 Ballrace Pilot for small engine bearing

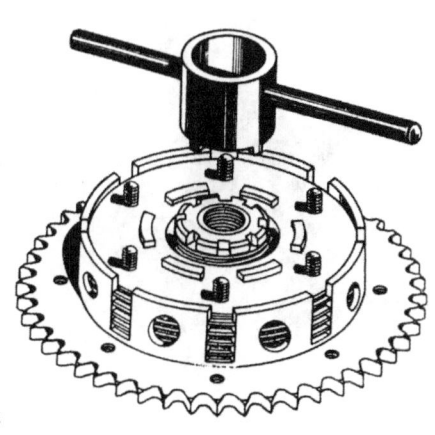

61-1915 Clutch Spring Nut Tube Spanner.

B.S.A. SERVICE SHEET No. 711—continued

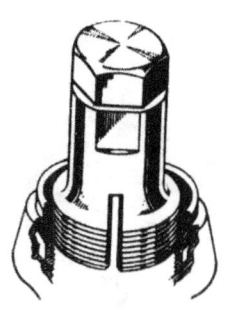

61-3060 Ballrace Extractor (steering head) for all 3/16" balls

61-3063 Ballrace Extractor (steering head) for all 1/4" balls

61-3006 Oil Seal Extractor

61-3007 Oil Seal Assembly Tool

61-3003 Spanner for Fork Plug Assembly

61-3002 Assembly Tool for Adjuster Sleeve
61-3008 Assembly Tool for Adjuster Sleeve

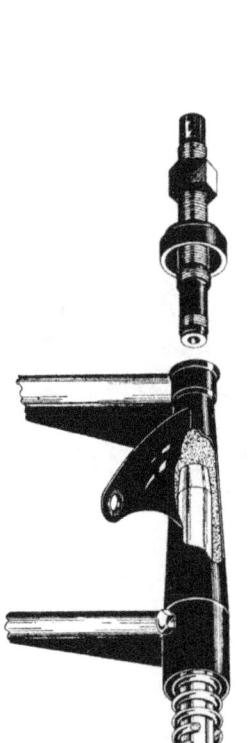
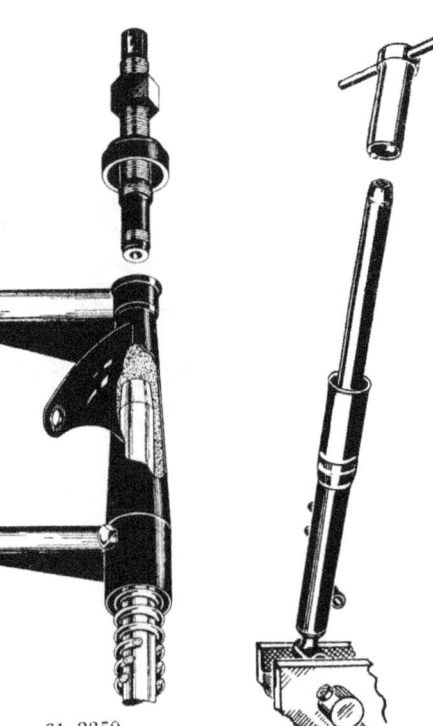

61-3350 Fork Shaft Dismantling and Assembly Tool

61-3005 Assembly Tool for Oil Seal Holder

61-3001 Spanner for Fork Top Nut Assembly

61-3222 Rear Suspension Strip and Assembly Tool

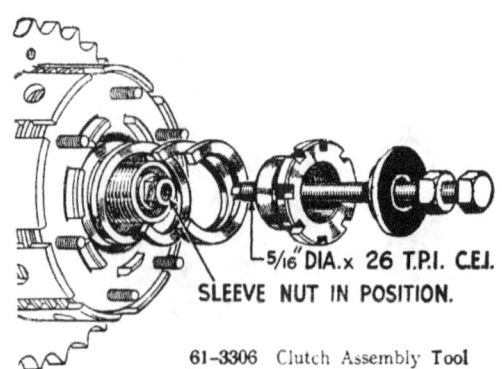

5/16" DIA. x 26 T.P.I. C.E.I. SLEEVE NUT IN POSITION.

61-3306 Clutch Assembly Tool

B.S.A. SERVICE SHEET No. 711—continued

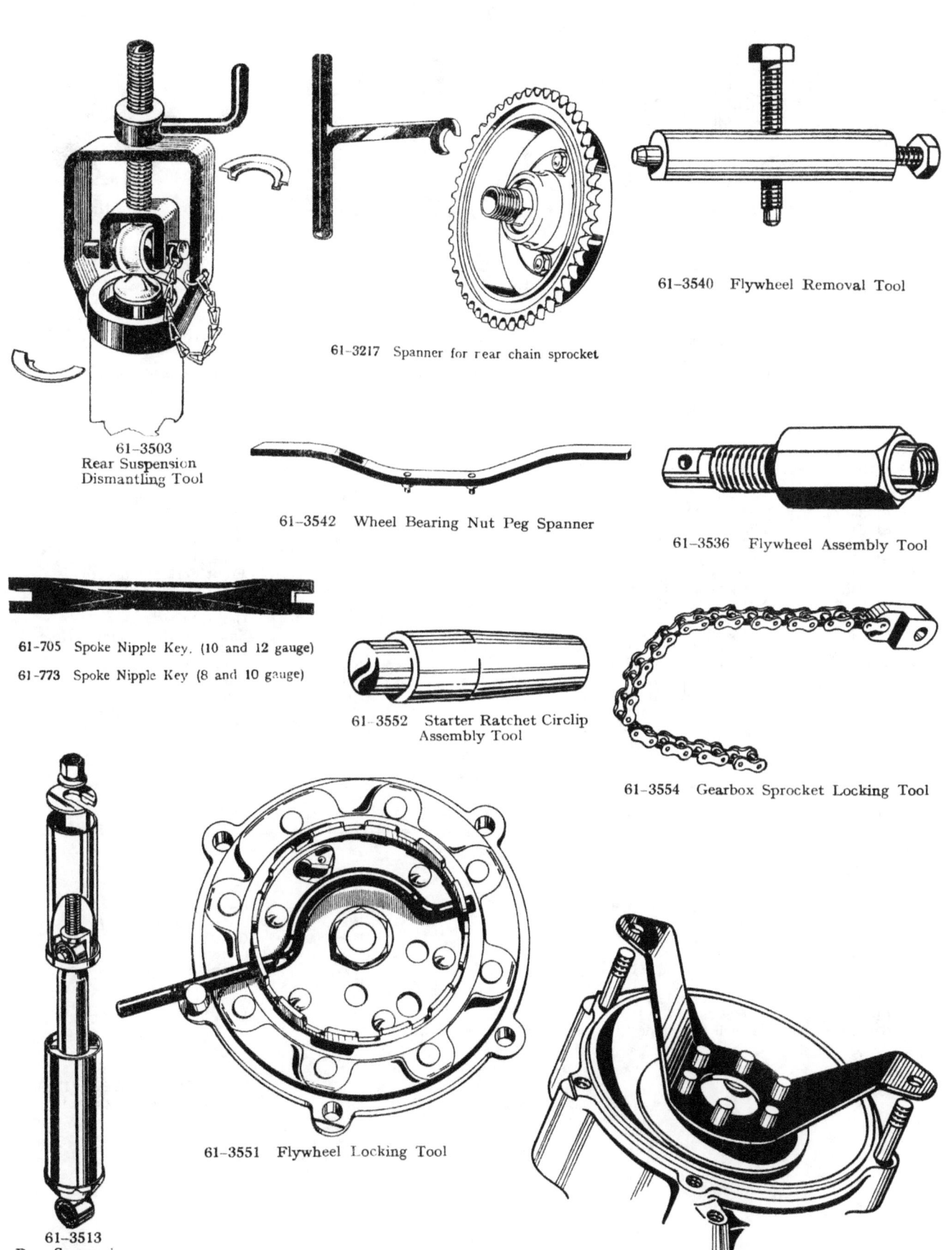

125

B.S.A. SERVICE SHEET No. 711—*continued*

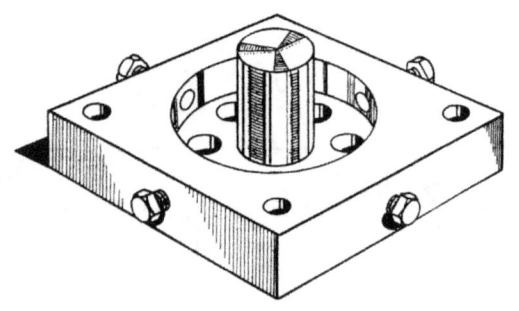

61-3499 Bench Die Holder

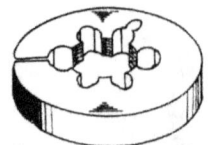

61-3483 Die

Tap

Die Nut

Part No.	Description	For
61-3574	Tap and Die Set in wooden case comprising tools listed below except 61-3483	General Workshop use
61-3575	Tap and Die Set in wooden case comprising all tools listed below	General Workshop use

TAPS.

Part No.	Taps.		For
61-3461	3/8" x 19 TPI B.S.P.	(R/H)	Petrol Tap Hole.
61-3462	3/8" x 20 TPI B.S.F.	(L/H)	Sunbeam Dynamo.
61-3463	7/16" x 20 TPI C.E.I.	(R/H)	General.
61-3464	1/2" x 20 TPI C.E.I.	(R/H)	General.
61-3502	9/16" x 20 TPI C.E.I.	(R/H)	General.
61-3465	9/16" x 20 TPI C.E.I.	(L/H)	Front Fork Spindle Hole.
61-3466	5/8" x 20 TPI C.E.I.	(R/H)	General.
61-3467	3/4" x 20 TPI C.E.I.	(R/H)	General.
65-3468	3/4" x 20 TPI B.S.W.	(R/H)	General.
61-3469	3/4" x 12 TPI B.S.F.	(L/H)	Sunbeam Rear Spindle Hole.
61-3470	7/8" x 20 TPI B.S.W.	(R/H)	Rear Suspension Shaft.
61-3471	1-1/16" x 20 TPI C.E.I.	(R/H)	Fork Shaft Top.
61-3472	1 1/8" x 28 TPI B.S.F.	(R/H)	Fork Shaft Bottom.
61-3473	1 1/2" x 20 TPI B.S.W.	(R/H)	Filler Caps.
61-3531	14 mm. x 1.25 mm.	(R/H)	14 mm. Spark Plug Hole
61-3533	1.250" x 20 TPI B.S.W.	(R/H)	Bantam Fork Tube (90-5021)

DIES.

Part No.	Dies.		For
61-3474	7/16" x 20 TPI C.E.I.	(R/H)	General.
61-3475	1/2" x 20 TPI C.E.I.	(R/H)	General.
61-3476	9/16" x 20 TPI C.E.I.	(R/H)	Gearbox Mainshaft.
61-3477	9/16" x 20 TPI C.E.I.	(L/H)	"A" Group Mainshaft.
61-3478	5/8" x 20 TPI C.E.I.	(R/H)	General.
61-3479	3/4" x 20 TPI C.E.I.	(R/H)	General.
61-3480	3/4" x 12 TPI B.S.F.	(L/H)	Sunbeam Rear Spindle.
61-3481	1" x 24 TPI C.E.I.	(R/H)	Fork Stem.
61-3482	1.120" x 24 TPI C.E.I.	(R/H)	Fork Stem.
61-3483	1 1/4" x 28 TPI WHIT.	(R/H)	Fork Sliding Tube Top.
61-3499	Bench Die Holder (for use with 61-3483)		

B.S.A. MOTOR CYCLES LTD.
Service Dept., Birmingham 11
Printed in England

B.S.A. Service Sheet No. 711A

Revised Sept., 1958

PRICE LIST

for

SERVICE TOOLS

1946 to 1958 Inclusive

Use in conjunction with Service Sheet No. 711

Part No.	Description	Used on Model	Retail Price Per Unit £ s. d.
15–832	Rear Hub Nut Spanner	A, B, C and M	4 5
61–317	Stud Box 5/16" c.e.i.	General	3 0
61–545	Stud Box 3/8" c.e.i.	General	3 0
61–658	Gudgeon Pin Bush Extractor	All Models	10 6
61–691	Cam Pinion Post Extractor	B and M	4 6
61–692	Flywheel "V" Blocks (used with 61–1821)	B, C and M	2 5 4
61–696	Socket Nut (used with 61–1817)	B, C and M	1 5
61–698	Crankpin Nut Spanner only (used with 61–1817)	B, C and M	1 1 0
61–699	Stud Box 1/4" c.e.i.	General	3 0
61–705	Nipple Key (10 and 12 gauge)	General	3 10
61–773	Nipple Key (8 and 10 gauge)	General	3 10
61–1747	Flywheel Bolster Ring	C Group	4 1 3
61–1749	Flywheel Bolster Ring	B and M 500 c.c.	4 1 3
61–1750	Flywheel Bolster Gauge Rod (2 per set)	B, C and M	7 7
61–1751	Flywheel Bolster	B, C and M	3 11 9
61–1754	Crankpin Nut Socket (used with 61–1817)	C Group	8 0
61–1755	Crankpin Nut Socket (used with 61–1817)	B and M	8 0
61–1817	Crankpin Nut Spanner complete	B, C and M	2 7 6
	Comprising:—		
	61–696 Socket Nut		1 5
	61–698 Spanner		1 1 0
	61–1754 Socket	C Group	8 0
	61–1755 Socket	B and M	8 0
	61–3228 Socket	Gold Star	9 1

BSA SERVICE TOOLS

Part No.	Description	Used on Model	Per Unit Retail Price
			£ s. d.
61-1821	"V" Block Base Plate (used with 61-692)	B, C and M	1 10 3
61-1822	Cush Drive Spring Assembly Tool (2 per set)	A, B, C and M	4 6
61-1903	Magdyno Drive Pinion Extractor	B and M	3 0
61-1912	Clutch Extractor	M to 1948	6 0
61-1915	Clutch Spring Nut Tube Spanner	M to 1948	4 6
61-1922	Reamer (used with 61-1932) (mainshaft bush)	C Group	3 5 0
61-1932	Reamer and Holder complete (used with 61-1922)	C Group	4 4 9
61-3001	Fork Top Nut Spanner	A, B, C and M	13 6
61-3002	Adjuster Sleeve Assembly Tool (steering head)	B, C and M	12 1
61-3003	Fork Plug Spanner (front fork)	A, B, C and M	13 6
61-3005	Oil Seal Holder Assembly Tool (front fork)	A, B, C and M	1 1 2
61-3006	Oil Seal Extractor (front fork)	A, B, C and M	15 1
61-3007	Oil Seal Assembly Tool (front fork)	A, B, C and M	6 0
61-3008	Adjuster Sleeve Assembly Tool (steering head)	A7/10, S7/8	12 1
61-3049	Cylinder Head Spanner	M20/21	10 6
61-3052	Cylinder Base Nut Spanner	M20/21	1 1 2
61-3055	Clutch Testing Tool	M to 1948	15 1
61-3060	Steering Head Ballrace Extractor	For 3/16" Balls	8 3
61-3061	Piston Ring Slipper (2 per set)	A7 to 1950	7 6
61-3063	Steering Head Ballrace Extractor	For 1/4" Balls	8 3
61-3064	Pinion Sleeve Extractor	B, C and M	2 11 5
61-3069	Inlet Tappet Guide Extractor	A7 to 1950	7 7
61-3159	Camshaft Bush Extractor	A7, A10	12 8
61-3167	Camshaft Bush Reamer (used with 61-3275/81)	A Group	3 0 6
61-3185	Gearbox Bush Extractor	M Group	15 9
61-3188	Flywheel Magneto Removal Tool (Wico Pacy)	D1, D3 and D5	6 8
61-3191	Clutch Plate Circlip Removal Tool	D1, D3 and D5	1 10 3
61-3199	Gearbox Bush Line Reaming Plate (used with 61-3205)	D1, D3 and D5	2 1 6
61-3205	Layshaft Bush Reamer only (used with 61-3199)	D1, D3 and D5	2 1 11
61-3206	Flywheel Dismantling and Assembly Tool	D1, D3 and D5	3 15 6

Comprising:—
    61-3207   Jig Body
    61-3208(2) Dismantling Bar
    61-3209   Dismantling Punch
    61-3210   Assembly Bridge
(*Note:—* Press as illustrated is not included).

Part No.	Description	Used on Model	Per Unit Retail Price
61-3212	Ballrace Pilot for large engine bearing	D1, D3 and D5	7 7
61-3213	Ballrace Pilot for small engine bearing	D1, D3 and D5	6 8
61-3214	Ballrace Pilot for gearbox pinion bearing	D1, D3 and D5	7 7
61-3215	Ballrace Pilot for gearbox mainshaft bearing	D1, D3 and D5	6 8
61-3217	Spanner for rear wheel sprocket	A7, A10	11 3
61-3220	Tube Spanner for cush drive nut	A, B, C and M	3 6
61-3222	Rear Suspension Strip and Assembly Tool	A, B and M	13 6
61-3228	Crankpin Nut Socket (used with 61-1817)	B32/4 G/S	9 1
61-3246	Reamer Gudgeon Pin Bush	D1, D3	14 6
61-3256	Extractor Set complete	All Models	1 12 7

Comprising:—
    61-351(1)   Plate
    61-776(1)   Bolt
    61-1732(2) Extractor Leg (A Group cam pinion)
    61-1733(2) Extractor Leg (engine pinion B, C and M).
    61-3187(2) Extractor Leg (crankshaft pinion A7/10).
    61-3198(2) Extractor Leg (engine sprocket etc., D, C and A).
    61-3548(2) Extractor Leg (Dandy flywheel)

BSA SERVICE TOOLS

Part No.	Description	Used on Model	Retail Price Per Unit
			£ s. d.
61-3257	Gearbox Sprocket Locknut Spanner	A, B and M	15 1
61-3258	Gearbox Sprocket Locknut Spanner	C	15 1
61-3262	Piston Ring Slipper (2 per set)	A10	6 0
61-3263	Valve Guide Punch (used on B33/34, exhaust and G/Stars with .374 dia. valve stems).		3 0
61-3264	Valve Guide Punch (comprising 61-3265/66 and 61-3307)	C10 In. and Ex.	12 8
61-3265	Valve Guide Punch (B31/32 inlet, A7/10, C11, C12 inlet and exhaust and G/Stars with .310" dia. valve stems)		6 0
61-3267	Valve Guide Punch (comprising 61-3268/9/70)	M20, M21 In. and Ex.	8 3
61-3268	Valve Guide Punch (B31/32 exhaust, B33/34 inlet and G/Stars with .348" dia. valve stems)		6 0
61-3275	Mainshaft and Camshaft Bush Reaming Jig	A7 to 1950	2 12 11
61-3281	Mainshaft and Camshaft Bush Reaming Jig	A10, AA7 onwards	2 12 11
61-3284	Reamer (mainshaft used with 61-3275/81)	A7, A10	4 6 2
61-3285	Pilot for 61-3275	A7 to 1950	15 1
61-3286	Pilot for 61-3281	A10, AA7 onwards	15 1
61-3287	Reamer Holder (used with 61-3284)	A7, A10	9 1
61-3290	Valve Seat Cutter Holder	A, B, C and M	5 3
61-3293	Valve Seat Cutter Pilot (5/16")	A, B and C	6 8
61-3294	Valve Seat Cutter Pilot (.350")	B and M	6 8
61-3295	Valve Seat Cutter Pilot (.375")	B, and M33	6 8
61-3298	Valve Seat Cutter (1 7/16" dia x 45° x 20°)	A7 and C	2 6 2
61-3299	Valve Seat Cutter (1 1/2" dia. x 45° x 20°)	A10 and C	2 6 2
61-3300	Valve Seat Cutter (1 5/8" dia. x 45° x 20°)	B	2 6 2
61-3301	Valve Seat Cutter (1 3/4" dia. x 45° x 20°)	B and M	2 6 2
61-3302	Valve Seat Cutter (1 7/8" dia. x 45° x 20°)	B and M	2 6 2
61-3305	Valve Seating Tool complete	A, B, C and M	12 16 2
61-3306	Clutch Assembly Tool	M to 1948	3 0
61-3308	Reamer for 61-3199 (comprising 61-3205 and 61-3309)	D1, and D3	2 8 1
61-3311	Crankshaft Balance Weight (18 ozs., 12 drms.)	A7 1951 onwards	15 1
61-3312	Crankshaft Balance Weight (16 ozs., 14 drms.)	A7 to 1951	15 1
61-3334	Piston Ring Slipper (2 per set)	A7 1951 onwards	6 0
61-3340	Valve Spring Compressor complete	A, B, C and M	1 1 2
61-3350	Front Fork Dismantling and Assembly Tool	A, B, C, M and S7/8	15 1
61-3362	Clutch Extractor Tool	A, B, C and M 1949 onwards	6 8
61-3366	Gudgeon Pin Bush Reamer (.750")	B, M and A10	1 1 10
61-3367	Gudgeon Pin Bush Reamer (.625")	C only	1 2 8
61-3487	Valve Guide Assembly Punch	S7 and S8	15 1
61-3497	Crankshaft Balance Weight (19 ozs. 8 drms.)	A10R/R and S/R	13 9
61-3499	Bench Die Holder (used with 61-3483)	A, B, C and M	2 18 6
61-3503	Rear Suspension Dismantling Tool	A and B S/A	1 17 10
61-3513	Rear Suspension Dismantling Tool	C12 and D3 S/A	1 14 4
61-3536	Flywheel Assembly Tool	Dandy	5 6
61-3540	Flywheel Removal Tool	Dandy	6 3
61-3542	Wheel Bearing Nut Peg Spanner	A and B, S/A	10 4
61-3548	Flywheel Removal Tool (2) (used with 61-3256)	Dandy	4 7
61-3551	Flywheel Locking Tool	Dandy	1 2
61-3552	Starter Ratchet Circlip Assembly Tool	Dandy	5 3
61-3553	Clutch Back Plate Locking Tool	Dandy	9 2
61-3554	Gearbox Sprocket Locking Tool	Dandy	5 5
61-3556	Gudgeon Pin Bush Reamer (11/16")	A7	1 17 10
61-3558	Locking Ring Spanner	8" Brake	11 10
61-3580	Gudgeon Pin Bush Reamer (7/16")	Dandy	1 0 0
61-3581	Gudgeon Pin Bush Reamer (9/16")	D5	1 6 10
65-9240	Valve Grinding Tool	A, B, C and M	1 10
65-9243	Combined "C" and Fork Top Nut spanner	A, B, C and M	1 10
67-9114	Push Rod Assembly Tool	A7/10 1951 onwards	1 5
90-297	Lucas Rotor Removal Tool	D1	1 3

BSA SERVICE TOOLS

Part No.	Description	Used on Models	Retail Price £ s. d.
61-3574	Tap and Die Set in wood case comprising taps and dies listed below except 61-3483	General	23 15 0
61-3575	Tap and Die Set in wood case comprising taps and dies listed below	General	32 7 0

TAPS

Part No.	Taps	Description	Retail Price £ s. d.
61-3461	3/8" x 19 T.P.I. B.S.P. R/H	Petrol Tap Hole	7 7
61-3462	3/8" x 20 T.P.I. B.S.F. L/H	Sunbeam Dynamo	7 7
61-3463	7/16" x 20 T.P.I. C.E.I. R/H	General	13 1
61-3464	1/2" x 20 T.P.I. C.E.I. R/H	General	14 6
61-3502	1/16" x 20 T.P.I. C.E.I. R/H	General	18 7
61-3465	9/16" x 20 T.P.I. C.E.I. L/H	Front Fork Spindle Hole ...	1 0 0
61-3466	5/8" x 20 T.P.I. C.E.I. R/H	General	17 3
61-3467	3/4" x 20 T.P.I. C.E.I. R/H	General	18 7
61-3468	3/4" x 20 T.P.I. B.S.W. R/H	General	18 7
61-3469	3/4" x 12 T.P.I. B.S.F. L/H	Sunbeam Rear Spindle Hole ...	1 0 0
61-3470	7/8" x 20 T.P.I. B.S.W. R/H	Rear Suspension Shaft ...	1 7 6
61-3471	1 1/16" x 20 T.P.I. C.E.I. R/H	Fork Shaft Top ...	1 5 6
61-3472	1 1/8" x 28 T.P.I. B.S.W. R/H	Fork Shaft ...	1 14 4
61-3473	1 1/2" x 20 T.P.I. B.S.W. R/H	Filler Cap ...	2 14 7
61-3531	14 mm. x 1.25 mm. R/H	Spark Plug ...	1 0 7
61-3533	1.250" x 20 T.P.I. B.S.W. R/H	D1 Fork Tube ...	1 11 0

DIES

Part No.	Dies	Description	Retail Price £ s. d.
61-3474	7/16" x 20 T.P.I. C.E.I. R/H	General	11 0
61-3475	1/2" x 20 T.P.I. C.E.I. R/H	General	12 4
61-3476	9/16" x 20 T.P.I. C.E.I. R/H	Gearbox Mainshaft ...	13 9
61-3477	9/16" x 20 T.P.I. C.E.I. L/H	A Group Mainshaft ...	17 3
61-3478	5/8" x 20 T.P.I. C.E.I. R/H	General	13 9
61-3479	3/4" x 20 T.P.I. C.E.I. R/H	General	18 7
61-3480	3/4" x 12 T.P.I. B.S.F. L/H	Sunbeam Rear Spindle ...	1 2 0
61-3481	1" x 24 T.P.I. C.E.I. R/H	Fork Stem	1 4 1
61-3482	1.120" x 24 T.P.I. C.E.I. R/H	Fork Stem	1 13 9
61-3483	1 7/8" x 28 T.P.I. Whit. R/H ... ... (Used with holder 61-3499)	Fork Sliding Tube Top ...	9 9 1

B.S.A. Motor Cycles Ltd., Service Department, Birmingham 11

Printed in England. Sept. 1958

B.S.A. Service Sheet No. 711B

Supplement to No. 711 and 711A

July 1960

SERVICE TOOLS

for

MOTOR CYCLES

B.S.A. SERVICE SHEET No. 711B (contd.)

Removing the Clutch Centre with Extractor No. 61-3583 (Model C15).

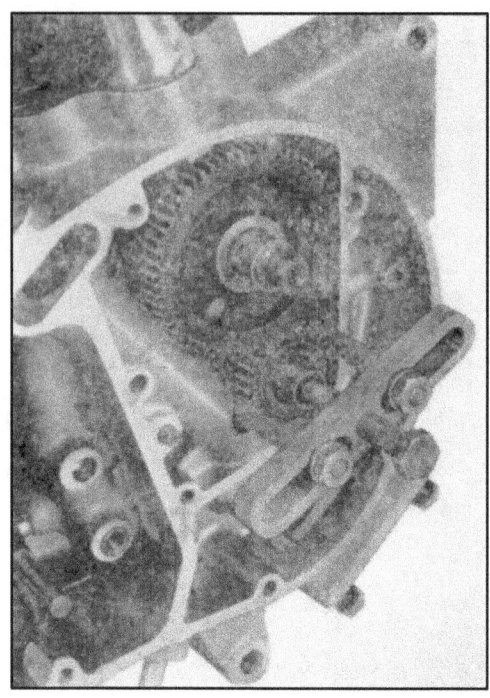

Removing the Crankshaft Pinion with Extractor No. 61-3681 using Legs No. 61-3588 (fitted with Legs 61-3585 for removing the Worm Wheel) (Model C15).

Parting the Flywheels using Bolster 61-3589, Stripping Bars 61-3590 and Punch 61-3601 (Model C15).

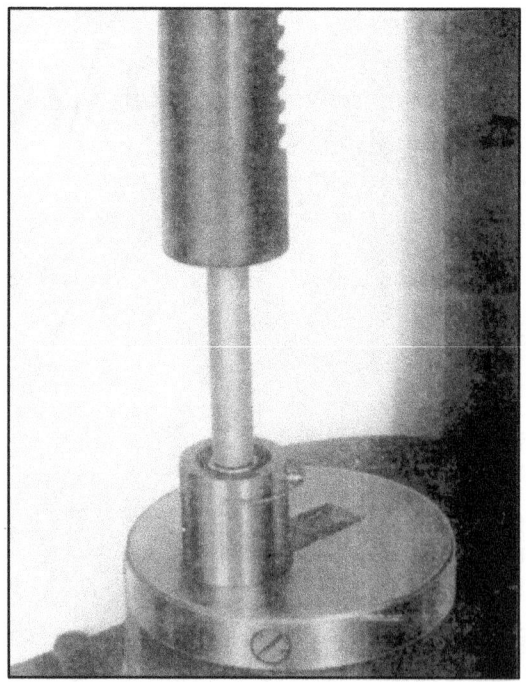

Assembling the Crankpin into the Gear Side Flywheel using Locating Gauge No. 61-3597 and Punch No. 61-3601 (Model C15).

B.S.A. SERVICE SHEET No. 711B (contd.)

Assembling the Drive Side Flywheel on to the Gear Side, using Bolster No. 61–3589, Bridge Piece No. 61–3591 and Punch No. 61–3601 (Model C15).

Flywheel Truing Sleeve No. 61–3592 used with Drive Side bearing on "V" blocks No. 61–692 (Model C15).

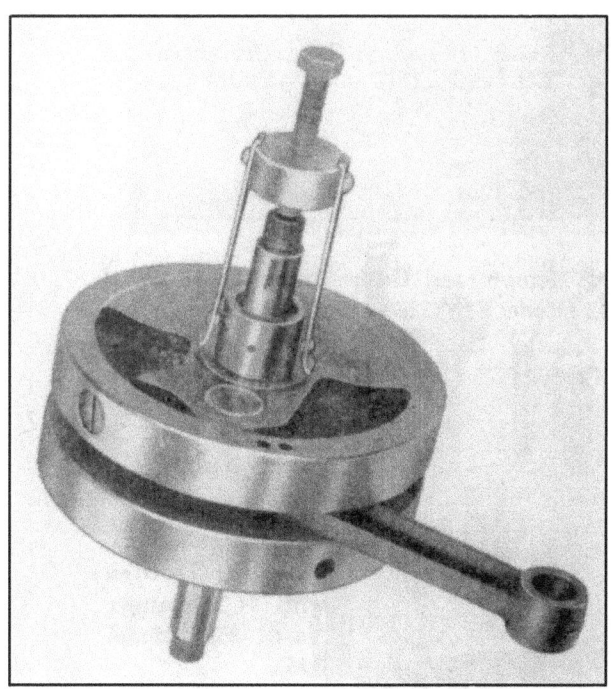

Removing the Gear Side Sleeve with Tool No. 61–3593 (Model C15).

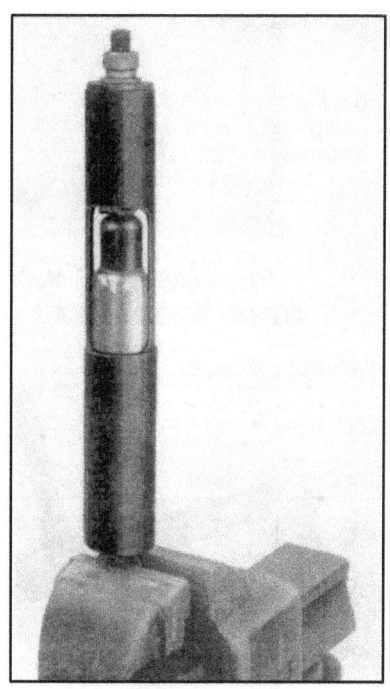

Dismantling the Rear Damper with Tool No. 61–3642 (for Models C15 and D7).

B.S.A. SERVICE SHEET No. 711B (contd.)

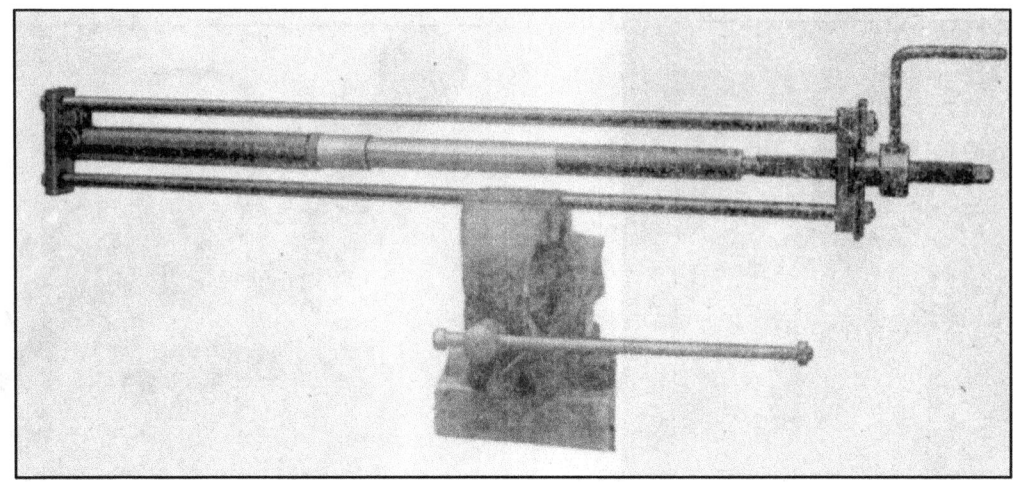

Withdrawing the Fork Main Member and Bushes from the Sliding Member using Tool No. 61-3587.

Reassembling the Fork Main Member, Sliding Member and Bushes using Tools No. 61-3587 and 61-3602 (Model C15).

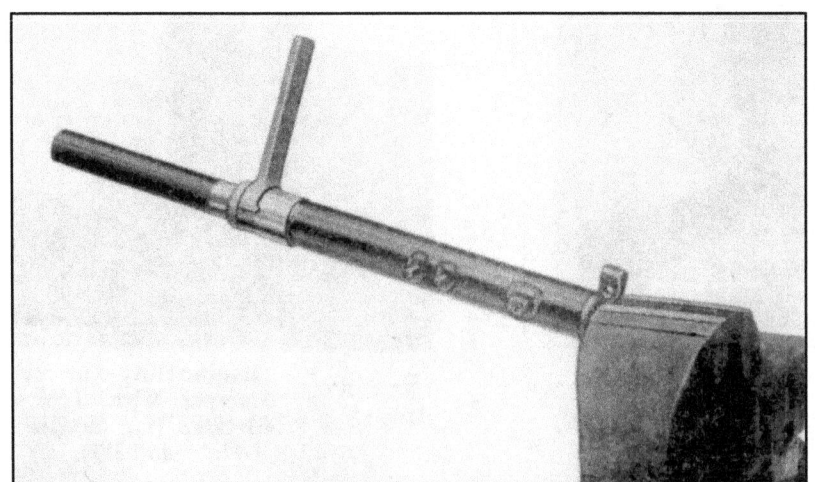

Removing the Fork Oil Seal Holder with "C" Spanner No. 61-3586 (Model C15).

B.S.A. SERVICE SHEET No. 711B (contd.)

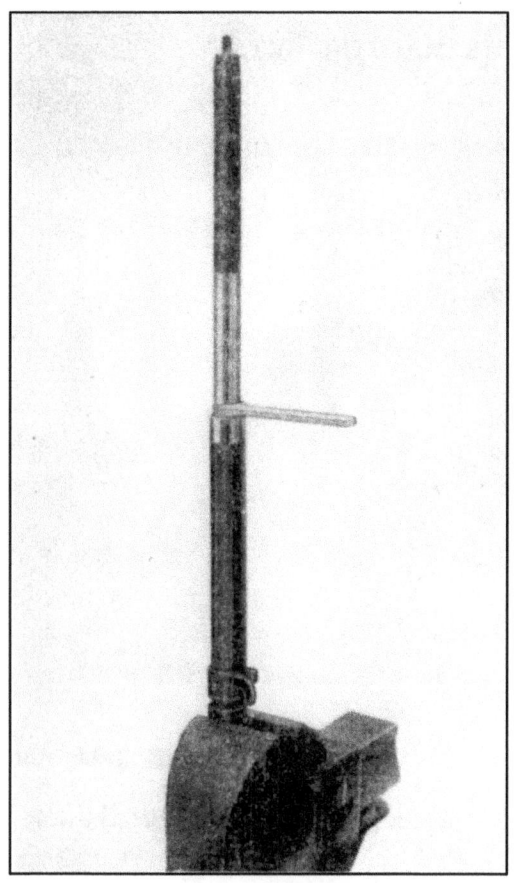

Taking off the Fork Leg Oil Seal Holder with Tool No. 3633 (Model D7).

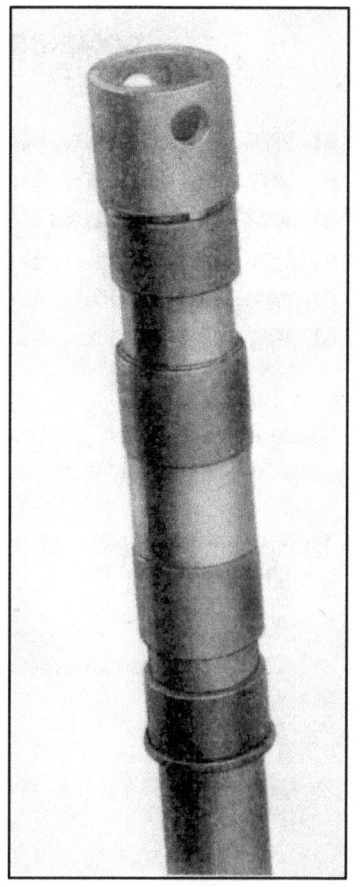

(Model C15). Removing the Fork Leg Bottom Nut with Dog Spanner No. 61–3606 (Tommy Bar not supplied).

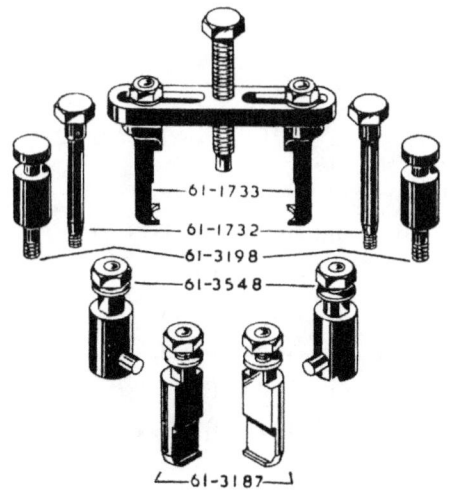

Pinion Extractor showing some of the special Legs.

PINION EXTRACTOR SETS

A Group	Part No. 61–3676
B and M Groups	Part No. 61–3677
C Group (excepting C15)	Part No. 61–3678
C15	Part No. 61–3681
D Group	Part No. 61–3679
Dandy	Part No. 61–3680
Complete Set	Part No. 61–3256

Details of comprising parts and applications are given overleaf.

B.S.A. SERVICE SHEET No. 711B (contd.)

COMPRISING PARTS OF EXTRACTOR SETS

61-3676 = 61-351 Plate, 61-776 Bolt, 61-1732 Leg (2), 61-3187 Leg (2), 61-3198 Leg (2).
61-3677 = 61-351 Plate, 61-776 Bolt, 61-1733 Leg (2).
61-3678 = 61-351 Plate, 61-776 Bolt, 61-1732 Leg (2), 61-1733 Leg (2), 61-3198 Leg (2).
61-3679 = 61-351 Plate, 61-776 Bolt, 61-3198 Leg (2).
61-3680 = 61-351 Plate, 61-776 Bolt, 61-3548 Leg (2).
61-3681 = 61-351 Plate, 61-776 Bolt, 61-3585 Leg (2), 61-3588 Leg (2).

These extractors are extremely useful for the removal of timing, worm or other gears, the legs being specially designed for the particular models.

They can also be used for other jobs of a like nature where a puller is required. All the legs are interchangeable and can be purchased separately if required.

61-358 GUDGEON PIN BUSH EXTRACTOR

is now cancelled and replaced by 61-3672.

This tool is now available for the individual models as detailed below:—

Tool No.	Model	Comprising
61-3651	—	Holder, Rod and Nut only.
61-3652	A7, A10	61-3651, and Bushes 61-3319/20.
61-3653	B Group	61-3651, and Bushes 61-3654/5.
61-3656	C10, C11, C12	61-3651, and Bushes 61-3657/8.
61-3659	C15, A7 (Steel Rod)	61-3651, and Bushes 61-3660/1.
61-3662	D1, D3	61-3651, and Bushes 61-3663/4.
61-3665	D5, D7	61-3651, and Bushes 61-3666/7.
61-3668	M20, M21	61-3651, and Bushes 61-654/5.
61-3669	Dandy	61-3651, and Bushes 61-3670/71.

B.S.A. SERVICE SHEET No. 711B (contd.)

Using a piston Ring Slipper makes replacement easier.

Piston Ring Slippers (Terry).

Now available for the following models:—

61–5004	55–60 mm. Bore	Models D1, D3.
61–5051	60–65 mm. Bore	Models C10L, C11, C12, D5, D7.
61–3682	65–70 mm. Bore	Models A Group, C15.

Additional Tools not illustrated

61–5035 valve grinding tool (Suction type). This tool is similar to 65–9240 shown on Service Sheet No. 711 but is suitable for valves with $\frac{3}{4}$ in. to 1 in. diameter heads.

61–3673 clutch nut screwdriver, designed specially for the moded C15.

BSA SERVICE SHEET No. 712X

ALL GROUPS
FLYWHEEL BALANCING (STATIC)

Revised and Reprinted October 1956.
Revised May 1958.

Flywheel balancing should not be undertaken except by an expert mechanic, who is fully equipped with the tools described in this Service Sheet.

Unless very great care is exercised, excessive engine vibration may result from any change of balance, and unless extreme care is practised in flywheel drilling, flywheels may be seriously weakened.

All flywheel assemblies are accurately balanced before leaving the Works and there should be no need to re-balance when fitting new big end assemblies unless the difference in weight between the old and new assembly is more than 1 to $1\frac{3}{4}$ozs.

When a fabricated crankshaft is employed as on the "C", "B" and "M" Group models, the method of flywheel truing is described in Service Sheet No. 607 in the case of "M" group machines and No. 305 in the case of "B" group and No. 407 for "C" group machines.

The equipment required for balancing is a drilling machine and knife edge rollers (see Fig. X10) which must be set up perfectly horizontal and sufficiently high to allow the flywheels to revolve with the Con Rod hanging.

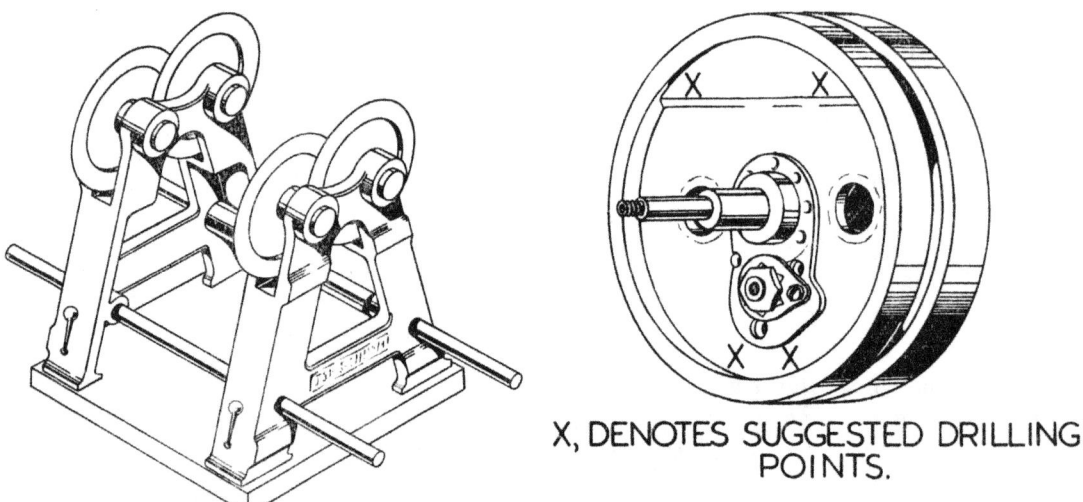

X, DENOTES SUGGESTED DRILLING POINTS.

Fig. X10. Knife Edge Rollers.   Fig. X11. "B" and "M" Group Flywheels.

For balancing purposes a small weight equivalent to part of the reciprocating weight must be attached to the small end of the Con Rod. A table of these weights is given below.

Place the assembly on the knife edges and allow to revolve till it stops, mark the lowest spot with chalk and check again two or three times.

To find the amount of the out-of-balance apply plasticine to the rim of the wheels diametrically opposite the heaviest point until the wheels remain stationary when placed in any position.

The wheels must now be drilled at the heaviest spot to remove metal equal to the weight of plasticine. Care must be taken to drill each wheel equally (see Fig. X11).

B.S.A. Service Sheet No. 712x (continued).

BALANCING "A" GROUP FLYWHEELS.

A group flywheels are treated similarly to the single cylinder models except that the Con Rods are not fitted, a balance weight being attached to each crank pin. These are available as Service Tools, 61-3310 for A7, 61-3312 for A7 after Engine No. AA7-101, 61-3311 for A10 and 61-3497 for A10 Road Rocket. New bolts and nuts must be used to secure the flywheel and the ends of the bolts peined over after locking.

Drilling is carried out on the periphery of the flywheel instead of the webs and care must be taken to keep the holes central and not too deep, the maximum depth should not be more than 3/16" (see Fig. X12). It is preferable to start with a smaller diameter hole which can be opened out if necessary, rather than a large diameter to then find that too much metal has been removed.

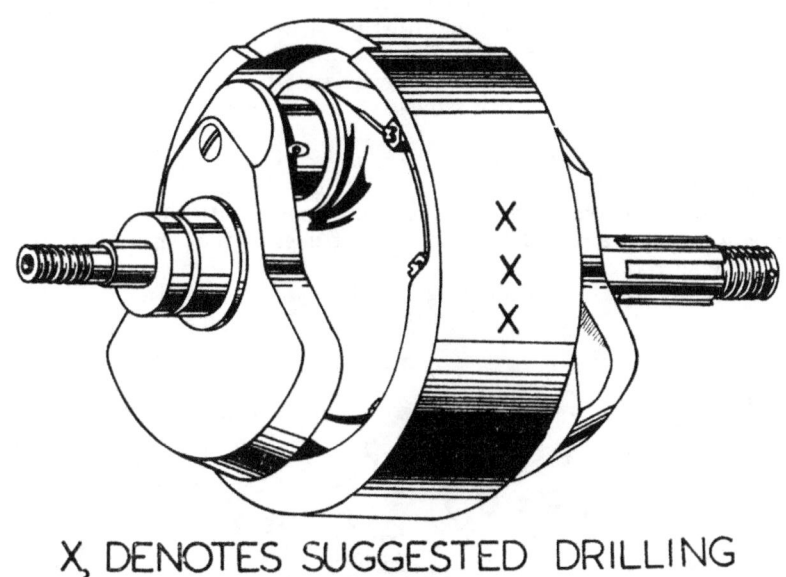

X, DENOTES SUGGESTED DRILLING POINTS.

Fig. X12. "A" Group Crankshaft.

Model	Weight attached	Model	Weight attached
A7	2 @ 19 ozs. 10 drams	B32 Competition	5 ozs. 4 drams
A7 after AA7-101	2 @ 16 ozs. 12 drams	B34 Competition	9 ozs. 9 drams
A10	2 @ 18 ozs. 10 drams	B32 Gold Star	6 ozs. 5 drams
A10 Road Rocket	2 @ 19 ozs. 8 drams	B34 Gold Star	11 ozs. 4 drams
C Group	3 ozs. 5 drams	M20	7 ozs.
B31	4 ozs. 6 drams	M21	5 ozs. 10 drams
B33 and M33	8 ozs. 8 drams		

Note:- Service Tool No. 61-3497 should be used on Crankshaft No. 67-1218 which is fitted to the Super Rocket and A10 machines after Eng. No. CA10R-4650 and DA10-101 respectively.

B.S.A. MOTOR CYCLES LIMITED, Service Dept., Birmingham, 11
(PRINTED IN ENGLAND)

BSA SERVICE SHEET No. 713

ALL MODELS EXCEPT "D" GROUP AND C15
DISMANTLING OF STEERING HEAD

Remove the headlamp from the forks after undoing the two retaining bolts, and allow it to hang in a position where it cannot be damaged. If a headlamp cowl is fitted, it should be removed complete with the headlamp.

On later models of the type shown in Fig. C31A the lamp is not removed, but it is necessary to take off the lamp front by unscrewing pin (F) and to disconnect the speedometer cable and the leads to the switch.

Detach the handlebars complete with controls, and lay them on top of the petrol tank, using a piece of rag to protect the enamel. Remove the chromium-plated top caps (A) and (B) Fig. C31. Slacken the pinch bolt (C) and remove the adjusting sleeve (D) or (E) Fig. C31A. Tap off the fork top yoke by striking it with a mallet underneath its two sides alternately.

The steering column can now be drawn downwards from the head, and the top ballrace removed. **Note.**—If the bearings are dry a means of catching the steel balls should be arranged as they will fall as the column is drawn out.

The cups which remain in the head can be withdrawn by means of extractor No. 61-3060 for "C" Group, and 61-3063 for "A", "M" and "B" Groups. This is screwed firmly into the cup, then extractor and cup are driven out from the opposite end with the aid of a suitable bar.

If the cups and cones are pitted to even a slight degree, they must be replaced, otherwise steering will be adversely affected and will rapidly become worse.

Pitting is invariably due to "hammering" of the balls in their tracks, caused by slack adjustment.

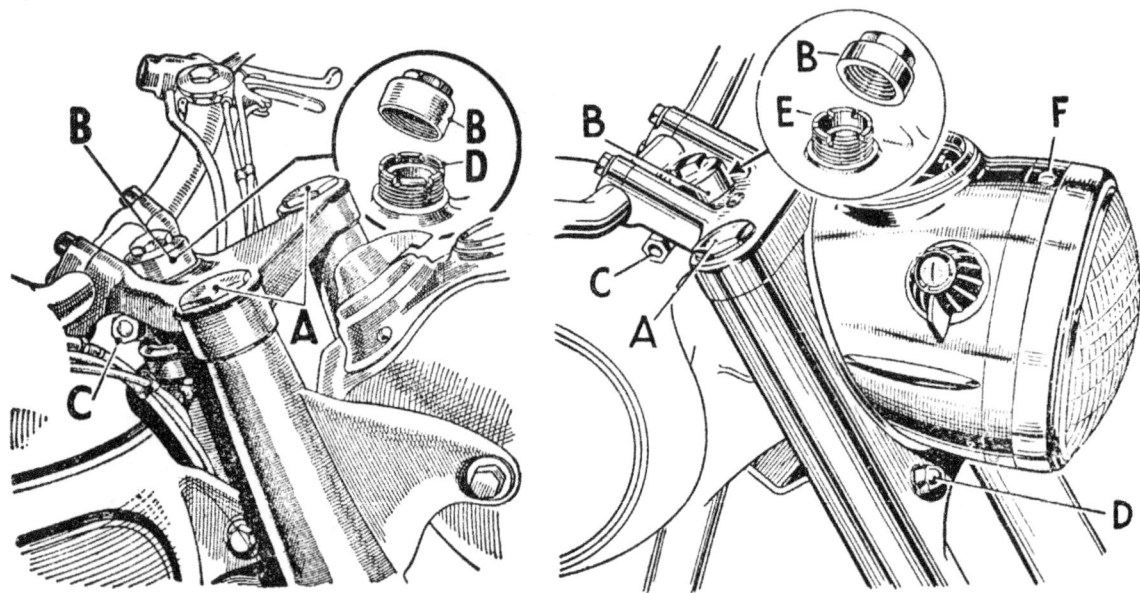

Fig. C31. The Front Fork & Steering Head.   Fig. C31A.

Reassembly of Steering Head.

When fitting new ballrace cups make sure that they are driven in squarely and that they are pressed well home. Replace the steering column balls, cone, adjusting sleeve and top-yoke. If any difficulty is experienced in retaining the balls in position, smear the tracks heavily with grease.

Adjust the column so that it turns freely without play and tighten the pinch bolt (C).

Finally replace headlamp and handlebar controls.

B.S.A. Motor Cycles Ltd., Service Dept., Armoury Road, Birmingham 11
B.S.A. Press.

Printed September, 1956
Revised October, 1957

SPOKE SIZES.

NOTE.—All Models use Forty Spokes per Wheel except "D" Group which have Thirty-six.

YEAR	MODEL	FRONT RIM SIZE	FRONT LEFT Length	FRONT LEFT Gauge	FRONT LEFT Part Number	FRONT RIGHT Length	FRONT RIGHT Gauge	FRONT RIGHT Part Number	REAR RIM SIZE	REAR LEFT Length	REAR LEFT Gauge	REAR LEFT Part Number	REAR RIGHT Length	REAR RIGHT Gauge	REAR RIGHT Part Number
1947	C10	WM1-19	8¾″	10	24-7012	8¾″	10	24-7012	WM1-19	8¾″	10	24-7012	6⅞″	10	24-7014
	C11	WM1-20	9¼″	10	24-6912	9 3/16″	10	29-5772	WM2-20	9¼″	10	24-6912	7⅜″	10	65-5873
	B31-B33	WM2-19	8 11/16″	10	65-5872	7½″	10	65-5910	WM2-19	8 3/16″	8/10	65-6072	8¾″	10	24-7012
	B32-B34	WM1-21	9 11/16″	10	65-5537	8 3/16″	10	90-5584	WM2-19	8 3/16″	8/10	65-6027	8¾″	10	24-7012
	M20-M21 Girder Fork	WM3-19	8¾″	10	24-7012	6¾″	8/10	24-6899	WM3-19	8⅝″	8/ 5/16	15-7037	8¾″	8	26-6824
	A7	WM2-19	7 29/32″	10/12	67-6008	8 1/16″	10/12	67-6007	WM3-19	7 29/32″	10/12	67-6008	8 1/16″	10/12	67-6007
1948	C10	WM1-19	8¾″	10	24-7012	8¾″	10	24-7012	WM1-19	8¾″	10	24-7012	6⅞″	10	24-7014
	C11	WM1-20	9¼″	10	24-6912	9 3/16″	10	29-5772	WM1-20	9¼″	10	24-6912	7⅜″	10	65-5873
	B31	WM2-19	8 11/16″	10	65-5872	7½″	10	65-5910	WM2-19	8 3/16″	8/10	65-6027	8¾″	10	24-7012
	B32	WM1-21	9 11/16″	10	65-5537	8 3/16″	10	29-5846	WM2-19	8 3/16″	8/10	65-6027	8¾″	10	24-7012
	B33	WM2-19	8 11/16″	10	65-5872	7½″	10	65-5910	WM2-19	8 3/16″	8/10	65-6027	8¾″	10	24-7012
	B34	WM1-21	9 11/16″	10	65-5537	8 3/16″	10	90-5584	WM2-19	8 3/16″	8/10	65-6027	8¾″	10	24-7012
	M20-M21 Girder Fork	WM3-19	8¾″	10	24-7012	6¾″	8/10	24-6899	WM3-19	8⅝″	8/ 5/16	15-7037	8¾″	8	26-6824
	M33-G.F.	WM3-19	8¾″	10	24-7012	6¾″	8/10	24-6899	WM3-19	8⅝″	8/ 5/16	15-7037	8¾″	8	26-6824
	A7	WM2-19	7 29/32″	10/12	67-6008	8 1/16″	10/12	67-6007	WM3-19	7 29/32″	10/12	67-6008	8 1/16″	10/12	67-6007
1949	D1	WM1-19	8 3/16″	10	90-5584	7½″	10	90-5583	WM1-19	8 3/16″	10	15-7072	8 3/16″	10	29-5846
	D1 Comp	WM1-19	8 3/16″	10	90-5584	7½″	10	90-5583	WM2-19	8 3/16″	10	15-7072	8 3/16″	10	29-5846
	C10	WM1-19	8¾″	10	24-7012	8¾″	10	24-7012	WM1-19	8¾″	10	24-7012	6⅞″	10	24-7014
	C11	WM1-20	9¼″	10	24-6912	9 3/16″	10	29-5772	WM1-20	9¼″	10	24-6912	7⅜″	10	65-5873
	B32-B34 G/S Std. & Spg. Frame	WM1-21	9 11/16″	10	65-5537	8 3/16″	10	90-5584	R	8 3/16″	8/10	65-6027	8¾″	10	24-7012
									WM2-19S	7 29/32″	10/12	67-6008	7 29/32″	10/12	67-6008
	B31-B32 Std. & Spg Frame	WM2-19	8 11/16″	10	65-5872	7½″	10	65-5910	R	8 3/16″	8/10	65-6027	8¾″	10	24-7012
									WM2-19S	7 29/32″	10/12	67-6008	7 29/32″	10/12	67-6008
	M20-M21-M33 Tele. Forks	WM2-19	8 11/16″	10	65-5872	7½″	10	65-5910	WM2-19	8⅝″	8/ 5/16	15-7037	8⅝″	8	24-6896
	A7 Star Twin Std. & Spg. Frame	WM2-19	8 11/16″	10	65-5872	7½″	10	65-5910	WM2-19	7 29/32″	10/12	67-6008	7 29/32″	10/12	67-6008

B.S.A. Service Sheet No. 714—continued

SPOKE SIZES—continued.

YEAR	MODEL	RIM SIZE	FRONT LEFT Length	FRONT LEFT Gauge	FRONT LEFT Part Number	FRONT RIGHT Length	FRONT RIGHT Gauge	FRONT RIGHT Part Number	RIM SIZE	REAR LEFT Length	REAR LEFT Gauge	REAR LEFT Part Number	REAR RIGHT Length	REAR RIGHT Gauge	REAR RIGHT Part Number
1950	D1 Std. & Spg. D1 Comp. Spg.	WM1-19	$8\frac{3}{16}''$	10	90-5584	$7\frac{7}{8}''$	10	90-5584	WM1-19	$8\frac{3}{16}''$	10	15-7072	$8\frac{3}{16}''$	10	90-5584
	C10	WM1-19	$8\frac{7}{8}''$	10	24-7012	$8\frac{3}{8}''$	10	24-7012	WM1-19	$8\frac{3}{8}''$	10	24-7012	$6\frac{7}{8}''$	10	24-7014
	C11	WM1-20	$9\frac{1}{4}''$	10	24-6912	$9\frac{5}{16}''$	10	29-5772	WM1-20	$9\frac{1}{4}''$	10	24-6912	$7\frac{3}{8}''$	10	65-5873
	B31-B33 Std. & Spg. Frame	WM2-19	$8\frac{11}{16}''$	10	65-5872	$7\frac{1}{2}''$	10	65-5910	WM2-19S	$8\frac{9}{16}''$	8/10	65-6302	$8\frac{3}{8}''$	10	24-7012
	B32-B34 Comp. Models	WM1-21	$9\frac{11}{16}''$	10	65-5537	$8\frac{9}{16}''$	10	90-5584	WM2-19	$8\frac{3}{8}''$	8/10	65-6027	$8\frac{1}{4}''$	10	24-7012
	350 and 500 Scramble & Grass Track Models	Varies to Spec.	$9\frac{11}{16}''$	10	65-5537	$8\frac{9}{16}''$	10	90-5584	Varies to Spec.	$7\frac{29}{32}''$	10	65-6302	$7\frac{29}{32}''$	10	65-6302
	350 & 500 O.H.V. Gold Star, Clubmans and Road Racing	Varies to Spec.	$9\frac{11}{16}''$	10	65-5926	$6\frac{7}{8}''$	10	24-7014	WM3-19	$7\frac{29}{32}''$	10	65-6302	$7\frac{29}{32}''$	10	65-6302
	M20-M21-M33	WM2-19	$8\frac{11}{16}''$	10	65-5872	$7\frac{1}{2}''$	10	65-5910	WM3-19	$8\frac{5}{8}''$	8/$\frac{1}{16}$	15-7037	$8\frac{5}{8}''$	8	24-6896
	A7 Star Twin Rigid & Spg. Frame	WM2-19	$8\frac{11}{16}''$	10	65-5872	$7\frac{1}{2}''$	10	65 5910	WM3-19	$7\frac{29}{32}''$	10	65-6302	$7\frac{29}{32}''$	10	65-6302
	A10	WM2-19	$8\frac{7}{8}''$	10	67-5545	$5\frac{11}{16}''$	10	67-5544	WM3-19	$7\frac{29}{32}''$	10	65-6302	$7\frac{29}{32}''$	10	65-6302
1951 and 1952 (other models as 1950)	C10 Spring Frame	WM1-19	$8\frac{7}{8}''$	10	24-7012	$8\frac{3}{8}''$	10	24-7012	WM1-19	$8\frac{3}{8}''$	10	24-7012	$6\frac{7}{8}''$	10	24-7014
	C11 Spring Frame	WM1-20	$9\frac{1}{4}''$	10	24-6912	$9\frac{5}{16}''$	10	29-5772	WM1-20	$9\frac{1}{4}''$	10	24-6912	$7\frac{3}{8}''$	10	65-5873
	M20-M21-M33 Spring Frame	WM1-19	$8\frac{11}{16}''$	10	65-5872	$7\frac{1}{2}''$	10	65-5910	WM2-19	$7\frac{29}{32}''$	10	65-6303	$7\frac{29}{32}''$	10	65-6302
1953 (other models as 1950/52)	B33-A7-A10 Rigid	WM2-19	$8\frac{1}{8}''$	10	67-5545	$5\frac{11}{16}''$	10	67-5544	WM2-19	$8\frac{3}{4}''$	10	24-7012	$8\frac{3}{16}''$	10	65-6027
	B33-A7-A10 Spring	WM2-19	$8\frac{7}{8}''$	10	67-5545	$5\frac{11}{16}''$	10	67-5544	WM2-19	$7\frac{29}{32}''$	10	65-6303	$7\frac{29}{32}''$	10	65-6302
	GOLD STAR Clubmans, Road Racing & Touring	WM1-19	$9\frac{11}{16}''$	10	67-5537	$8\frac{9}{16}''$	10	90-5584	WM2-19	$7\frac{29}{32}''$	10	65-6303	$7\frac{29}{32}''$	10	65-6302
	B32-B34 Trials	WM1-21	$9\frac{11}{16}''$	10	67-5537	$8\frac{9}{16}''$	10	90-5584	WM3-19	$7\frac{29}{32}''$	10	65-6303	$7\frac{29}{32}''$	10	65-6302
	B32-B34 Scrambles	WM1-21	$9\frac{11}{16}''$	8	42-5524	$8\frac{7}{16}''$	8	31-6015	WM3-19	$7\frac{29}{32}''$	10	65-6303	$7\frac{29}{32}''$	10	65-6302

B.S.A. Service Sheet No. 714—continued

SPOKE SIZES—continued

YEAR	MODEL	FRONT RIM SIZE	FRONT LEFT Length	FRONT LEFT Gauge	FRONT LEFT Part Number	FRONT RIGHT Length	FRONT RIGHT Gauge	FRONT RIGHT Part Number	REAR RIM SIZE	REAR LEFT Length	REAR LEFT Gauge	REAR LEFT Part Number	REAR RIGHT Length	REAR RIGHT Gauge	REAR RIGHT Part Number
1954 and 1955	D1-D3 Rigid & Spring	WM1-19	$8\frac{9}{16}''$	10	90-5584	$7\frac{7}{8}''$	10	90-5584	WM1-19	$8\frac{9}{16}''$	10	90-6042	$8\frac{9}{16}''$	10	90-5584
	D1-D3 Comp.	WM1-19	$8\frac{9}{16}''$	10	90-5584	$7''$	10	90-5584	WM1-19	$8\frac{9}{16}''$	10	90-6042	$8\frac{9}{16}''$	10	90-5584
	C10L	WM1-19	$8\frac{9}{16}''$	10	90-5584	$7''$	10	90-5584	WM1-19	$8\frac{9}{16}''$	10	90-6042	$8\frac{9}{16}''$	10	90-5584
	C11G	WM1-19	$8\frac{3}{4}''$	10	24-7012	$8\frac{3}{4}''$	10	24-7012	WM1-19	$6\frac{7}{8}''$	10	24-7014	$8\frac{3}{4}''$	10	24-7012
	C11G (1955) Rigid & Spring	WM1-19	$8\frac{3}{4}''$	10	24-7012	$7\frac{1}{2}''$	10	65-5910	WM1-19	$6\frac{7}{8}''$	Butted 8/10	24-7014	$8\frac{3}{4}''$	10	24-7012
	B31-B33 Rigid	WM2-19	$8\frac{1}{4}''$	10	65-5872	$7\frac{1}{2}''$	10	65-5910	WM2-19	$8\frac{9}{16}''$	10	65-6027	$8\frac{3}{4}''$	10	24-7012
	B31-B33 Spring	WM2-19	$8\frac{1}{4}''$	10	65-5872	$7\frac{1}{4}''$	10	65-5910	WM2-19	$7\frac{22}{32}''$	10	65-6303	$7\frac{22}{32}''$	10	65-6302
	B32-B34 Comp. Rigid	WM1-21	$9\frac{1}{4}''$	10	65-5537	$8\frac{9}{16}''$	10	90-5584	WM2-19	$7\frac{1}{2}''$	10	65-6303	$7\frac{22}{32}''$	10	65-6302
	B31 Swinging Arm	WM2-19	$8\frac{1}{4}''$	10	65-5872	$7\frac{1}{2}''$	10	65-5912	WM2-19	$7\frac{22}{32}''$	10	65-6303	$7\frac{22}{32}''$	10	65-6302
	B32-B34 Swinging Arm	WM1-21	$9\frac{1}{4}''$	10	65-5537	$8\frac{9}{16}''$	10	90-5584	WM2-19	$7\frac{22}{32}''$	10	65-6303	$7\frac{22}{32}''$	10	65-6302
	B33 1954 Swinging Arm	WM2-19	$8\frac{7}{8}''$	10	67-5545	$5\frac{1}{4}''$	10	67-5544	WM2-19	$7\frac{22}{32}''$	10	65-6303	$7\frac{22}{32}''$	10	65-6302
	B33 1955 Swinging Arm	WM2-19	$8\frac{7}{8}''$	Butted 8/10	67-5606	$5\frac{1}{4}''$	10	67-5544	WM2-19	$7\frac{22}{32}''$	10	65-6303	$7\frac{22}{32}''$	10	65-6302
	GOLD STAR Clubmans, Road Racing & Touring	WM1-19	$8\frac{1}{8}''$	10	67-5545	$5\frac{11}{32}''$	10	67-5544	WM2-19	$7\frac{22}{32}''$	10	65-6303	$7\frac{22}{32}''$	10	65-6302
	GOLD STAR Trials	WM1-21	$9\frac{1}{4}''$	10	65-5926	$6\frac{7}{8}''$	10	65-5910	WM2-18	$7\frac{7}{8}''$	10	42-6011	$7\frac{7}{16}''$	10	42-6112
	GOLD STAR Scrambles	WM1-21	$9\frac{1}{4}''$	10	65-5537	$8\frac{9}{16}''$	8	31-6015	WM3-19	$7\frac{22}{32}''$	10	65-6303	$7\frac{22}{32}''$	10	65-6302
	M20-M21-M33 Rigid	WM2-19	$8\frac{1}{4}''$	10	42-5524	$8\frac{7}{16}''$	10	65-5910	WM2-19	$8\frac{9}{16}''$	Butted 8	15-7037	$8\frac{9}{16}''$	Butted 8	24-6896
	M20-M21-M33 Spring	WM2-19	$8\frac{1}{4}''$	10	65-5872	$7\frac{1}{2}''$	10	65-5910	WM2-19	$7\frac{22}{32}''$	10	65-6303	$7\frac{22}{32}''$	10	65-6302
	"A" GROUP Plunger & Swinging Arm 1954	WM2-19	$8\frac{7}{8}''$	10	67-5545	$5\frac{11}{32}''$	10	67-5544	WM2-19	$7\frac{22}{32}''$	10	65-6303	$7\frac{22}{32}''$	10	65-6302
	"A" GROUP Plunger & Swinging Arm 1955	WM2-19	$8\frac{7}{8}''$	Butted 8/10	67-5606	$5\frac{11}{32}''$	10	67-5544	WM2-19	$7\frac{22}{32}''$	10	65-6303	$7\frac{22}{32}''$	10	65-6302

B.S.A. Service Sheet No. 714—continued

SPOKE SIZES—continued.

YEAR	MODEL	RIM SIZE	FRONT LEFT Length	FRONT LEFT Gauge	FRONT Part Number	FRONT Length	FRONT RIGHT Gauge	FRONT Part Number	RIM SIZE	REAR LEFT Length	REAR LEFT Gauge	REAR Part Number	REAR Length	REAR RIGHT Gauge	REAR Part Number
1956/7	D1 Plunger	WM1-19	8 3/16"	10	90-5584	7 7/8"	10	90-5583	WM1-19	8 3/16"	10	90-6042	8 3/16"	10	90-5584
	D3 Swinging Arm	WM1-19	8 3/8"	10	90-5584	7 7/8"	10	90-5583	WM1-19	8 3/16"	10	90-6042	8 3/16"	10	90-5584
	C10L	WM1-19	8 3/4"	10	24-7012	8 3/8"	10	24-7012	WM1-19	8 3/4"	10	90-6042	8 3/8"	10	90-5584
	C12	WM1-19	6 5/8"	10	29-5976	6 5/8"	10	29-5976	WM1-19	7"	10	29-5940	7"	10	29-5940
	B31-B33	WM2-19	6 1/4"	Butted 8/10	42-5635	6 1/4"	Butted 8/10	42-5635	WM2-19	6 1/4"	Butted 8/10	42-5635	6 1/4"	Butted 8/10	42-5635
	GOLD STAR Clubmans, Road Racing & Touring	WM1-19	5 1/8"	10	42-5552	5 7/8"	10	42-5552	WM3-19	7 22/32"	10	65-6303	7 22/32"	10	65-6302
	B32-B34 Comp.	WM1-21	9 11/16"	10	65-5537	8 7/16"	10	90-5584	WM3-19	7 22/32"	10	65-6303	7 22/32"	10	65-6302
	GOLD STAR Scrambles	WM1-21	9 11/16"	8	42-5524	8 7/8"	8	31-6015	WM3-19	8 5/8"	Butted 8	15-7037	8 5/8"	Butted 8	24-6896
	M21 Rigid	WM2-19	8 3/4"	Butted 8/10	67-5606	5 11/16"	Butted 8/10	66-5560	WM2-19	7 22/32"	10	65-6303	7 22/32"	10	65-6302
	M21-M33 Plunger	WM2-19	8 3/8"	Butted 8/10	67-5606	5 11/16"	Butted 8/10	67-5606	WM2-19	6 1/4"	Butted 8/10	42-5635	6 1/4"	Butted 8/10	42-5635
	A7 and Shooting Star	WM2-19	6 1/4"	Butted 8/10	42-5635	6 1/4"	Butted 8/10	42-5635	WM2-19	6 1/4"	Butted 8/10	42-5635	6 1/4"	Butted 8/10	42-5635
	A10 Plunger	WM2-19	8 3/8"	Butted 8/10	67-5606	5 11/16"	Butted 8/10	66-5561	WM2-19	7 22/32"	Butted 8/10	67-6017	7 22/32"	Butted 8/10	67-6016
	A10 and Road Rocket	WM2-19	6 1/4"	Butted 8/10	42-5635	6 1/4"	Butted 8/10	42-5635	WM2-19	6 1/4"	8/10	42-5635	6 1/4"	Butted 8/10	42-5635
	Dandy 70	WM0-15	5 5/8"	12	64-5505	5 5/8"	12	64-5505	WM0-15	5 5/8"	Butted 11/12	64-5507	5 5/8"	Butted 11/12	64-5507

BSA SERVICE SHEET No. 802

Reprinted June 1966

"B" AND "M" GROUP MODELS

MAGDYNO

The magdyno is a combined generator and magneto unit the generator being mounted above the magneto and driven through gears from the magneto driving shaft. Details of the E3HM generator which is incorporated in the magdyno are given in Service Sheet No. 809. The magdyno is arranged for variable ignition by means of hand control.

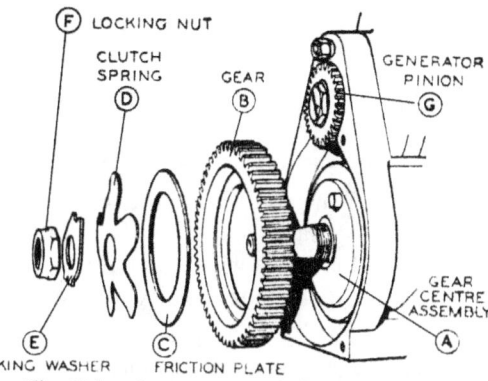

Fig. Y.5. Arrangement of slipping clutch.

A shock absorbing drive is incorporated in the larger of the two gears which take the drive from the magneto shaft to the generator. This considerably relieves the peak loading on the teeth of the driving gear and gives far longer life. The drive is taken from the gear centre *A* (Fig. Y5) which is keyed to the magneto shaft, through the fabric gear *B* which is held against the gear centre under the pressure of a star-shaped spring *D* to the pinion *G* on the generator shaft. The effect of a violent overload is to cause the fabric gear to slip relative to the gear centre and so prevent shock from being transmitted to the fabric gear.

ROUTINE MAINTENANCE

Lubrication

To be carried out every 3,000 miles.

The cam is lubricated from a wick contained in the contact breaker base. To reach the wick, take out the screw securing the spring arm carrying the moving contact and lift off the backing spring and spring arm. The screw carrying the wick can then be withdrawn. At the same time, unscrew the contact breaker securing screw, take the tappet which operates the contact spring from its housing and lightly smear with thin machine oil. When replacing, see that the backing spring is fitted on top of the spring arm and that its bent portion is facing outwards.

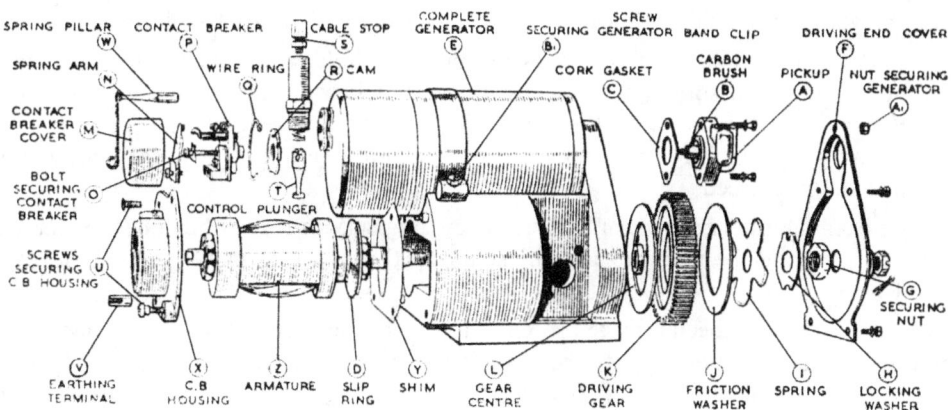

Fig. Y.6. The Magdyno (Exploded view)

B.S.A. Service Sheet No. 802—(contd.)

Adjustment

To be carried out every 3,000 miles.

Remove the contact breaker cover and turn the engine until the contacts are fully opened. Check the gap with a gauge having a thickness of .012 in. If the setting is correct, the gauge should be a sliding fit, but if the gap varies appreciably from the gauge it should be adjusted. Keep the engine in the position to give maximum opening of the contacts, slacken the locknut and turn the contact screw by its hexagon head until the gap is set to the gauge. Finally tighten the locknut and re-check the setting.

Cleaning

To be carried out every 6,000 miles.

Take off the contact breaker cover and examine the contact breaker. If the contacts are burned or blackened, clean them with fine carborundum stone or with very fine emery cloth, and afterwards wipe away any dust or dirt with a petrol-moistened cloth. Cleaning of the contacts is made easier if the moving contact arm is removed. Procedure is given above.

Remove the high-tension pick-up, wipe clean and polish with a fine dry cloth. The high-tension pick-up brush must move freely in its holder. If it is dirty, clean with a cloth moistened with petrol. If the brush is worn to within $\frac{1}{8}$ in. of the shoulder it must be renewed. While the high-tension pick-up is removed, clean the slip ring track and flanges by holding a soft cloth on the ring by means of a suitably shaped piece of wood while the engine is slowly turned.

Replacement of High-tension Cable

If, on inspection, the high-tension cable shows signs of perishing or cracking, it must be replaced by a suitable length of 7 mm. rubber-covered ignition cable.

To fit a new high-tension cable to a pick-up terminal, bare the end of the cable for about $\frac{1}{4}$ in., thread the knurled moulded nut over the cable, thread the bare wire through the washer removed from the end of the old cable and bend back the strands. Finally screw the nut into the pick-up.

SERVICING

Testing Magneto in position on Engine

Testing magneto in position to locate cause of misfiring or failure of ignition:—

Disconnect the cable from the sparking plug and hold it so that the terminal end is about $\frac{1}{8}$ in. from some part of the cylinder block while the engine is turned over. If the spark that jumps from the cable end is strong and regular, the fault lies in the sparking plug, which must be removed for examination and if necessary cleaned and adjusted, or replaced.

Next examine the high-tension cable. After long service it may have become cracked or perished and the magneto may be sparking through to a metal part of the engine or frame.

If the magneto has been replaced recently it may be incorrectly timed. For instructions on re-timing refer to Service Sheet No. 604. If the performance of the magneto is still not satisfactory, the contact breaker may require cleaning or adjustment (see *Routine Maintenance*).

B.S.A. Service Sheet No. 802—(contd.)

Carefully examine the slip ring and if it is damaged in any way it must be replaced. To do this take off the inner race of the bearing using an extractor, lift off the shims and the grease flinging plate and pull the slip ring off the shaft. (NOTE:—When removing the inner race the extractor must bear on the brass shaft extension and not on the electric contact or insulator down the centre of the shaft. A disc of appropriate diameter can be placed across the face of the shaft extension.) Carefully straighten the wire coming from the armature and see that the bared end is clean and then fit the new slip ring over the shaft, taking care that the wire enters the hole in the boss in the slip ring and that it goes fully home without bending. Seal the lead-in to the slip ring boss with varnish—a special air drying varnish is used at the works but shellac varnish can be used in an emergency.

Replace the grease flinging plate, the full number of shims and inner race of the bearing.

TESTING

If test apparatus is not available, a rough check of the armature windings can be made by means of a two-volt battery (a tapping across one cell of the motor cycle battery) and an ammeter.

To check the Primary Winding of the Armature

Screw the contact breaker retaining screw into the end of the armature shaft.

Connect one terminal of the battery to one terminal of the ammeter.

Connect the second terminal of the ammeter to the screw in the armature shaft.

Connect the second terminal of the battery to the metal body of the armature.

The ammeter will record the current taken by the armature primary winding and should be approximately four amperes.

To check the Secondary Winding of the Armature

Leave the connections as detailed above for the primary winding check.

Take a piece of high-tension cable about 15 in. long and bare one end back about $\frac{1}{2}$ in. and the other end about 4 in. Wrap the longer bared end round the brass insert of the slip ring and hold the other end about $\frac{1}{8}$ in. from the body of the armature.

If the lead from the battery which was connected to the armature body to test the primary winding is then flashed quickly on and off the body, a spark should occur between the high-tension wire and the armature body.

Failure to spark indicates a fault either in the armature windings or the condenser and a replacement armature must be fitted.

An armature test can be carried out by connecting in series an 8-volt accumulator, a four lobe cam and contact breaker (having 45° closed period) and the armature under test, the contact breaker to coil connection being at earth potential. A 0.2 mfd. condenser must be connected across the contacts. Run the contact breaker at 750 r.p.m., giving 3,000 operations of the contacts per minute, and connect the high-tension cable from the

B.S.A. Service Sheet 802—(contd.)

coil to either a 3-point spark gap or rotary gap set to 13 kv. Regular sparking should occur under these conditions. Explore the surface of the winding with an earthed pointer—no flashover must occur.

It should be noted that in the above test, sparking will occur, provided that the armature winding is in order, even if the condenser in-built with the armature is open-circuited. Disconnect the 0.2 mfd. condenser from the supply circuit above when regular sparking should continue. Failure to do so indicates that the armature condenser is faulty and a replacement armature must be fitted.

If satisfactory performance is not obtained during the above test, measurement should be made of the maximum primary running current. To do this, include also in the above series circuit a moving coil ammeter (of not more than 5 amperes full scale deflection) and a variable resistance of approximately 5 ohms (of adequate current rating for cool running). Connect the high-tension cable from the coil to a 3-point spark gap set to 5.5 mm. or a rotary gap set to 9.5 kv. Run the contact breaker as before, and adjust the variable resistance until occasional missing occurs, that is, when the coil is just failing to spark regularly. Under these conditions, the permissible primary current as read on the ammeter should be not more than 1.2 amperes.

In both the above tests, it is important that the supply voltage be maintained at 8 volts, that the cam speed be kept constant, and that the winding under test is not subjected to any external magnetic influence (e.g. it must not be tested on an iron bed-plate).

Reassembly

See that the bearings are clean and if necessary wash them in petrol and dry thoroughly. Lightly pack them with high melting point grease. Fit the inner races on the armature shaft using a hand press and a length of tube fitting over the shaft and locating on the race. Fit the balls and cages in position over the inner races and press the outer races into their housings with a mandrel of the type shown, taking care to ensure that a suitable serrated insulating washer is positioned between each race and its housing to ensure that the race is a tight fit in its housing.

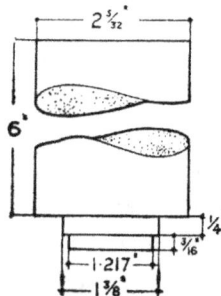

Fig. Y.11. Mandrel for replacement of outer races

See that the slip ring and metal insert are clean; if necessary carefully wipe it clean with a petrol moistened cloth. See that the inside of the magneto body is clean and free from swarf and insert the armature in the body, drive end first.

B.S.A. Service Sheet No. 802—(contd.)

If the contacts are badly burned they should be renewed by a replacement contact set. If the contact breaker is in good order, there may be an internal fault in the magneto.

To Dismantle

Take off the driving end cover F (Fig. Y6) by unscrewing the four countersunk head screws. To dismantle the slipping clutch it will be necessary to use a jig (Fig. Y7) to hold the larger gear whilst the securing nut is being undone. This consists simply of a length of $\frac{1}{4}$ in. diameter mild steel rod bent to a flat 'U' the ends being cut short with their centres $3\frac{3}{16}$ in. apart, so that one can be slipped in the hole in the wheel whilst the other is engaged with the hole in the top of the casting through which the dynamo securing stud usually goes. A $\frac{7}{16}$ in. box spanner can then be used on the securing nut G (Fig. Y6). Note that the tab of the locking washer H must be bent back first.

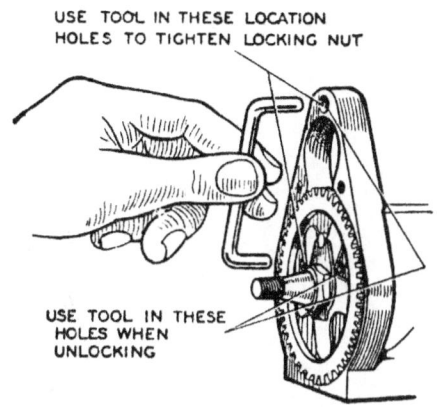

Fig. Y.7. Dismantling slipping clutch

Remove the locking washer H, clutch spring I, friction washer J, and driving gear K.

Take off the contact breaker cover M, remove the spring arm N carrying the contact, unscrew the bolt O securing the contact breaker P, and draw the contact breaker off the shaft. Spring the wire ring Q securing the cam R out of its location in the contact breaker housing, and remove the cam. The timing control barrel and cable will have been removed when taking the magdyno off the motor cycle. Remove the control plunger T.

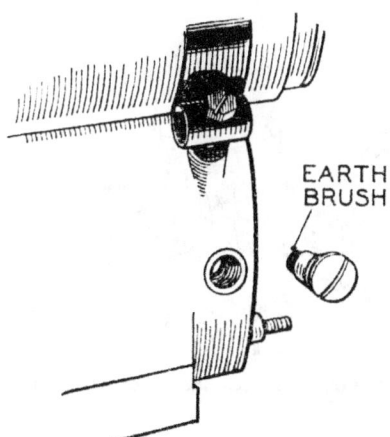

Fig. Y.8. Location of earthing brush

Remove the pick-up holder and the small earthing brush (Fig. Y8), which will be found on the side of the magdyno. Unscrew the screws U (Fig. Y6), earthing terminal V and pillar W from the contact breaker end plate X, and remove the plate from the magdyno

B.S.A. Service Sheet No. 802—(contd.)

together with the shims Y. The armature Z can then be removed from the machine by tapping the driving end of the shaft with a rawhide mallet to detach it from the gear centre L. There is no need to put a keeper across the magnet as it retains its magnetic properties more or less indefinitely. Although it loses a certain immaterial amount of power in the first removal of the armature, subsequent removals do not affect it. Do not allow the magneto body to come in close contact with any iron filings as they may become attracted to the magnet and cause the armature to bind.

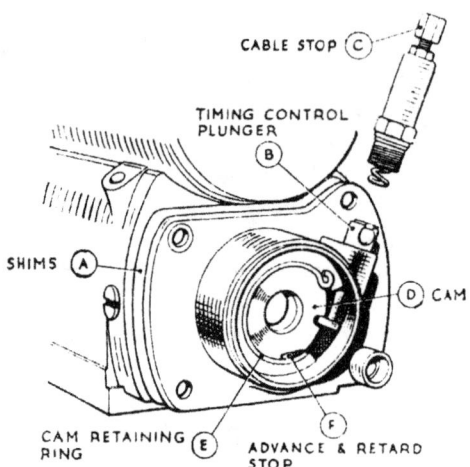

Fig. Y9. Contact breaker housing, showing timing control mechanism.

When the armature is removed, it should be examined for mechanical faults such as a cracked or bent shaft. Any defect in the winding or condenser needs special equipment to detect, and in the event of trouble being suspected, a complete service armature should be fitted.

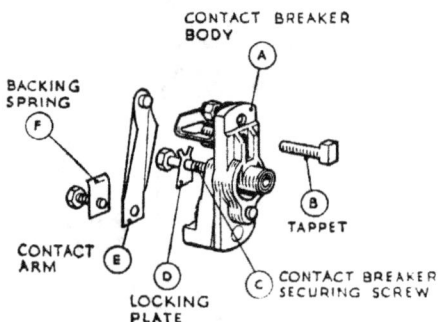

Fig. Y.10. Contact breaker tappet

It is important that the two ball bearings which support the armature shaft are in good condition. If they are packed on assembly with a suitable high melting point grease they will stand an almost unlimited amount of normal wear, but if they start to fail due to a bent shaft or other cause, they must be replaced. The balls and cages can readily be removed off the inner races which can then be pulled off the armature shaft using an extractor. The outer races can be removed with an expanding collet type extractor.

B.S.A. Service Sheet No. 802—(contd.)

Refit the contact breaker end plate, taking care that the end plate shims are in position, and replace and tighten the end plate fixing screws. Also replace the pillar carrying the cover fixing arm.

Check the armature for end play. It should revolve freely when turned by hand, but no end play should be felt. If necessary adjust by adding or removing shims behind the contact breaker plate until adjustment is correct.

Replace the cam and contact breaker as follows:—

Insert the timing control plunger in its housing, followed by the spring, and screw the timing control tube, together with cable stop, into the housing.

Place the cam in its housing with the formed surface facing outwards, position the broad slot in the cam over the timing range pin and locate the end of the control plunger in the appropriate slot in the cam. Secure the cam by springing the circlip into its location.
Note that a recess is provided for the "eye" at one end of the circlip.

See that the tappet moves freely in the contact breaker body, add a few drops of thin machine oil to the cam lubrication wick, and place the contact breaker body on the end of the armature shaft. Place the specially shaped tag washer over the contact breaker fixing screw and locating the flat side of the washer against the location provided for it in the contact breaker body, screw the bolt home and lock by bending the tags of the washer over the flats on the head of the bolt.

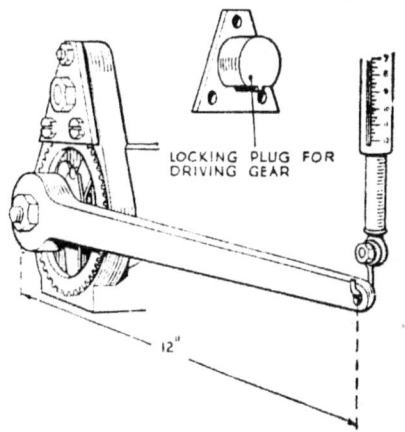

Fig. Y.12. Method of checking clutch setting

Fit the spring arm carrying the contact and also the backing spring (bent portion facing outwards), place a lockwasher over the fixing screw, and fully tighten it.

Adjust the contacts to the correct setting (see *Routine Maintenance*) and replace the contact breaker cover.

See that the pick-up is clean and the brush moves freely. Place the cork washer in position on the magneto body, followed by the pick-up and secure by means of the fixing screws or spring arm.

B.S.A. Service Sheet No. 802—(contd.)

Check that the earthing brush moves freely in its holder and screw it into the magneto body.

To reassemble the slipping clutch, key the gear centre *A* (Fig. Y5) on to the spindle, replace the driving gear *B*, friction washer *C*, clutch spring *D*, locking washer *E*, and secure by tightening the fixing nut *F* fully. The 'U'-shaped jig must be used to prevent rotation of the shaft while tightening the nut.

After assembling, the setting of the clutch must be checked. This can easily be done by locking the driving gear and applying a steady load on the driving spindle, as shown in Fig. Y12. The clutch should slip with a torque of 4–10 lbs. feet or more, i.e. a 4–10 lb. pull measured on a spring balance via a spanner 12 in. long. If slipping occurs at a value outside these limits, a new clutch spring must be fitted.

B.S.A. MOTOR CYCLES LTD., Service Department, Armoury Road, Birmingham 11.

B.S.A. PRESS

BSA SERVICE SHEET No. 804

C10, C11, "A", "B" AND "M" GROUP MODELS
REGULATOR UNIT—Models MCR1 and MCR2

This unit houses the generator voltage regulator unit and the cut-out. Although combined structurally, the regulator and cut-out are electrically separate.

On machines fitted with an E3L dynamo the regulator unit is type MCR2, this unit is slightly different in construction to the MCR1. The procedure for testing and adjusting is, however, unaltered.

Positive Earth Lighting System
Some machines have the battery positive terminal connected to the frame instead of the negative terminal. This does not affect the regulator adjustment except that the voltmeter connections should be reversed.

The Regulator
The regulator unit is arranged to work in conjunction with the shunt-wound generators described in Service Sheet No. 809. The regulator is set to maintain a pre-determined generator voltage at all speeds, the field strength being controlled by the automatic insertion of a resistance in the generator field circuit, and a current or series winding on the same regulator compensates this voltage figure in accordance with the output current, to ensure that the battery does no receive an excessive charging current when in a discharged condition. Hence the charging current depends upon the difference between the controlled generator voltage and the battery terminal voltage and is therefore at a maximum when the battery is discharged, automatically tapering off to a minimum as the battery becomes charged and its voltage rises. In addition, a form of temperature compensation ensures that the voltage characteristics of the regulator are matched to those of the battery for large variations in working temperature.

Normally, during day-time running, when the battery is in good condition, the generator gives only a trickle charge, so that the ammeter reading will seldom exceed 1—2 amperes.

The Cut-out
The cut-out is an automatic switch which is connected between the dynamo and battery. It consists of a pair of contacts held open by a spring and closed magnetically. When the engine is running fast enough to cause the voltage of the generator to exceed that of the battery, the contacts close and the battery is charged by the generator. On the other hand, when the speed is low or the engine is stationary, the contacts open, thus disconnecting the generator from the battery and preventing current flowing from the battery through the windings.

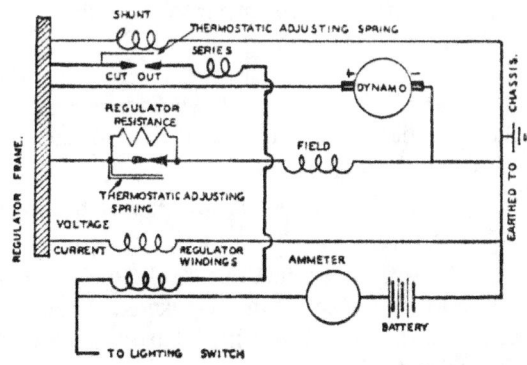

Fig. Y15. *Circuit diagram of Charging System.*

B.S.A. Service Sheet No. 804 (contd.)

Test Data

Cut-out	MCR.1	MCR.2
Cut-in voltage	6.2—6.6 volts	6.3—6.7 volts
Drop-off voltage	3.5—5.3 volts	4.5—5.0 volts
Reverse current	0.7—2.5 amperes	3.0—5.0 amperes

Regulator

SETTING IN OPEN CIRCUIT

10°C.	50°F.	8.0—8.4 volts	7.7—8.1 volts
20°C.	68°F.	7.8—8.2 volts	7.6—8.0 volts
30°C.	86°F.	7.6—8.0 volts	7.5—7.9 volts
40°C.	104°F.	7.4—7.9 volts	7.4—7.8 volts

Servicing

TESTING IN POSITION TO LOCATE FAULT IN CHARGING CIRCUIT

If the procedure given in Service Sheet No. 809 shows the generator to be in order, proceed to check further as follows:—

First ensure that the wiring between regulator and battery is in order. To do this disconnect the wire from the (A) terminal of the regulator (Fig. Y16). It may be necessary in some cases to remove the regulator from the motorcycle.

Connect the end of the wire removed to the positive terminal of a voltmeter, and connect the negative voltmeter terminal to an earthing point on the machine.

If a voltmeter reading is given, the wiring is in order and the regulator must be examined If there is no reading, examine the wiring for broken wires or loose connections.

Regulator Adjustment

Remove the cover of the regulator unit, insert a piece of paper between the cut-out contacts, and proceed as follows:—

Connect the positive terminal of the moving coil voltmeter (0—10 volts) to the (D) terminal on the regulator and connect the other lead of the voltmeter to an earthing point on the engine.

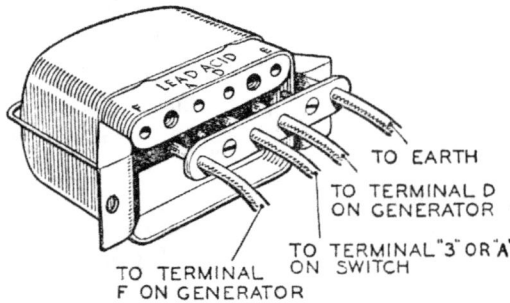

Fig. Y16. *Connections to Regulator Unit.*

Start the engine and slowly increase the speed until the voltmeter needle "flicks" and then steadies; this should occur at a voltmeter reading between the limits for the particular atmospheric temperature.

If the voltage at which the reading becomes steady is outside these limits, the regulator must be adjusted.

Shut off the engine, release the locknut (A) Fig. Y17, on the regulator adjusting screw (B) and turn the screw in a clockwise direction to raise the setting, or in an anti-clockwise direction to lower the setting. Turn the screw a fraction of a turn at a time and then tighten the locknut.

B.S.A. Service Sheet No. 804 (contd.)

When adjusting, do not run the engine up to more than half-throttle, as while the dynamo is on open circuit, it will build up to a high voltage if run at a high speed and so a false voltmeter reading would be obtained.

Remove paper from between cut-out contacts.

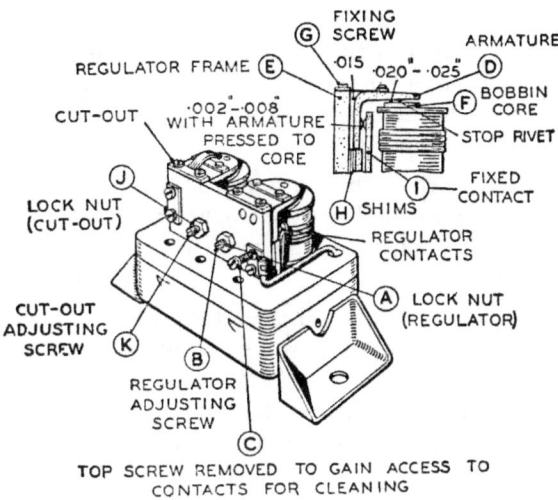

Fig. Y17. *Regulator and Cut-out Adjustment and Setting.*

Cleaning the Regulator Contacts

After long periods of service it may be found necessary to clean the vibrating contacts of the regulator. These are accessible if the top screw (C) securing the fixed contact is removed and the bottom screw slackened to permit the fixed contact to be swung outwards. The contacts can then be polished with fine emery cloth.

Mechanical Setting of Regulator

The armature carrying the moving contact of the regulator is accurately set and should no be removed. If, however, it does become necessary to re-set the contacts, slacken the two fixing screws (G) Fig. Y17, and proceed as follows:—

Insert a .015 in. (0.20 in.) feeler gauge between the back of the armature (D) and the regulator frame (E).

Press back the armature against the frame and down on to the top of the bobbin core with the gauge in position, and lock the armature by tightening the two fixing screws (G). Check the air gap between the top of the bobbin core (F) and the underside of the armature (D)—not under the stop rivet. Adjust if necessary to .025 in. (.012—.020 in.), by removing shims (H) at the back of the fixed contact on an MCR1 regulator or by bending the fixed contact breaker on an MCR2 regulator. The gap between the regulator contacts when the armature is pressed down should now be .002—.008 in. (.006—.017 in.). Finally check, and if necessary re-set, the electrical adjustment of the regulator.

The figures in brackets refer to the MCR2 regulator.

B.S.A. Service Sheet No. 804 (contd.)

Electrical Setting of Cut-out

If the regulator setting is within the correct limits, but the battery is still not receiving current from the dynamo, the cut-out may be out of adjustment or there may be an open circuit in the wiring of the cut-out and regulator unit.

Remove the cable from the terminal on the regulator marked (A). Remove the voltmeter lead from the (D) terminal of the regulator unit and connect it to terminal (A). Run the engine as before: at a fairly low engine speed, the cut-out should operate, when a voltmeter reading should be given of the same value as that when the voltmeter was connected to terminal (D). If there is no reading, the setting of the cut-out may be badly out of adjustment and the contacts not closing.

To check the voltage at which the cut-out operates, the voltmeter must be connected between the (D) terminal and earth. Start the engine and slowly increase its speed until the cut-out contacts are seen to close, noting the voltage at which this occurs. This should be 6.2—6.6 volts.

If operation of the cut-out is outside these limits, it will be necessary to adjust. To do this slacken the locknut (J) Fig. Y17, on the cut-out adjustment screw (K) and turn the screw in a clockwise direction to raise the voltage setting or in an anti-clockwise direction to reduce the setting, testing after each adjustment by increasing the engine speed until the cut-out is seen to operate, and noting the corresponding reading.

Tighten the locknut after making the adjustment. If the cut-out contacts appear burnt or dirty, place a strip of fine glasspaper between the contacts then, with the contacts closed by hand, draw the paper through. This should be done two or three times with the rough side towards each contact.

Mechanical Setting of Cut-out

If, for any reason, the armature has to be removed from the cut-out frame, care must be taken to obtain the correct air-gap settings on reassembly. These can be obtained as follows:—

Slacken the two armature fixing screws, adjusting screw (K) and the screw securing the fixed contact. Insert a .014 in. gauge between the back of the armature and the cut-out frame. (The air-gap between the core face and the armature shim should now measure .011—.015 in. If it does not, fit a armature assembly). Press the armature back against the gauge and tighten the fixing screws. With the gauge still in position, set the gap between the armature and the stop plate arm to .030—.034 in. be carefully bending the arm. Remove the gauge and tighten the screw securing the fixed contact.

Insert a .025 in. gauge between the core face and the armature. Press the armature down on to the gauge. The gap between the contacts should now measure .002—.006 in, and the drop-off voltage should be between the limits given in the test data. If necessary, adjust the gap by carefully bending the fixed contact breaker.

B.S.A. MOTOR CYCLES LTD., Service Department, Armoury Road, Birmingham 11.
Printed in England
B.S.A. Press

BSA SERVICE SHEET No. 804A

"A", "B" AND "M" GROUP MODELS
CONTROL BOX - MODEL BR107

General

The regulator and cut-out contacts are positioned, for ease of access, above their respective armatures. It will be noticed that some of the internal electrical joints are resistance brazed.

SETTING DATA
Cut-out

Cut-in voltage	... 6.3—6.7 volts
Drop-off voltage	... 4.8—5.3 volts
Reverse current	... 3.0—5.0 volts

Regulator

Setting on open circuit relative to ambient temperature.

10°C.	50°F.	...	7.7—8.1 volts
20°C.	68°F.	...	7.6—87.0 volts
30°C.	86°F.	...	7.5— .9 volts
40°C.	104°F.	...	7.4— .8 volts

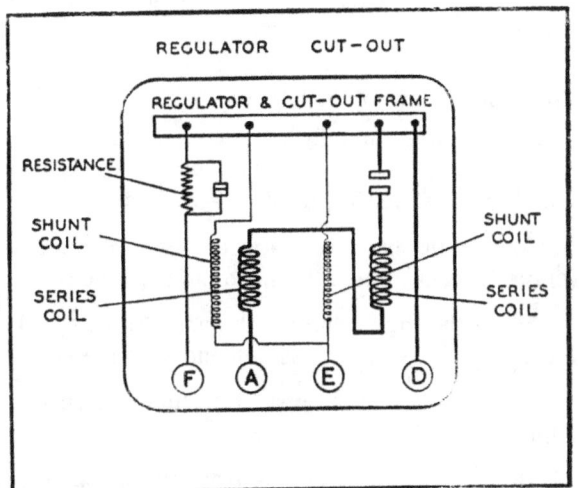

Fig. Y15a. *Internal Connections of Control Box.*

Servicing

Before making any adjustment to the regulator, ensure that the dynamo, dynamo drive and battery are in order.

If the machine is used regularly and a sound battery does not keep in a charged condition, or if the dynamo output does not fall when the battery is fully charged, the following procedure should be adopted:—

Withdraw the cable from terminal (A) Fig. Y16a, and connect it to the negative terminal of a voltmeter. Connect the positive voltmeter terminal to an earthing point on the machine. If a voltmeter reading is given, the circuit from the battery to terminal (A) is in order.

If there is no reading, examine the wiring for defective cables or loose connections. Reconnect the cable to terminal (A).

Check that the wiring between dynamo terminal (D) and control box terminal (D), and between dynamo terminal (F) and control box terminal (F), is in good condition.

B.S.A. Service Sheet No. 804A (contd.)

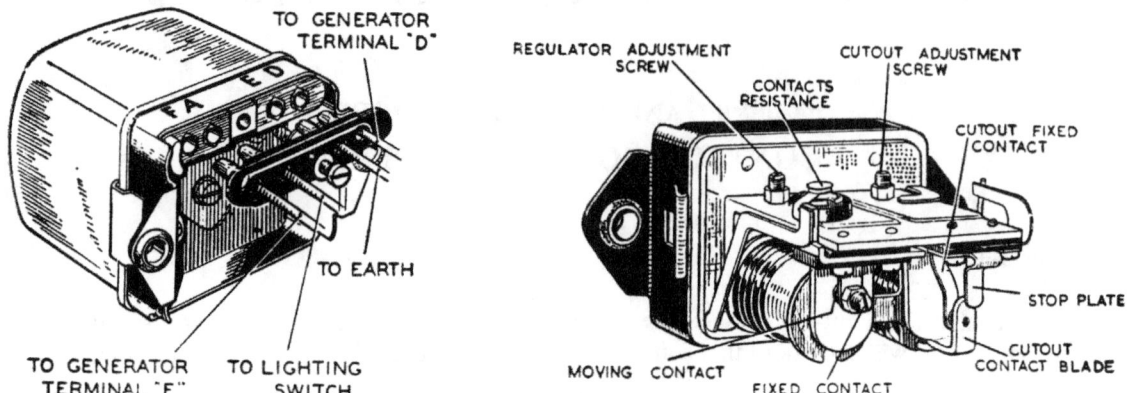

Fig. Y16a. *Control Box Connections and Internal Layout*

Electrical Setting of Regulator

The regulator is carefully set during manufacture and it should not be necessary to make further adjustment. If the charging system is suspect, it is important that only a good quality moving coil voltmeter (0—20 volts) is used for checking.

Connect the negative voltmeter lead to terminal (D) and the positive lead to terminal (E) on the control box. Remove the negative cable from the battery.

Start the engine and slowly increase the speed until the voltmeter needle "flicks" and then steadies. Note the reading and stop the engine.

If the voltage lies outside the limits given in the setting data, the regulator must be adjusted.

Remove the control box from the machine and take off the cover. It is importan that adjustments are carried out with the control box supported in a similar position to that in which it is mounted on the machine. Re-start the engine.

Slacken the locknut of the adjusting screw, Fig. Y17a, and turn the screw clockwise to raise, or anti-clockwise to lower the setting. Turn the screw only a fraction of a turn at a time and then tighten the locknut. Repeat until the correct setting is obtained. Then stop the engine.

Adjustment should be completed within 30 seconds, otherwise heating of the shunt-winding will cause false settings to be made. A dynamo run at high speed on open circuit will build up a high voltage; therefore, do not run the engine up to more than half full speed.

Mechanical Setting of Regulator

If the armature has been removed, the air-gap settings will have to be re-adjusted. Otherwise they should not be altered. To adjust, proceed as follows:—

Slacken the locknut on the voltage adjusting screw and unscrew the adjuster until it is well clear of the armature tension spring. Also slacken the two armature securing screws, Fig. Y17a.

B.S.A. Service Sheet No. 804A (contd.)

Insert a .015 in. feeler gauge wide enough to cover completely the core face between the armature and the core shim, taking care not to damage the shim. Press the armature squarely down against the gauge and tighten the two securing screws. With the gauge still in position, screw the adjustable contact down until it just touches the armature contact.

Tighten the locknut, and re-set the voltage adjusting screw as described above.

Cleaning Contacts

After long periods of service it may be found necessary to clean the contacts. Use a fine carborundum stone or fine emery cloth. Wipe away all traces of dust or other foreign matter with methylated spirits.

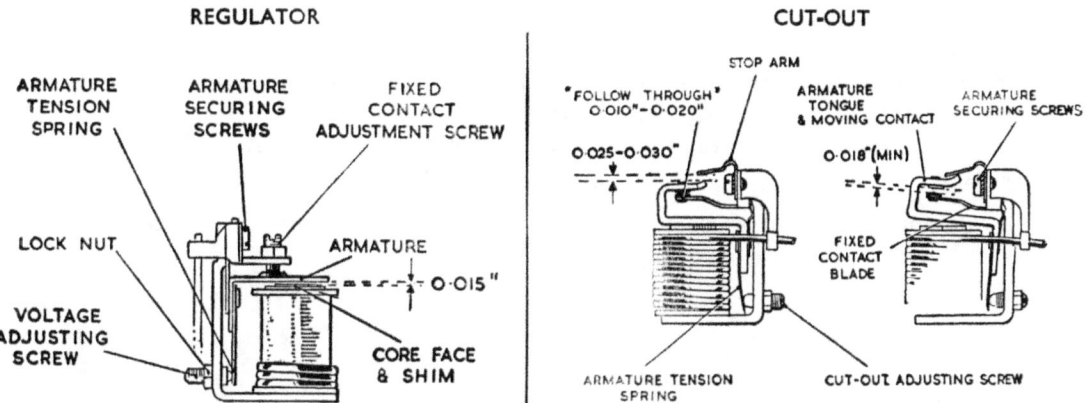

Fig. Y17a. *Regulator and Cut-out Adjustment and Setting.*

Electrical Setting of Cut-out

If the regulator is correctly set but the battery is still not being charged, the cut-out may be out of adjustment.

Connect a voltmeter between terminals (D) and (E) on the control box, start the engine and slowly increase the speed until the contacts close. Note the reading, and stop the engine. If outside the limits of 6.3—6.7 volts, it will be necessary to adjust the cut-out.

Re-start the engine, and slacken the locknut securing the cut-out adjusting screw, Fig. Y17a. Turn the screw clockwise to raise, or anti-clockwise to lower the setting. Move the screw only a fraction of a turn at a time and then retighten the locknut. Test after each adjustment by increasing engine speed and noting the voltmeter reading at the instant of contact closure. Stop the engine.

Setting of the cut-out, like that of the regulator, must be made as quickly as possible because of temperature rise effects.

If the cut-out fails to operate, there may be an open circuit in the wiring of the control box, in which case the unit should be replaced.

B.S.A. Service Sheet No. 804A (contd.)

Mechanical Setting of Cut-out

If, for any reason, the armature has been removed from the frame, the correct air-gap settings must be obtained on reassembly.

Slacken the adjusting screw locknut and unscrew the adjuster until it is well clear of the tension spring. Press the armature squarely down on the core face and tighten the securing screws. Adjust the gap between the armature tongue and the stop arm by carefully bending the arm. The gap must be .025—.030 in. when the armature is pressed down, Fig. Y17a. Similarly, the fixed contact blade must be bent so that, when the armature is pressed down, there is a minimum "follow-through" or blade deflection of .010 in. To prevent contact chatter, the "follow-through" must not exceed .020 in.

With the armature in the free position, the contact gap must be .018 in. minimum.

Finally, re-set the cut-out adjusting screw.

Cleaning Contacts

If the cut-out contacts appear rough or burnt, place a strip of fine glasspaper between them, close the contacts by hand and draw the paper through two or three times with the rough side towards each contact in turn. Wipe away dust or other foreign matter with methylated spirits.

Do not use emery cloth or carborundum stone for cleaning cut-out contacts.

B.S.A. MOTOR CYCLES LTD., Service Department, Armoury Road, Birmingham 11.
Printed in England
B.S.A. Press.

BSA SERVICE SHEET No. 805

Reprinted June, 1960

All Models

BATTERY — LEAD-ACID TYPES

The range of Lucas batteries listed here covers those models fitted to B.S.A. motor cycles in recent years.

PU5E and LVW5E Small capacity batteries for light-weight machines.

PU7E .. .. Standard battery for cradle mounting.

GU11E .. .. Larger capacity battery for sidecar machines.

SC7E .. .. Large capacity lightweight battery for machines fitted with starting motors or two-way radio equipment, e.g. police machines.

All current Lucas motor cycle batteries are 'dry charged', and do not require initial charging. Except that these batteries have porous rubber separators, they are identical with earlier models supplied wet or uncharged and require the same routine maintenance when in service.

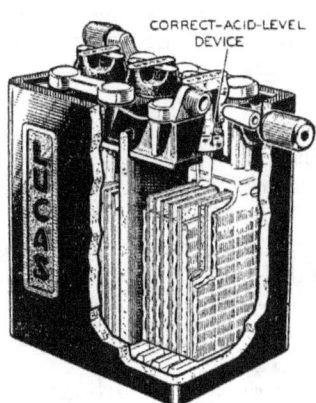

Fig. Y18. Sectioned battery, model PU7E/9

STORAGE

Used batteries must be fully charged before storing. In temperate climates they should be examined fortnightly, or weekly in the case of model LVW5E and all models when stored in the tropics. If necessary, give them a short refreshing charge.

After a long period of storage, the condition of the battery will often improve if it is put through a 'cycle', as described on page 4.

MAINTENANCE

Every fortnight, or more frequently in hot climates, examine the condition of the battery. Examine five-plate batteries every week.

Never use a naked light when examining the condition of the cells, as there is a **danger** of igniting the gas coming from the active materials.

Cleaning

Remove the battery cover and clean the cell tops. Examine the connections. If they are loose or dirty, remove them and scrape the contact surfaces clean. Coat them with petroleum jelly before replacing.

Remove the filler plugs and check that the vent holes are clear and that the rubber washer fitted under some plugs is in good condition.

Topping-up

During charging, water is lost by gassing and evaporation. Examine the electrolyte level in each cell and, if necessary, add distilled water to raise the electrolyte level with the top edges of the separators.

SC7E batteries have a woven glass pad fitted in each cell to reduce splashing when the battery is gassing during charging. When 'topping-up' this type of battery it is useful to note that the correct electrolyte level is reached when moisture appears through the porous glass pad.

B.S.A. Service Sheet No. 805 (continued)

The Lucas Battery Filler

The use of a Lucas motor cycle Battery Filler will be found helpful in this 'topping-up' process, as it ensures that the correct electrolyte level is automatically attained and also prevents distilled water from being spilled over the battery top.

Correct-Acid-Level-Devices

The correct-acid-level-device fitted to some Lucas batteries consists of a central tube with a perforated flange which rests on a ledge in the filling orifice.

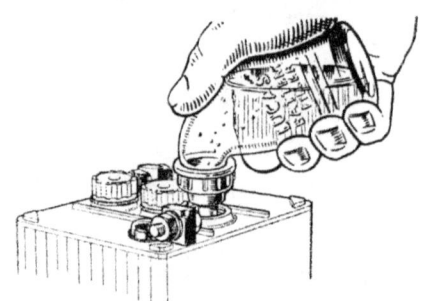

Fig Y19. The Lucas battery filler

When 'topping-up' a battery fitted with these devices, pour distilled water round the flange (not down the tube) until no more drains through into the cell. This will happen when the electrolyte level reaches the bottom of the central tube and prevents further escape of air displaced by the 'topping-up' water. Lift the tube slightly to allow the small amount of water in the flange to drain into the cell. The electrolyte level will then be correct.

If a battery requires 'topping-up' too frequently, the voltage regulator (on machines fitted with d.c. generators) may be out of adjustment, i.e. set too high, and should be checked. Conversely, a persistently low state of charge may be due to a regulator being set too low.

If one cell in particular needs 'topping-up' more than another, it is likely the container is cracked, in which event replace the battery and clean the carrier, using a solution of ammonia or bi-carbonate of soda in water. After cleaning and drying, paint the battery carrier and other surfaces affected by the electrolyte with anti-sulphuric paint.

TABLES OF SPECIFIC GRAVITIES AND CHARGING RATES

Battery	Plates per cell	Amp. Hr. Capacity		Electrolyte to fill one two-volt cell		Home Trade and Climates Ordinarily below 90°F. (32°C.) Specific Gravity of Acid (corrected to 60°F.)		Climates frequently over 90°F. (32°C.) Specific Gravity of Acid (corrected to 60°F.)		Initial Charge Current	Re-charge Current
1	2	3		4		5	6	7	8	9	10
		At 10 hour rate	At 20 hour rate	Pint	c.c.	Filling	Fully Charged	Filling	Fully Charged	Amp.	Amp.
LVW5E	5	5	5.7	1/8	71	1.270	1.270–1.290	1.210	1.210–1.230	0.3	0.5
PU5E	5	8	9	1/6	94	1.270	1.270–1.290	1.210	1.210–1.230	0.6	1.0
PU7E	7	12	13.5	1/5	113	1.270	1.270–1.290	1.210	1.210–1.230	0.8	1.5
GU11E	11	20	22.8	1/3	189	1.270	1.270–1.290	1.210	1.210–1.230	1.3	2.2
SC7E	7	22.5	26	—	250	1.270	1.270–1.290	1.210	1.210–1.230	1.5	2.5

The maximum permissible electrolyte temperature during charging is given below. Should the temperature of the electrolyte exceed this value interrupt the charge and allow the battery temperature to fall at least 10°F. (5.5°C.) before charging is resumed.

Climates normally below 80°F. (27°C.)	Climates between 80°–100°F. (27°–38°C.)	Climates frequently above 100°F. (38°C.)
100°F. (38°C.)	110°F. (43°C.)	120°F. (49°C.)

The specific gravity of the electrolyte varies with temperature. For convenience in comparing specific gravities, they are always corrected to 60°F., which is adopted as the reference temperature. The method of correction is as follows:

For every 5°F. *below* 60°F., *deduct* 0.002 from the observed reading to obtain the true specific gravity at 60°F. For every 5°F. *above* 60°F., *add* 0.002 to the observed reading to obtain the true specific gravity at 60°F.

The temperature must be that indicated by a thermometer having its bulb actually immersed in the electrolyte, and not the ambient temperature.

B.S.A. Service Sheet No. 805 (continued)

SERVICING
Battery Persists in Low State of Charge
First consider the conditions under which the battery is used. If the battery is subject to continuous discharge, e.g. long periods of night parking with lights on without suitable opportunities for recharging, a low state of charge is inevitable.

A fault in the dynamo or regulator, or neglect during a period out of commission, may also be responsible.

Vent Plugs
See that the ventilating holes in each vent plug are clear, and that the rubber washer fitted under the plug is in good condition.

Level of Electrolyte
The surface of the electrolyte should be level with the tops of the separators. If necessary, top-up with distilled water. Any loss of acid from spilling or spraying (as opposed to normal loss of *water* by evaporation) should be made good by dilute acid of the same specific gravity as that already in the cell.

Cleanliness
See that the top of the battery is free from dirt or moisture which might provide a discharge path. Check that the battery connections are clean and tight.

Hydrometer Tests
The space between each separator is not wide enough to permit the nozzle of an hydrometer to be inserted. Before taking a sample, tilt the battery to bring sufficient electrolyte above the separators. If the level of the electrolyte is so low that an hydrometer reading cannot be taken, no attempt should be made to take a reading after adding distilled water until the battery has been on charge for at least 30 minutes.

Measure the specific gravity of the acid in each cell in turn. The reading given by each cell should be approximately the same; if one cell differs appreciably from the others, an internal fault in that cell is indicated.

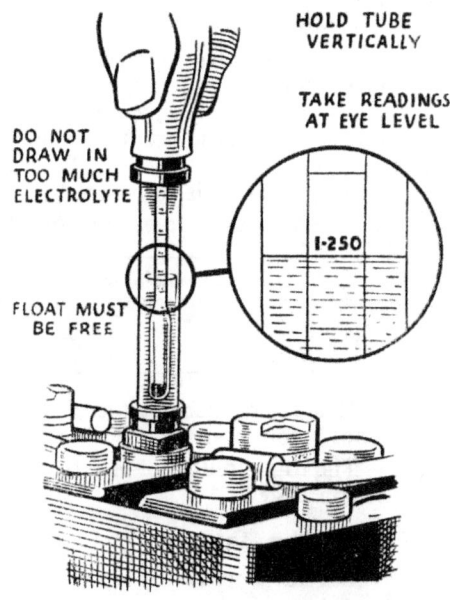

Fig Y20. Taking hydrometer readings

Specific gravity readings and their indications are as follows:

Climates under 90°F.				Climates over 90°F.
1.270—1.290	..	Cell fully charged	..	1.210—1.230
1.190—1.210	..	Cell about half discharged	..	1.130—1.150
1.110—1.130	..	Cell fully discharged	..	1.050—1.070

The appearance of the electrolyte drawn into the hydrometer when taking a reading gives a useful indication of the state of the plates: if it is very dirty, or contains small particles in suspension, it is possible that the plates are in a bad condition.

Discharge Test
Motor-cycle batteries must *not* be subjected to the heavy discharge test, as recommended for motor-car and commercial vehicle batteries.

RECHARGING FROM AN EXTERNAL SUPPLY
If the hydrometer test indicates that the battery is merely discharged, and is otherwise in a good condition, it should be recharged, either on the motor-cycle by a period of daytime running, or on the bench from an external supply.

B.S.A. Service Sheet No. 805 (continued)

If the latter, the battery should be charged at the rate given in the table until the specific gravity and voltage show no increase over three successive hourly readings. During the charge the electrolyte must be kept level with the tops of the separators by the addition of distilled water.

A battery that shows a general falling-off in efficiency, common to all cells, will often respond to the process known as 'cycling'. This process consists of fully charging the battery by passing through it from an external source the appropriate re-charge current given in the table. The battery is then discharged by connecting to a lamp board, or other load, taking a current equal to the normal re-charge current. The battery should be capable of providing this current for at least 7 hours before it is fully discharged, as indicated by the voltage of each cell falling to 1.8. If the battery discharges in a shorter time, repeat the 'cycle' of charge and discharge.

PREPARING BATTERIES FOR SERVICE

All new batteries are supplied without electrolyte but with the plates in a charged condition. When they are required for service it is only necessary to fill each cell with sulphuric acid of the correct specific gravity. No initial charging is required.

Preparation of Electrolyte

The electrolyte is prepared by mixing together distilled water and concentrated sulphuric acid. The mixing must be carried out either in a lead-lined tank or in suitable glass or earthenware vessels. Slowly add the acid to the water, stirring with a glass rod. *Never add water to acid*, as the resulting chemical reaction causes violent and dangerous spurting of the concentrated acid. The specific gravity of the filling electrolyte depends on the climate in which the battery is to be used.

The approximate proportions of acid and water are indicated in the following table:

To obtain Specific Gravity (corrected to 60°F.) of	Add 1 vol. of acid 1.835 S.G. (corrected to 60°F.) to
1.270	2.8 vols. of water
1.210	4.0 vols. of water

Heat is produced by the mixture of acid and water, and the electrolyte should be allowed to cool before pouring it into the battery.

The total volume of electrolyte required can be estimated from the figures quoted in the table on page 2.

Filling the Battery

Carefully break the seals in the cell filling holes and fill each cell with electrolyte to the top of the separators, *in one operation*. The temperature of the filling room, battery and electrolyte should be maintained between 60°F. and 100°F. If the battery has been stored in a cool place, it should be allowed to warm up to room temperature before filling.

Putting into Use

Batteries filled in this way are 90 per cent charged. If time permits, however, a freshening charge of four hours at the normal recharge rate given in the table would be beneficial.

During the charge the electrolyte must be kept level with the top edge of the separators by the addition of distilled water. Check the specific gravity of the acid at the end of the charge; if 1.270 acid was used to fill the battery, the specific gravity should now be between 1.270 and 1.290; if 1.210, between 1.210 and 1.230.

Maintenance in Service

After filling, the battery needs only the recommended attention.

B.S.A. MOTOR CYCLES LTD.
Service Dept., Waverley Works,
Birmingham, 10.

JU/B5029

Printed in England.

BSA SERVICE SHEET No. 806

Reprinted April, 1960

All Models

LAMPS

LUCAS LIGHTING

Headlamps

Although the headlamps fitted to individual models may vary in detail, they remain similar with regard to the general features described below. All headlamps are fitted with a double filament main bulb and a pilot bulb. One of the double filaments provides the main riding beam while the second, brought into operation by means of the dipper switch, provides the dipped beam.

On some models the headlamp incorporates a panel containing the ammeter and lighting switch but if a cowl is fitted then it carries these components externally to the headlamp shell.

Other headlamps contain wire wound resistances for the purpose of reducing the charging rates under certain conditions and these are described under the appropriate lighting circuit.

Setting and Focusing

The best way of checking the setting of the lamp is to park the motor cycle in front of a light coloured wall at a distance of about 25 feet. If necessary, slacken the bolts securing the headlamp and move the lamp until, with the main driving light switched on, the beam is projected straight ahead and parallel with the ground. With the lamp in this position, the height of the beam centre from the ground should be the same as the height of the centre of the headlamp from the ground.

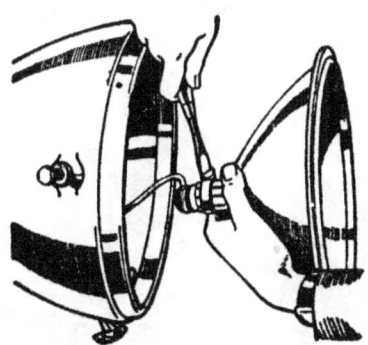

Fig. Y.22 Headlamp Focusing.

The headlamp must be focused so that, when the main driving light is switched on, a uniform beam without any dark centre is given. If the bulb needs adjusting, remove the lamp front and reflector, as described below, and slacken the bulb holder clamping clip at the back of the reflector. Move the bulb holder backwards and forwards until the correct position is obtained, and then tighten the clamping clip.

More sealed beam light units are fitted with the pre-focus type of bulb and therefore no focusing is necessary.

Removal of Front and Reflector, pre-1948 models

Press back the fixing clip at the bottom of the lamp. The front and reflector can now be taken off. The bulb holder is secured to the reflector by means of two fixing springs. When replacing the front, locate the top of the rim first, then press on at the bottom and secure with the fixing clip.

B.S.A. Service Sheet No. 806 (cont.)

1948 Models (Fig. Y.23)

Press back the fixing clip at the bottom of the lamp, and remove the lamp front. The reflector is secured to the lamp body by means of a rubber bead. When refitting the rubber bead, locate its thinner lip between the reflector rim and the edge of the lamp body. To replace the front, locate the metal tongue in the slot at the top of the lamp, press the front on, and secure by means of the fixing catch.

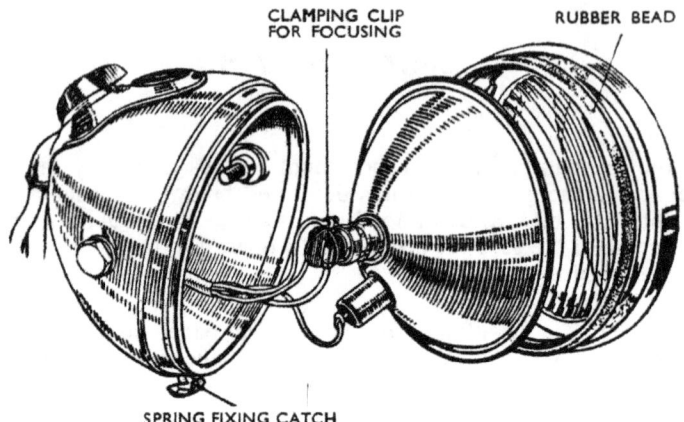

Fig. Y.23.

Sealed Beam Headlamps

Later models are fitted with a sealed light unit having the reflector and glass sealed together. After slackening the securing screw on the top of the headlamp, the rim, complete with light unit, may be removed. To replace, locate the rim on the lip at the bottom of the lamp body, press the light unit assembly and rim into position and tighten the securing screw. The main headlamp bulb in some of these headlamps is of the pre-focus type and is held in position by a cap with bayonet type fitting. In all cases access to the main or pilot bulbs is obtained by removal of the light unit assembly.

Breakage of the headlamp glass with this type of unit involves replacement of the glass and reflector complete. The light unit may be removed from the headlamp rim after prising out the retaining clips.

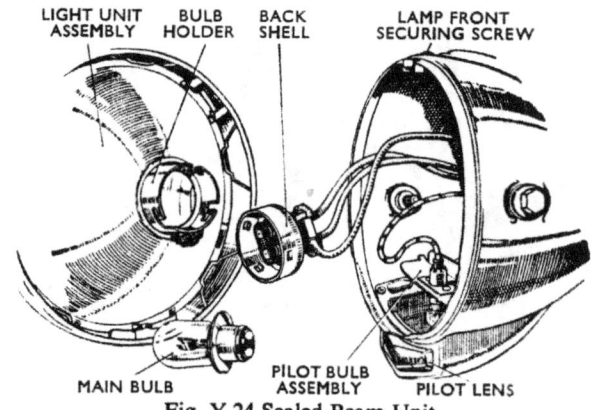

Fig. Y.24 Sealed Beam Unit.

Replacement of Bulbs

When the replacement of a bulb is necessary, it is important not only that the same size bulb is fitted, but that it has a high efficiency and will focus in the reflector. Cheap and inferior replacement bulbs often have the filament of such a shape that it is impossible to focus correctly; for example, the filament may be to the one side of the axis of the bulb resulting in loss of range and light efficiency.

Lucas Genuine Spare Bulbs are specially tested to check that the filament is in the correct position to give the best results with Lucas lamps. To assist in identification, Lucas bulbs are marked on the metal cap with a number. When fitting a replacement, see that it has the same number as the original bulb.

B.S.A. Service Sheet No. 806 (cont.)

When fitting a main headlamp bulb, care must be taken to insert it the correct way round, i.e. with the dipped beam filament above the centre filament.

The pre-focus type bulb is located by a flange and there is a notch which engages on a raised portion of the bulb holder to ensure correct positioning.

Where the pilot bulb is contained in an underslung cowl, the metal strip on which the bulb is mounted should be pushed to the rear and lifted away in order to provide access to the bulb.

Tail Lamps

Where the tail lamp is of the metal type the body or back should be removed by pushing it in, rotating to the left, and pulling away, thus providing access to the bulb. The moulded plastic type of rear lamp can be dismantled by unscrewing the two screws in the cover.

When a stop lamp is fitted, a two-filament type of bulb is employed with offset bayonet type fixing pins to ensure that it can only be fitted correctly.

MAIN BULBS

Models A7, A10, B31, 32, 33, 34, C12, C15 and M20, M21.

Lucas No. 168, 6v. 24/24w. (with E3H Dynamo). Lucas No. 169, 6v. 30/30w. (with E3L Dynamo). Lucas No. 312, 6v. 30/24w. (Pre-focus type Bulb).

Models C10 and C11.

Lucas No. 180, 6v., 18/18w. (with E3H Dynamo). Lucas No. 168, 6v. 24/24w. (with E3L Dynamo).

Models C11G and D1 (early) Lucas

Lucas No. 312, 6v. 30/24w. (Pre-focus type Bulb).

PILOT

Lucas No. 200, 6v. 3w. Lucas No. 988, 6v. 3w. (with Sealed Beam Light Unit).

TAIL

Lucas No. 205, 6v. 6w.
Lucas No. 384, 6v. 6/18w. (Stop/Tail Lamp).

JU/B4780

B.S.A. MOTOR CYCLES LTD.
Service Dept., Waverley Works,
Birmingham, 10
Printed in England.

BSA SERVICE SHEET No. 807

Reprinted June 1960

All Models

ELECTRIC HORN—HIGH FREQUENCY MODELS

General

Electric horns are adjusted to give their best performance before leaving the Works, and will give long periods of service without any attention.

Servicing

If the horn becomes uncertain in action or does not vibrate, it does not follow that the horn has broken down. The trouble may be due to a discharged battery or a loose or broken connection in the horn wiring.

The performance of the horn may be upset by the fixing bolt working loose, or by the vibration of some part adjacent to the horn. To check this, remove the horn from its mounting, hold it firmly in the hand by its bracket and press the push. If the note is still unsatisfactory, the horn may require adjustment, but this should only be necessary after a very long period of service.

Method of Adjusting

The adjustment of a horn does not alter the characteristics of the note but merely takes up wear of vibrating parts.

If the horn is used repeatedly when badly out of adjustment, due usually to unsuccessful attempts at adjustment, the horn may become damaged, due to the excessive current which it will take. When testing, do not continue to operate the push if the horn does not sound. If, when the push is operated, the horn does not take any current (indicated by an ammeter connected in series with the horn) it is possible that the horn has been adjusted so that its contact breaker is permanently open.

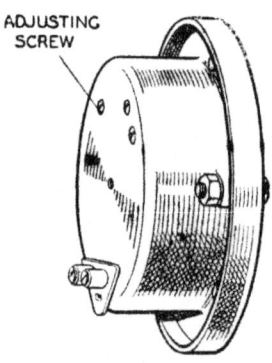

Fig. Y26.
Typical electric horn, showing adjustment screw.

After adjusting, note the current consumption, which must not exceed 3—4 amperes. A horn may give a good note, yet be out of adjustment and taking an excessive current. When adjusting do not attempt to unscrew the nut securing the tone disc or any other screw in the horn.

The adjustment is made by turning the adjustment screw, usually in a clockwise direction. The underside of the screw is serrated, and the screw must not be turned for more than 2 or 3 notches before re-testing. If the adjustment screw is turned too far in a clockwise direction, a point will occur at which the armature pulls in but does not separate the contacts.

B.S.A. Service Sheet No. 807 (contd.)

Some models have no adjustment screw at the back of the horn. Adjustment is carried out by means of the grub screw and locking collar which are revealed upon removal of the large domed nut on the front of the horn. Take care that the large nut securing the sounding disc is not disturbed. The locking collar requires a special tool, or a large screwdriver with the blade ground so as to leave two projecting prongs, in order that it may be undone. No attempt should be made to loosen the collar without a proper tool as it is very tight and may become damaged so that it cannot be removed. The adjustment should be carried out in a similar manner to that described for the other type of horn, but the locking collar should be firmly tightened after each adjustment as this affects the note.

B.S.A. MOTOR CYCLES LTD.,
Service Dept., Waverley Works.
Birmingham, 10.
Printed in England.

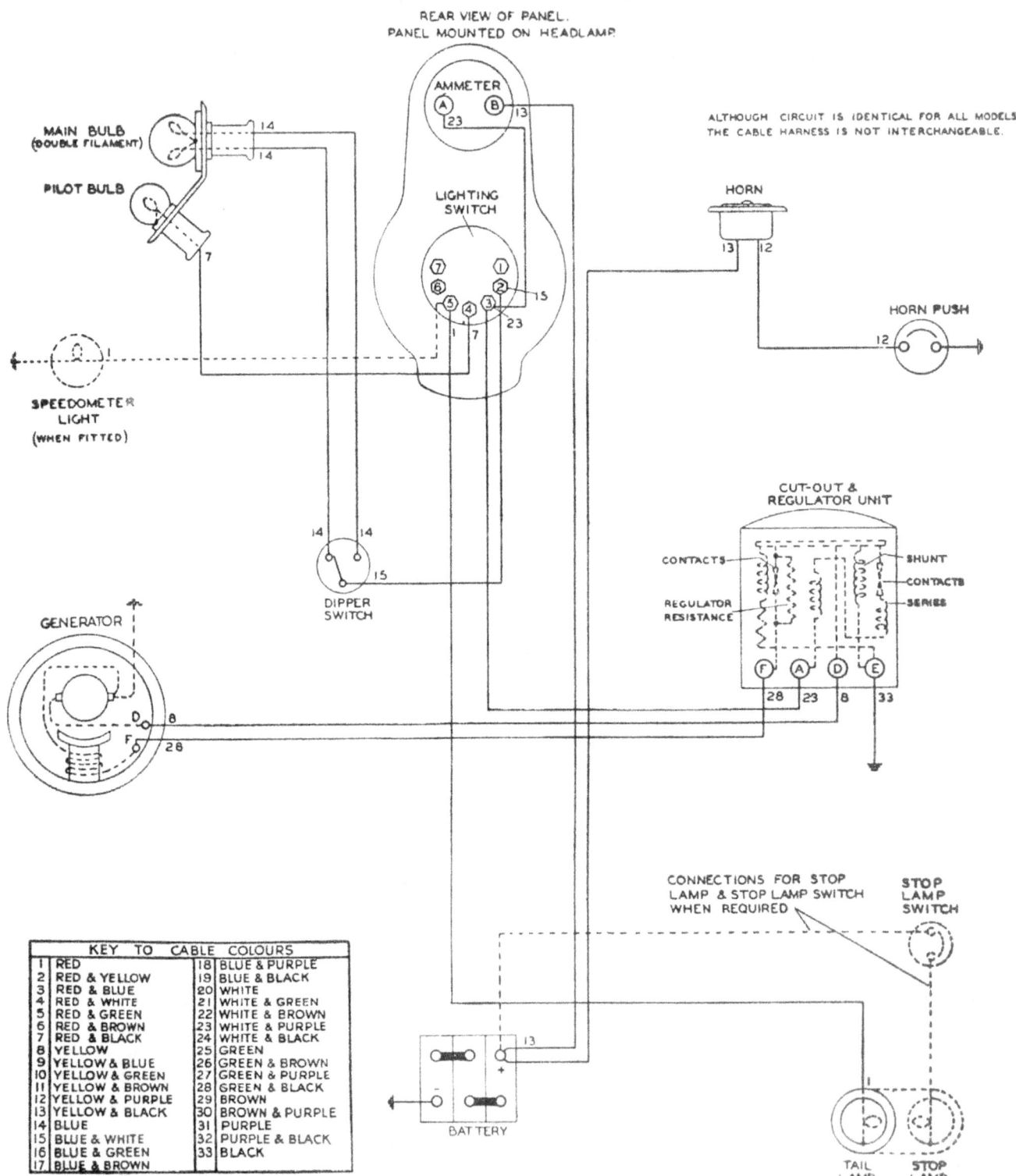

B.S.A. Service Sheet No. 808 (cont.)

C10 and C11 Models
WIRING DIAGRAM
(NEGATIVE EARTH)

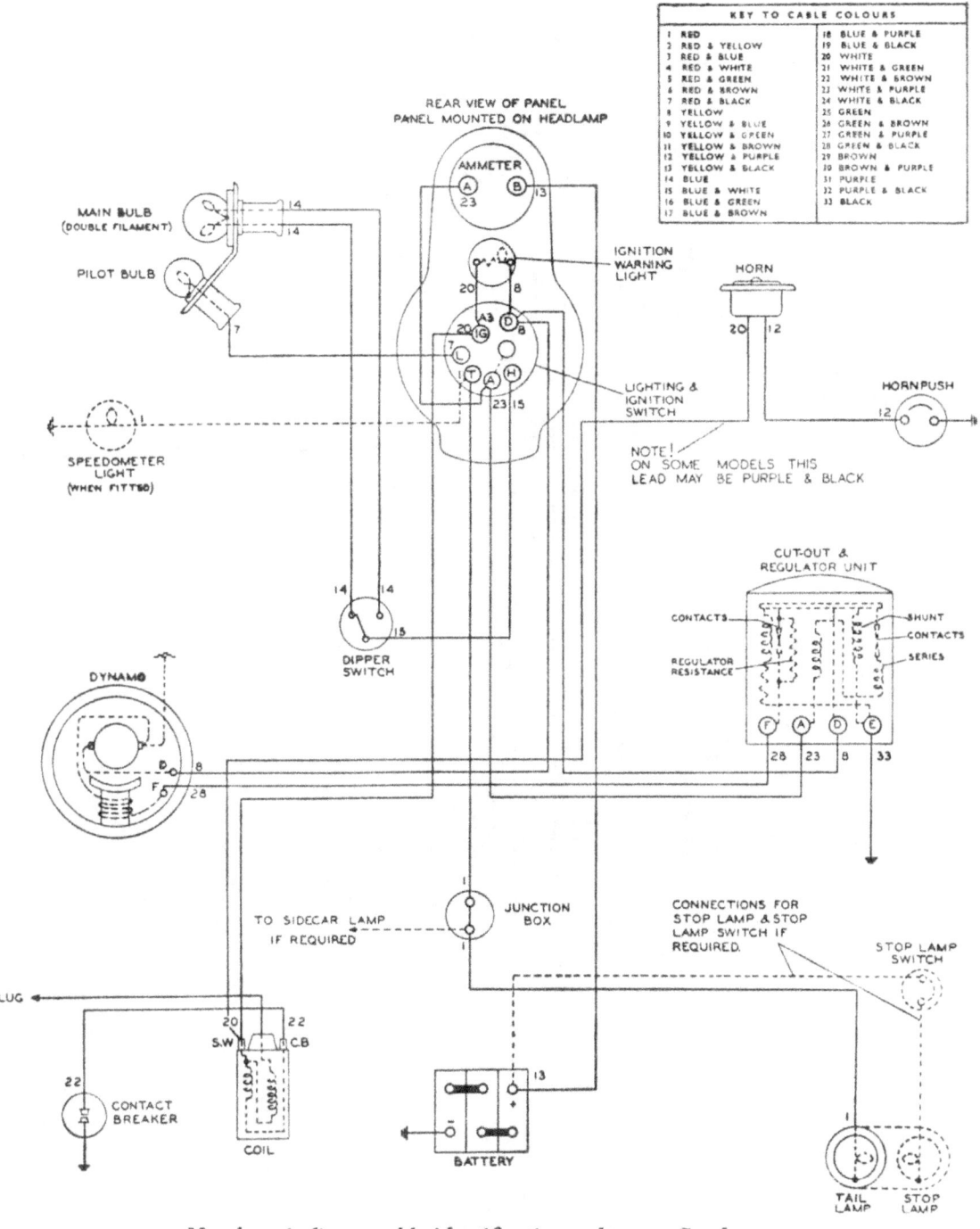

Numbers indicate cable identification colours. See key.

B.S.A. MOTOR CYCLES LTD.
Service Dept., Armoury Road,
Birmingham, 11

Printed in England.

BSA SERVICE SHEET No. 808A

A, (except A50/A65) B and M Group Models
WIRING DIAGRAM
(Positive Earth System)

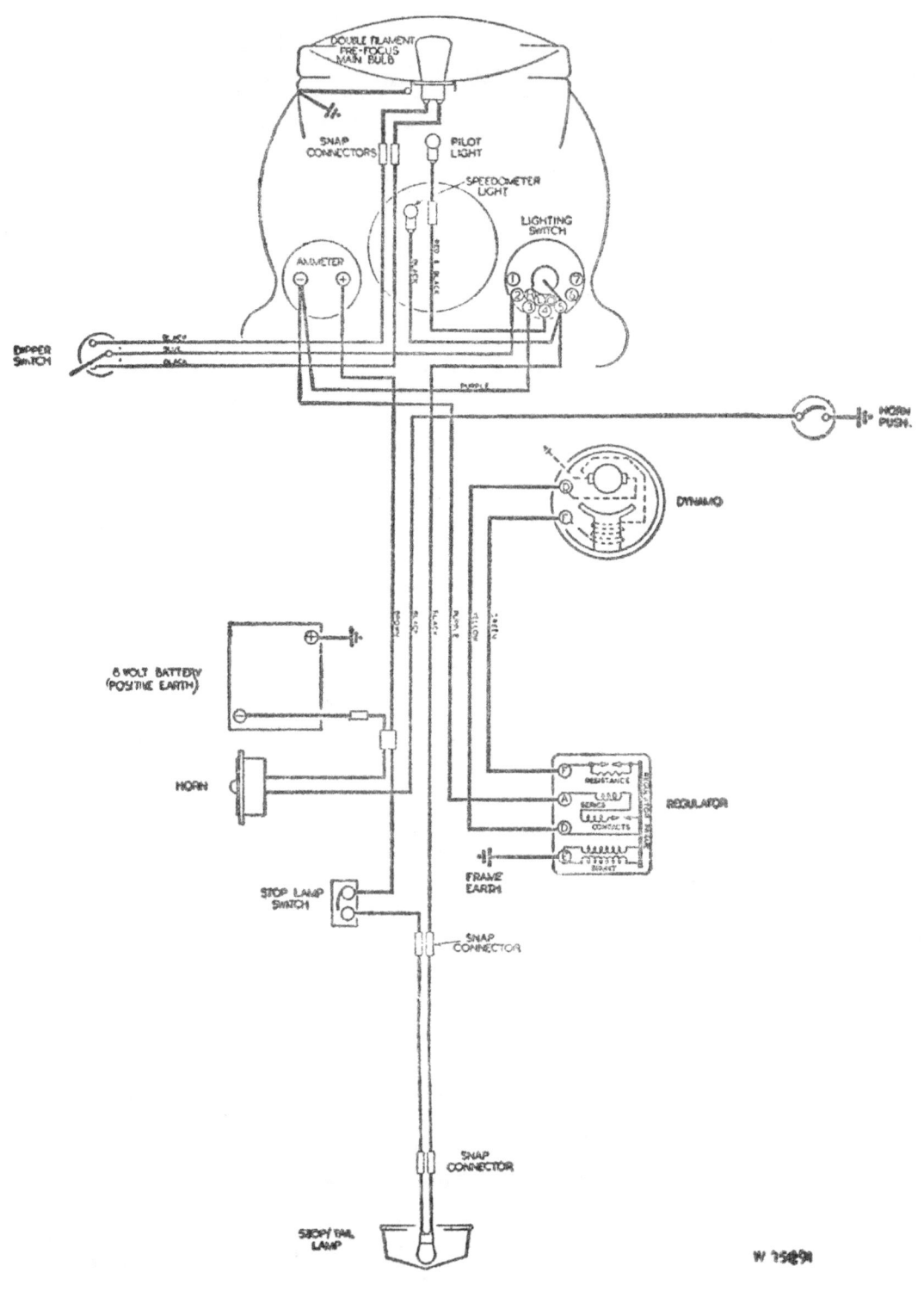

B.S.A. Service Sheet No. 808A (contd.)

C Group Models
WIRING DIAGRAM
(Positive Earth System)

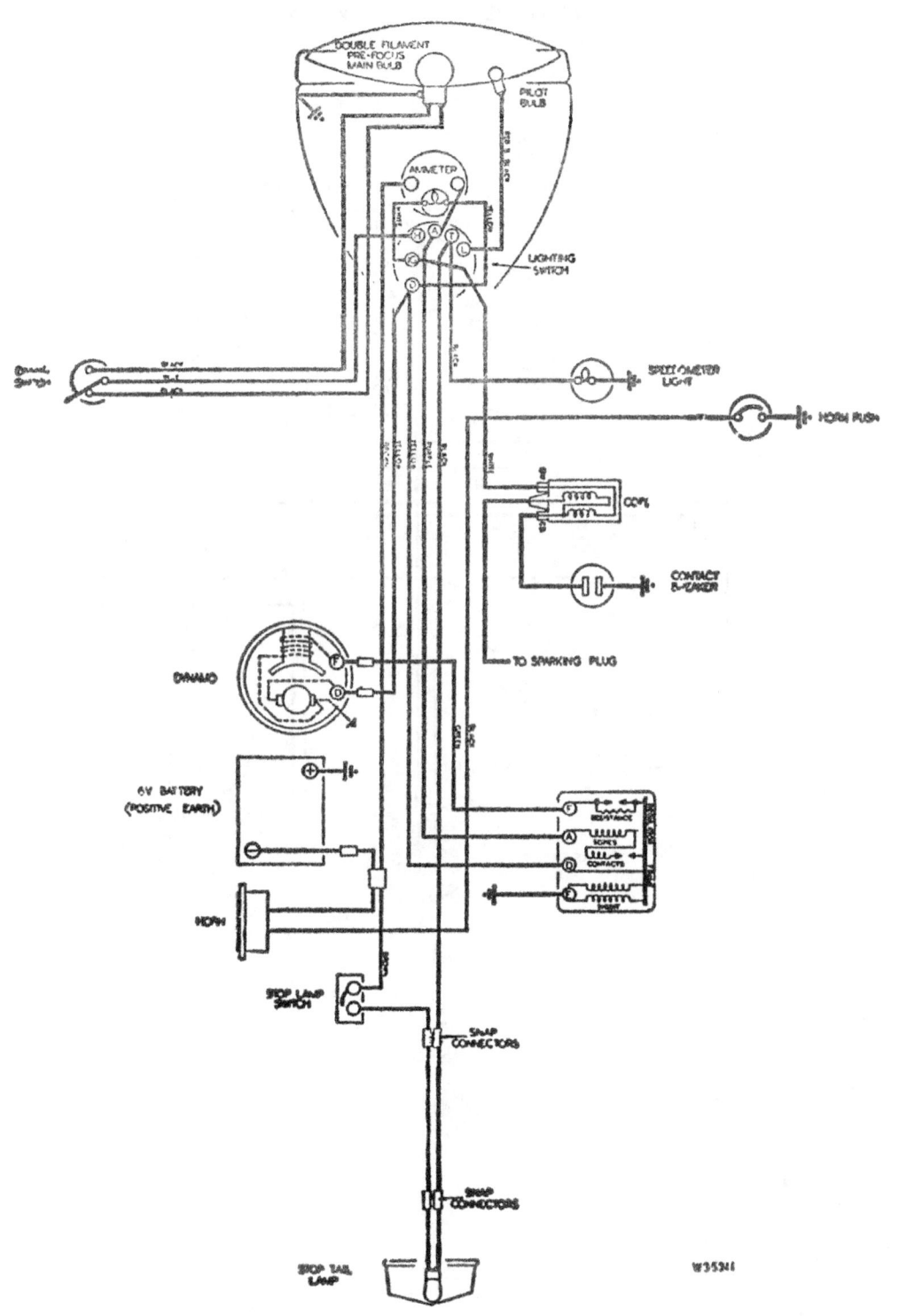

B.S.A. MOTOR CYCLES LTD.,
Service Dept., Armoury Road, Birmingham 11,

Printed in England.

BSA SERVICE SHEET No. 808F

M Group Models

WIRING DIAGRAM (Positive Earth System)

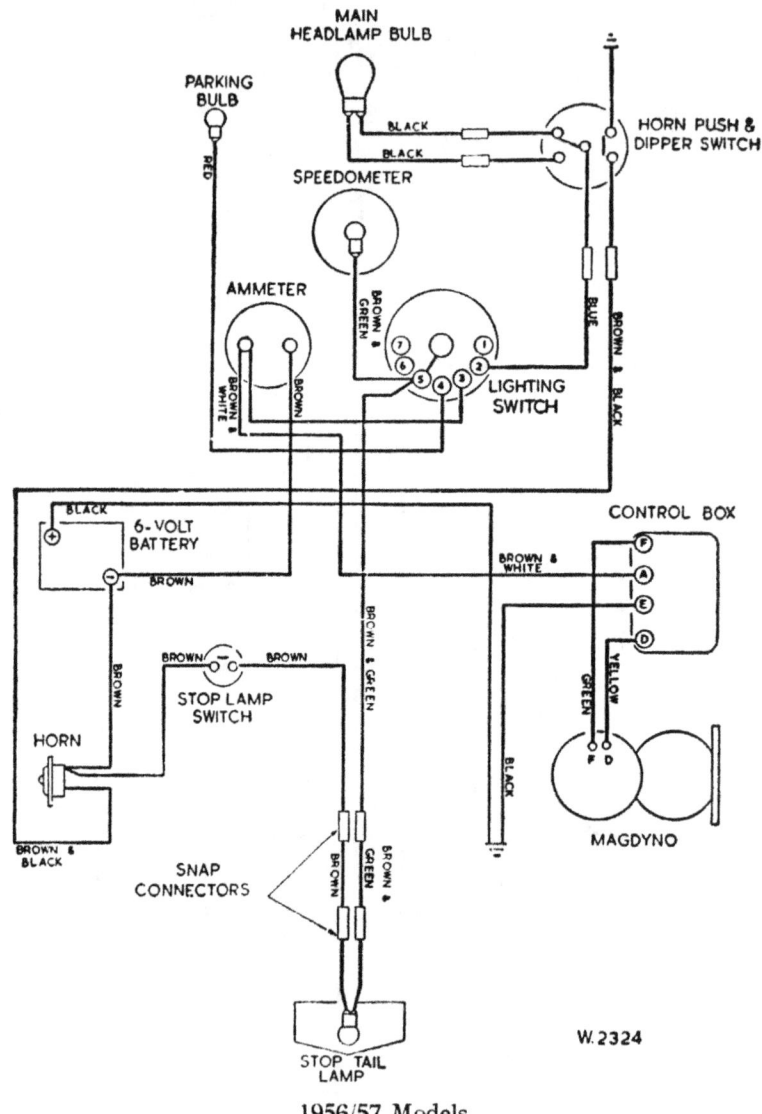

1956/57 Models

B.S.A. Service Sheet No. 808F—*continued*

A and B Group Models Wiring Diagrams

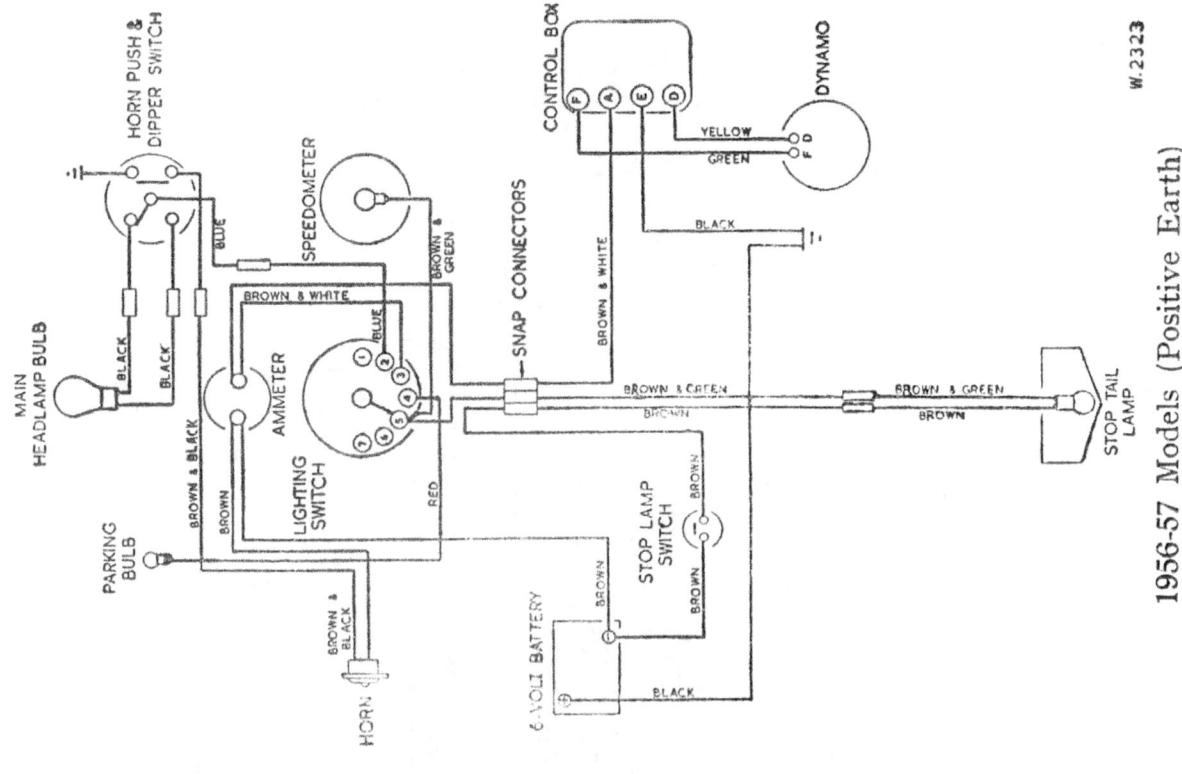

1956-57 Models (Positive Earth)

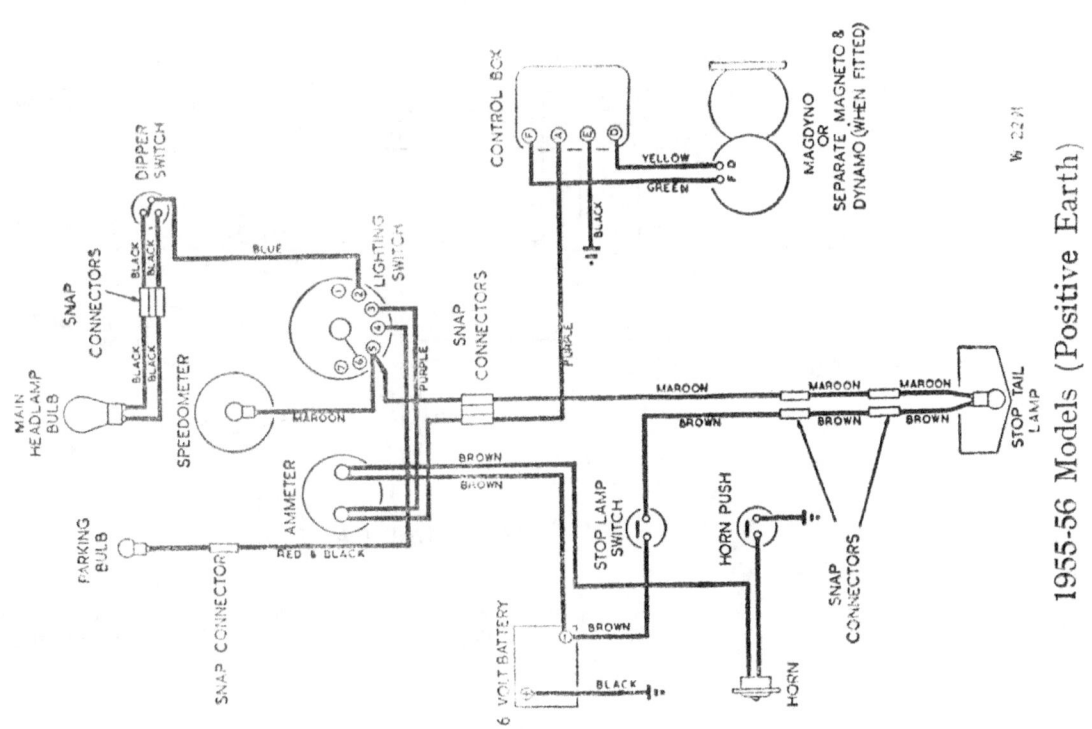

1955-56 Models (Positive Earth)

B.S.A. Press.

B.S.A. MOTOR CYCLES LTD
Service Dept., Armoury Road,
Birmingham 11

BSA SERVICE SHEET No. 808H

B Group Models
(FITTED WITH ALTERNATOR)

WIRING DIAGRAM (Positive Earth System)

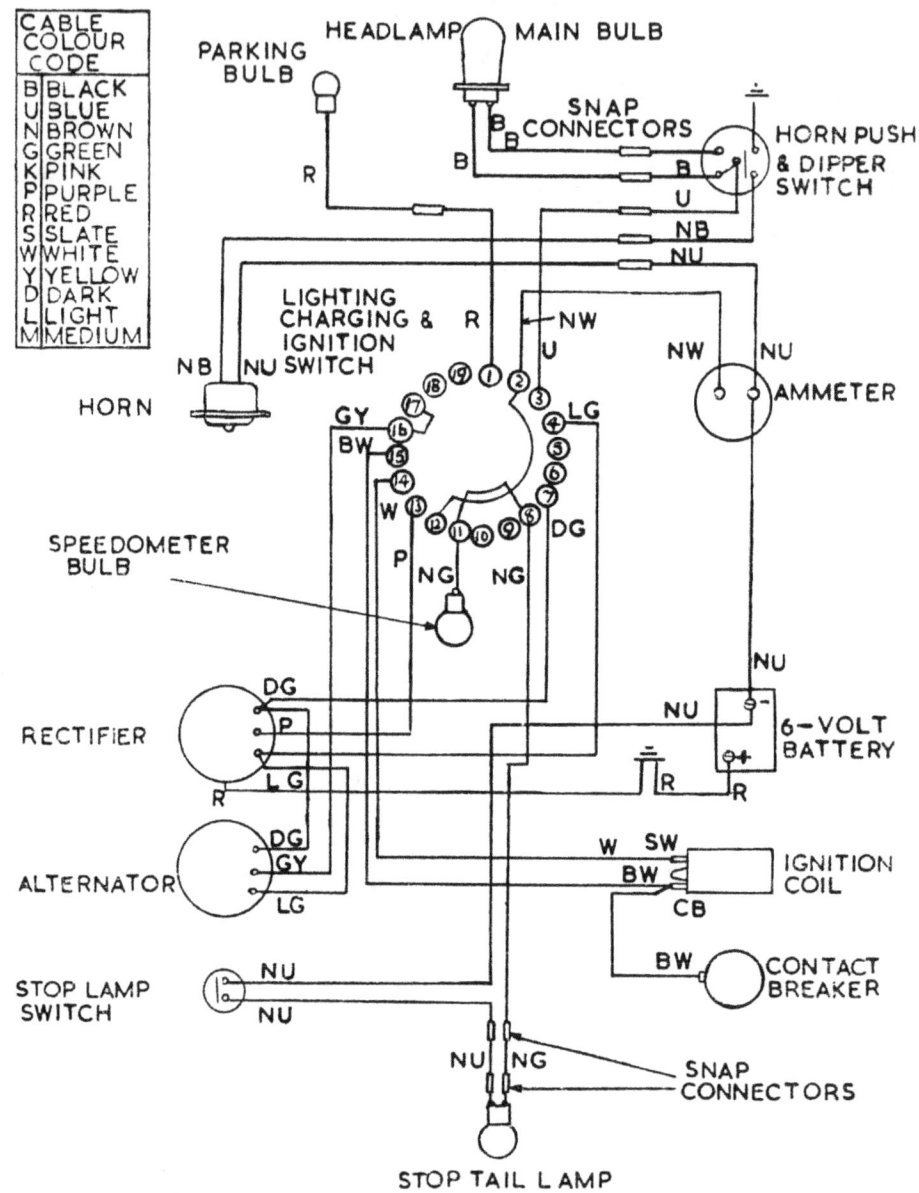

B.S.A. MOTOR CYCLES LTD.
Service Dept., Armoury Road, Birmingham, 11
Printed in England

BSA SERVICE SHEET No. 809

All Models except D1, C10L, C11G, C12, C15 and "B" Group fitted with Alternators

GENERATORS–MODELS E3H and E3HM

The generator is a shunt-wound two pole machine, arranged to work in conjunction with a regulator unit to give an output which is dependent on the state of charge of the battery and the loading of the electrical equipment in use. When the battery is in a low state of charge, the generator gives a high output, whereas if the battery is fully charged the generator gives only a trickle charge to keep the battery in a good condition without overcharging. In addition, an increase of output is given to balance the current taken by the lamps when in use.

Models E3H and E3HM are similar in construction. The former will be found on motor cycles having separate magneto or coil ignition, while model E3HM is the generator portion of the combined unit known as the "magdyno".

ROUTINE MAINTENANCE

Lubrication

The lubricator at the commutator end bracket must be given a few drops of good grade thin machine oil every 1,000—2,000 miles. The bearing at the driving end is packed with H.M.P. grease and will last until the machine is taken down for a general overhaul, when the bearing should be repacked.

Inspection of Commutator and Brush Gear

About once every six months remove the cover band for inspection of commutator and brushes. The brushes are held in contact with the commutator by means of springs. Move each brush to see that it is free to slide in its holder; if it sticks, remove it and clean with a

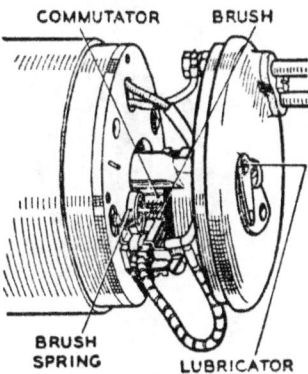

Fig. Y30. *Commutator and Bracket Assembly.*

cloth moistened with petrol. Care must be taken to replace the brushes in their original positions, otherwise they will not "bed" properly on the commutator. If, after long service, the brushes have become worn to such an extent that the brush flexible is exposed on the

B.S.A. Service Sheet No. 809 (contd.)

running face, or if the brushes do not make good contact with the commutator, they must be replaced by genuine Lucas brushes. The commutator should be free from any trace of oil or dirt and should have a highly polished appearance. Clean a dirty or blackened commutator by pressing a fine dry cloth against it while the engine is slowly turned over by means of the kickstarter crank. (It is an advantage to remove the sparking plug before doing this). If the commutator is very dirty, moisten the cloth with petrol.

Test Data

Cutting-in speed: 1,250—1,500 r.p.m. at 7 generator volts.

Output: 6.5 amps at 1,900—2,200 r.p.m. at 7 generator volts, taken on 1.1 ohm resistance load. Resistance to be capable of carrying 10 amps without overheating.

Field resistance: 3.2 ohms.

SERVICING

Testing in position to locate fault in Charging Circuit

In the event of a fault in the charging circuit, adopt the following procedure to locate the cause of trouble.

Check that the generator and regulator unit are connected correctly. The generator terminal (D) should be connected to the regulator unit terminal (D) and generator terminal (F) to regulator unit terminal (F).

Remove the cables from the generator terminals (D) and (F) and connect the two terminals with a short length of wire. Start the engine and set to run at normal idling speed.

Connect the positive lead of a moving coil voltmeter, calibrated 0—10 volts, to one of the generator terminals and connect the negative lead to a good earthing point on the generator yoke or engine.

Fig. Y31. *Testing Brush Spring Tension.*

Gradually increase the engine speed, when the voltmeter reading should rise rapidly and without fluctuation. Do not allow the voltmeter reading to rise above 10 volts, and do not race the engine in an attempt to increase the voltage. It is sufficient to run the generator up to a speed of 1,000 r.p.m. If there is no reading, check the brush gear as

B.S.A. Service Sheet No. 809 (contd.)

described below. If there is a low reading of approximately ½ volt, the field winding may be at fault. If there is a reading of approximately 1½ to 2 volts, the armature winding may be at fault.

Remove the cover band and examine the brushes and commutator. Hold back each of the brush springs and move the brush by pulling gently on its flexible connector. If the movement is sluggish, remove the brush from its holder and ease the sides by lightly polishing on a smooth file. Always replace brushes in their original positions. If the brushes are worn so that they do not bear on the commutator, or if the brush flexible is exposed on the running face, new brushes must be fitted.

Test the brush spring tension with a spring scale. The correct tension is 10—15 oz. and new springs must be fitted if the tension is low.

If the commutator is blackened or dirty, clean it by holding a petrol-moistened cloth against it while the engine is turned slowly by means of the kickstart (with sparking plug removed).

Re-test the generator as above. If there is still no reading on the voltmeter, there is an internal fault and the complete unit, if a spare is available, should be replaced. Otherwise the unit must be dismantled for internal examination.

If the generator is in good order, restore the original connections. Connect regulator unit terminal (D) to generator terminal (D) and regulator terminal (F) to generator terminal (F). Proceed to test the regulator unit as described in Service Sheet No. 804.

To Dismantle

Remove the generator from the motor cycle. To remove the generator from the magdynos unscrew the hexagon-headed nut from the driving end cover and slacken the two screws securing the band clip. Proceed to dismantle, as follows:—

On E3HM machines, bend back the tag on the washer (B) Fig. Y33, locking the screw (A) securing the driving gear (C) and remove the screw. On E3H machines, withdraw the cotter pin (A) and remove the nut (B) from the armature shaft. Withdraw the gear from

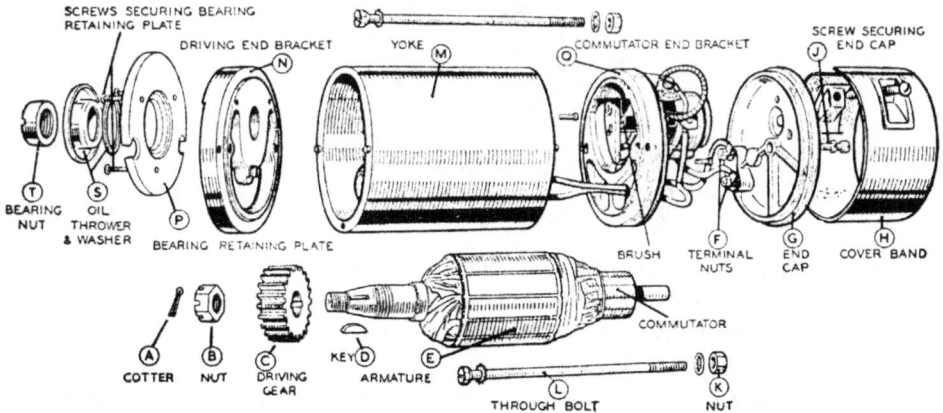

Fig. Y32. *Generator, model E3H (with oil seal).*

B.S.A. Service Sheet No. 809 (contd.)

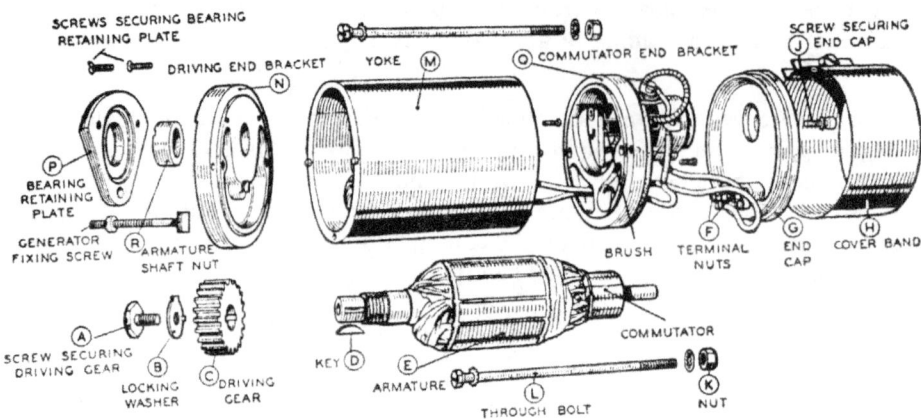

Fig. Y33. *Generator, model E3HM.*

the shaft by carefully levering it off or by means of an extractor. Remove the key(s) (D), from the shaft.

Remove the cover band (H), hold back the brush springs and lift the brushes from their holders.

Take out the screw (J), with spring washer, from the centre of the black moulded end cap (G). Draw the cap away from the end bracket, take off terminal nuts (F), and spring washers, and lift the connections off the terminals.

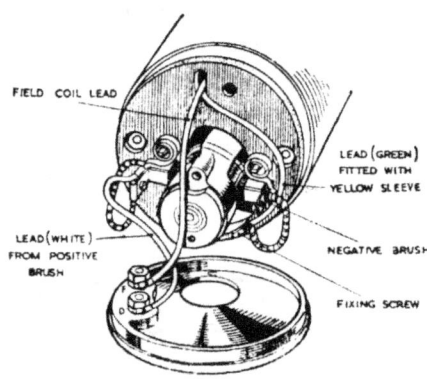

Fig. Y34. *Generator Connections.*
Note:- On later machines, the white lead is omitted, the brush
flexible lead being connected direct to terminal "D"

Unscrew and remove from the driving end bracket the two through bolts (L) securing the driving end bracket (N) and commutator end bracket (Q) to the yoke (M). Hold the nuts (K) at the commutator end while unscrewing the bolts, and take care not to lose the nuts.

On E3HM Machines.—Remove the bearing retaining plate (P) from the driving end bracket secured by two screws and a long threaded bolt. Unscrew the nut (R) from the end of the armature shaft and the armature can then be removed from the driving end bracket (N) by means of a hand press.

B.S.A. Service Sheet No. 809 (contd.)

On E3H Machines.—Remove the bearing nut (T) and the oil thrower and washer (S). Withdraw the three screws securing the retaining plate (P). The armature can then be removed from the driving end bracket (N) by means of a hand press.

Take out the screw securing the green field coil lead with the yellow sleeve to commutator end bracket and remove the end bracket (Q), withdrawing the connectors through the slot in the insulating plate.

Unscrew the three screws securing the insulating plate to the commutator end bracket and remove the plate complete with brush gear.

Commutator

Examine the commutator. If it is in good condition, it will be smooth and free from pits or burned spots. Clean with a petrol-moistened cloth. If this is ineffective, carefully polish with a strip of very fine glasspaper while rotating the armature. To remedy a badly worn commutator, mount the armature with or without the drive end bracket in a lathe, rotate at high speed and take a light cut with a very sharp tool. Do not remove more metal than is necessary. Polish the commutator with very fine glasspaper.

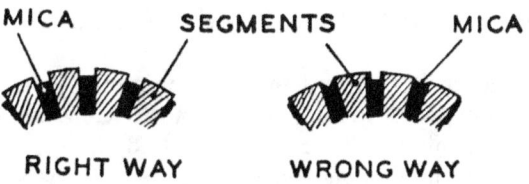

Fig. Y35. *Method of Undercutting Commutator Insulation.*

Undercut the mica insulation between the segments to a depth of $\frac{1}{32}$ in. with a hacksaw blade ground down until it is only slightly thicker than the mica.

Field Coil

Measure the resistance of the field winding by means of an ohm meter. If this is not available, connect a 6-volt D.C. supply with an ammeter in series across the coil. The ammeter reading should be approximately 1.9 amperes. No reading on the ammeter indicates an open circuit in the field winding.

To check for earthed coil, connect a mains test lamp between one end of the coil and the yoke. If the bulb lights, there is an earth between coil and yoke.

In either case, unless a replacement generator is available, the field coil must be replaced but this should only be attempted if a wheel-operated screwdriver and pole shoe expander are at hand, the latter being especially necessary to ensure that there will not be any air-gap between the pole shoe and the inner face of the yoke.

To replace the field coil, proceed as follows:—

Unscrew the pole shoe retaining screw (Fig. Y36) by means of the wheel-operated screwdriver.

Draw the pole shoe and field coil out of the yoke and lift off the coil.

B.S.A. Service Sheet No. 809 (contd.)

Fit the new field coil over the pole shoe and place it in position inside the yoke. Take care to ensure that the taping of the field coil is not trapped between the pole shoe and the yoke.

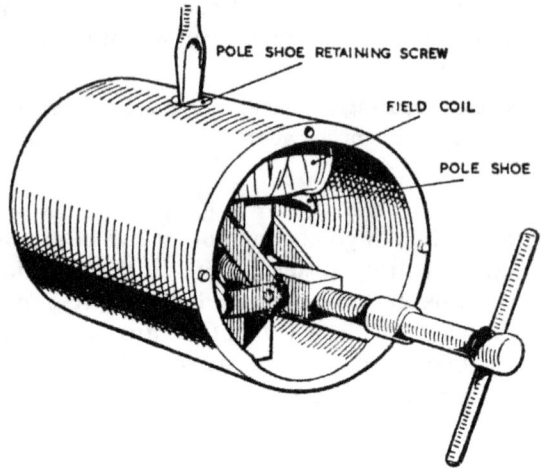

Fig. Y36. *Pole Shoe and Field Coil Assembly.*

Locate the pole shoe and field coil by lightly tightening the fixing screw. Insert the pole shoe expander, open to its fullest extent and tighten the screw. Remove the expander and give the screw a final tightening with the wheel-operated screwdriver. Lock the screw in position by caulking, that is, by tapping some of the metal of the yoke into the slot in the head of the screw.

Armature
The testing of the armature winding requires the use of a voltdrop test or growler. If these are not avilable, the armature should be checked by substitution. No attempt should be made to machine the armature core or to true a distorted armature shaft.

Bearings
A ball bearing is fitted at the driving end and a plain porous bronze bearing bush at the commutator end.

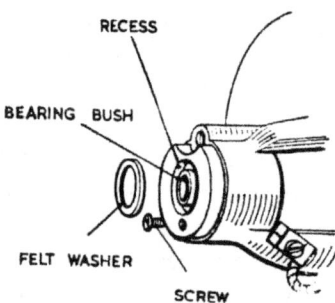

Fig. Y37. *Commutator End Bracket with Bearing Bush.*

Bearings which are worn to such an extent that they will allow side movement of the armature shaft must be replaced. To replace the bearing bush at the commutator end, proceed as follows:—

B.S.A. Service Sheet No. 809 (contd.)

Remove the screw, press the bearing bush out of the commutator end bracket and remove the felt washer (see Fig. Y37).

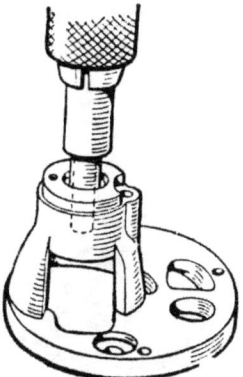

Fig. Y38. *Fitting Bearing Bush using a shouldered Mandrel.*

Press the new bearing bush into the end bracket using a shouldered mandrel (Fig. Y38) of the same diameter as the shaft which is to fit in the bearing. (NOTE:—Before use, new bearing bushes should be stored in a covered container and fully covered with oil of a grade equivalent to Mobiloil Arctic, or other good thin mineral oil. The minimum time of soaking should normally be 24 hours, but in cases of extreme urgency this period may be shortened by heating the oil to 100°C., when the time of immersion may be reduced to 2 hours). The bush should be pressed in until it is flush with the face of the end bracket. Fit the felt washer in the space between the bearing and the wall of the bearing housing.

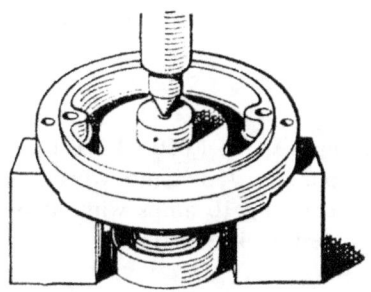

Fig. Y39. *Removing the Ball Race.*

The ball bearing at the driving end is replaced as follows:—

Remove bearing retaining plate from driving end bracket as previously described.

Press the bearing out of the end bracket, using a metal drift locating on the inner journal of the bearing (Fig. Y39).

Wipe out the bearing housing and pack the new bearing with H.M.P. grease.

Position the bearing in its housing and press it squarely home, applying pressure on the outer journal of the bearing (Fig. Y40).

B.S.A. Service Sheet No. 809 (contd.)

Reassembly

In the main, the reassembly of the generator is a reversal of the operations described in the paragraph on dismantling, bearing in mind the following points.

The field coil lead fitted with the short length of yellow tubing must be connected together with eyelet of the negative brush to the commutator end bracket by means of the screw provided.

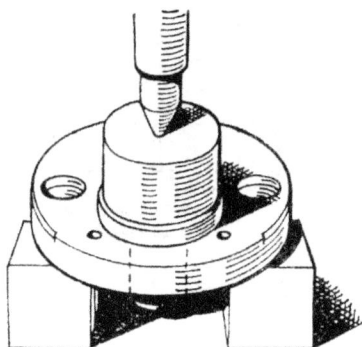

Fig. Y40. *Fitting the Ball Race.*

The second field coil lead must be connected to terminal (F) on the mouled end cap

The lead (coloured white) from the terminal on the positive brush box must be connected to terminal (D) on the mouled end cap.

(NOTE:—On later machines, the brush flexible lead is connected direct to terminal (D) and the white lead is omitted).

Take care to refit cover band in original position and make sure that the securing screw, when of flush-fitting pattern, does not short on brush gear.

E3L Dynamo

On some models an E3L dynamo is fitted. This is a higher output machine and the test figures are as follows. Cutting in speed 1,050—1,200 r.p.m. at 6.5 dynamo volts. Output 8.5 amps at 1,850—2,000 r.p.m. at 7 dynamo volts taken on .8 ohm resistance load. Resistance to be capable of carrying 10 amps without overheating. Field resistance 2.8 ohms. The dismantling and testing instructions are similar to those given for the E3H dynamo except for the following:—

1. Ball bearing fitted at commutator end.
2. Brush spring tension, 13—20 ozs.
3. Testing field coils, the ammeter reading will be 2.1 amperes.

B.S.A. MOTOR CYCLES LTD., Service Department, Armoury Road, Birmingham 11

BSA SERVICE SHEET No. 813

"C" AND "B" GROUP MODELS (EXCEPT C15 COMPETITION)

FITTED WITH CRANKSHAFT MOUNTED ALTERNATORS

LUCAS LIGHTING

The electrical system used on these models provides D.C. for the battery, ignition coil and lights, by passing the A.C. output of the generator through a bridge type rectifier.

The alternator is connected to a section of the headlamp switch so that the output is automatically matched to the demands of the lighting circuit and the characteristics of the alternator prevent overcharging.

"C" Group except C15
Cable Colours
Light Green
Dark Green
Middle Green or Green/Yellow

"B" Group & C15
Cable Colours
Green/Black or Dark Green
Green/Yellow
Green/White or Light Green

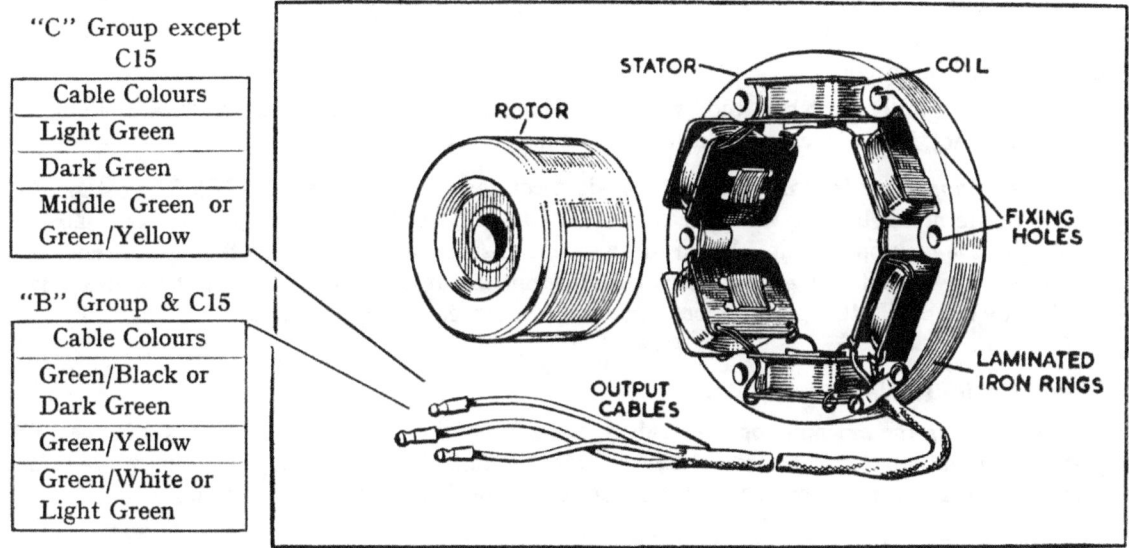

Stator and Rotor of Lucas Motor Cycle Alternator
(RM 13 on C11G and C15, RM 13/15 on C12, and RM 15 on new series "B" group machines)

Output Control

The standard circuit has the output wires from the generator connected by their snap connectors to similarly coloured wires on the wiring harness and provides the following output control.

Lighting Switch in "OFF" Position

The output is taken from one pair of coils by means of the Light Green and Dark Green wires, and the remaining coils (Light Green and Middle Green wires) (Light Green and Green/Yellow on "B" group) are open-circuited.

Lighting Switch in "PILOT" Position

Output taken from one pair of coils by Light Green and Dark Green wires as before and the remaining coils are on open-circuit.

B.S.A. SERVICE SHEET No. 813 (contd.)

Lighting Switch in "HEAD" Position

All three pairs of coils are connected in parallel and the maximum output is obtained. Note.—To provide an increased charging rate with the lighting switch in the "OFF" position, some models will be found to have the wire joining terminals 5 and 6 of the headlamp switch removed. This means that no coils are shorted out in this switch position and the charging rate is slightly increased.

In circumstances where a considerable amount of low speed running is necessary or there are long periods of parking with the lights on, it is possible to increase the charging rate with the lighting switch in the "OFF" and "PILOT" positions by connecting the Medium Green alternator cable (Green/Yellow for C15) by its snap connector to the Dark Green harness cable and the Dark Green alternator cable to the Medium Green harness cable (Green/Yellow for C15).

The Light Green cables should not be disturbed. These alternative connections considerably increase the charging rate in these switch positions, and the connections should be returned to standard for normal conditions of use or long runs.

Owing to the effects of the above modifications it is essential that the wiring circuit is returned to standard before checking the charging rates during fault finding.

Emergency Starting

With the ignition switch in the "EMG" position, the battery is not isolated from the alternator and will, in fact, receive a charge whilst the machine is being run.

This arrangement is also a safeguard against continuous running in the "EMG" position. The back pressure of the battery will increase as it is charged, until it is sufficiently strong to affect the working of the ignition system. When this happens misfiring will occur, resulting in poor engine performance. In view of this, always check that the machine is not being run with the ignition switch continually in the "EMG" position, before testing the system for other faults.

Motor Cycle Trials Events, etc.

When using the machine for trials riding, the alternator can be used continuously in the "EMG" position without a battery, providing the lead from the main harness to the battery negative terminal is earthed to the machine, but contact breaker points are liable to become badly burned.

Test Procedure

As the lights and other equipment are operated on a normal D.C. circuit they can be checked by normal continuity tests with a battery and bulb.

The following equipment is required to satisfactorily test the charging circuit. The meters used should be accurate moving coil instruments.

A.C voltmeter scale 0–15 volts.
D.C. ammeter scale 0–15 amps.
D.C. voltmeter scale 0–15 volts.

1 ohm. load resistance.
12 volt battery and 36 watt bulbs.

When checking the alternator output the engine should be run at approximately 3,000 r.p.m.

If the performance of the alternator has proved unsatisfactory, it is advisable to first check the wiring to make sure that good contact is being made at the various connections and that none of the wiring of alternator coils are shorting to the frame.

B.S.A. SERVICE SHEET No. 813 (contd.)

CHECKING D.C. INPUT TO BATTERY

Test 1. Ammeter connected in series with main lead and battery.

Test 2. Disconnect main lead from battery. Connect 1 ohm resistor in place of battery. Feed ignition coil separately from battery. Turn ignition switch to IGN position.

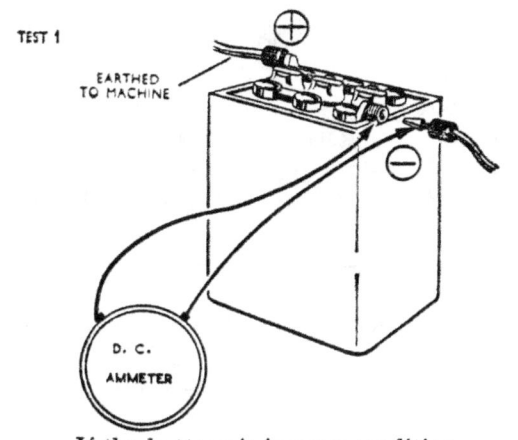

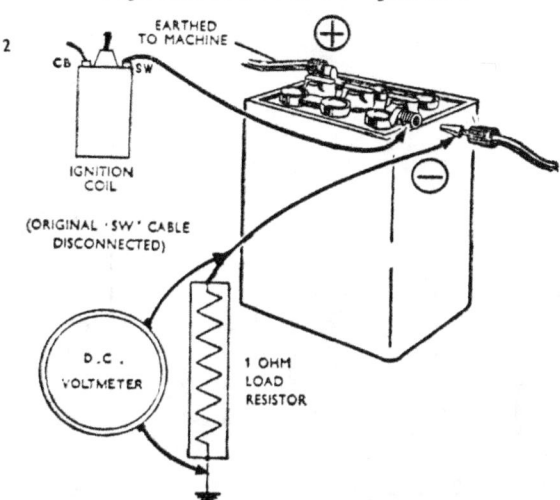

If the battery is in poor condition or low state of charge use Test 2.

Test	Switch Position	Reading Amps. at 3,000 r.p.m.		
		RM13	RM13/15	RM15
1	OFF	1.5 (min.)	1.75 (min.)	2.5 (min.)
	PILOT	0.5 (min.)	0.75 (min.)	1.5 (min.)
	HEAD	0.25 (min.)	0.5 (min.)	2.5 (min.)

Test	Switch Position	Reading Volts at 3,000 r.p.m.		
		RM13	RM13/15	RM15
2	OFF	1.5 (min.)	1.75 (min.)	2.5 (min.)
	PILOT	1.5 (min.)	1.75 (min.)	2.0 (min.)
	HEAD	3.0 (min.)	3.25 (min.)	3.0 (min.)

Conclusion from these Tests

Test 1. If meter readings are as stated, the charging circuit and alternator are satisfactory. No reading; check the generator.

A low reading can be caused by a faulty battery.

Proceed with Test 2. If readings still low check battery with hydrometer and discharge tester.

Test 2. If meter readings are lower or higher than values stated, check the generator. No reading on meter; check the rectifier.

Important

Inaccurate readings can be due to faulty wiring, bad connections at the snap connectors or poor earths. Make a quick visual check of all connections before proceeding with the tests.

Remember it is no use carrying out Test 1 if the battery is faulty or in a low state of charge; if in doubt proceed with Test 2.

B.S.A. SERVICE SHEET No. 813 (contd.)

Testing the RM13 Alternator on the Machine, using an A.C. Voltmeter and 1 Ohm Load Resistor

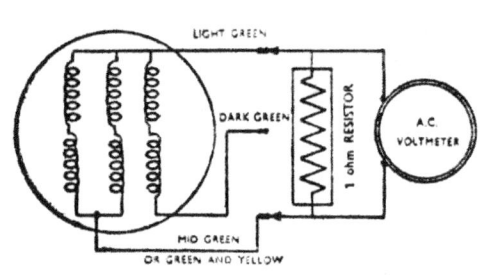

Test	Voltmeter and Resistor Connected Across	Reading Volts at 3,000 r.p.m.		
		RM13	RM13/15	RM15
1	Dark Green and Light Green	3.0 (min.)	3.25 (min.)	4.25 (min.)
2	Light Green and Mid Green or Green/Yellow	6.0 (min.)	6.25 (min.)	6.75 (min.)
3	Dark Green and Light Green (with Mid Green or Green/Yellow connected to Dark Green).	8.5 (min.)	8.75 (min.)	9.25 (min.)
4	Any one lead and Generator Stator (Earth)	No Reading	No Reading	No Reading

Conclusions from these Tests.

Low reading on any group of coils indicates shorted turns.

Zero reading will indicate open circuit coil.

If all coils read low, partial de-magnetisation of rotor may have occured as a result of faulty rectifier. Check rectifier, and battery earth polarity before replacing rotor.

A reading between any one lead and the generator stator indicates an earthed coil. Replace stator or locate earth by isolating and testing individual coils.

Note.

With the engine running at 3,000 r.p.m. (approx.) the output voltages are steady, and even if the engine is running a few r.p.m. faster or slower the values stated will be obtained from a good generator.

B.S.A. SERVICE SHEET No. 813 (contd.)

Rectifier—Bench Testing

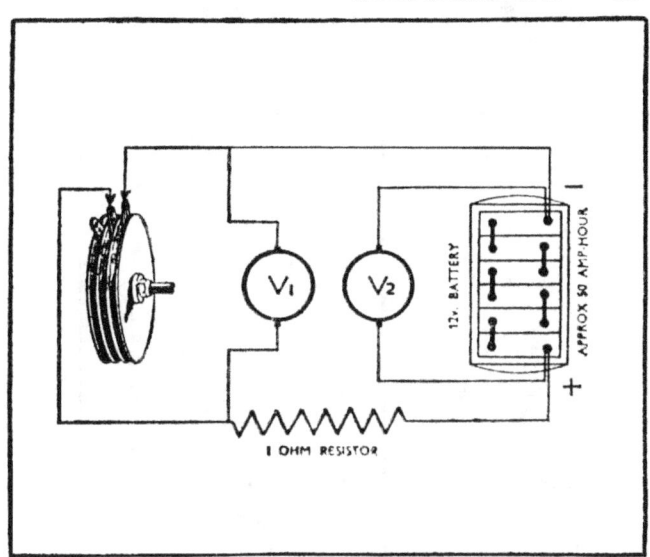
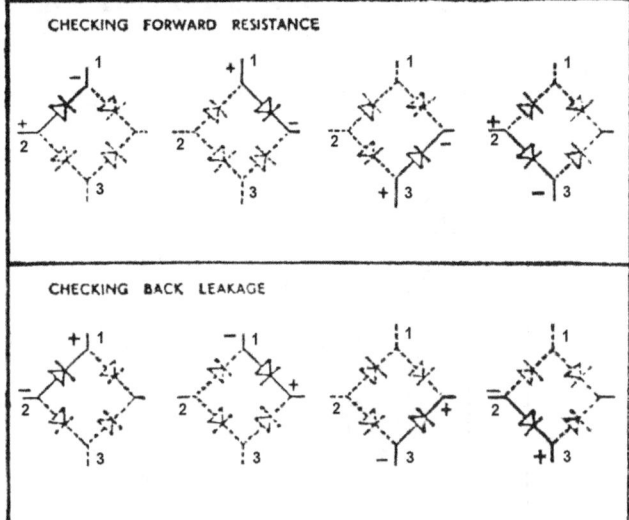

V1—will measure the volt drop across the rectifier plate.
V2—must be checked when testing the rectifier plate, to make certain the supply voltage is the recommended 12 volts on load.

It is essential that the supply is kept at 12 volts for these Tests.

Forward Resistance Test

Test 1. Connect test leads in turn to terminals 2 and 1, bolt and 1, bolt and 3, 2 and 3. Reading in all positions should not be greater than 2.5 volts. Keep the testing time as short as possible to avoid overheating the rectifier cell. Note.—If the later type of rectifier, which has no terminal markings, is fitted, the same test procedure is followed. The same voltage values also apply.

Back Leakage Test

Test 2. Proceed as for Test 1, and test each cell in turn, but reverse the test leads. Reading on V1 should not be less than 2 volts below the open-circuit reading on voltmeter No. 2, i.e., 10 volts.

Conclusion from these Tests

Test 1. If the voltage reading on V1 is more than 2.5 volts, on any cell, it is aged and the rectifier should be replaced.

Test 2. If the voltage reading on V1 is less than 10 volts, on any cell, the rectifier is shorted and should be replaced.

Important

Before fitting a replacement rectifier check the following points:—
1. Check that battery is correctly connected, **Positive to Earth**.
2. Check rectifier visually for signs of damage.

Never disturb the tension of the nut which holds the elements together on the through bolt. The efficiency of the rectifier depends upon the correct tension of the plates. The tension of the nut is set before leaving the works, and cannot be adjusted correctly in service.

B.S.A. SERVICE SHEET No. 813 (contd.)

Checking Rectifier in Position on Machine

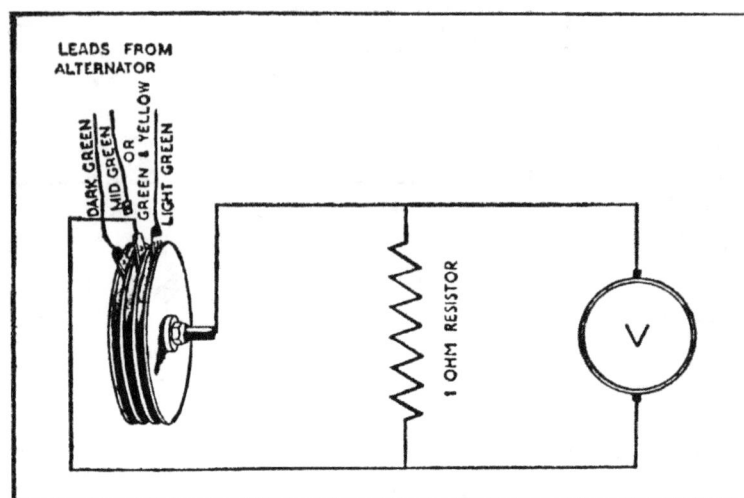
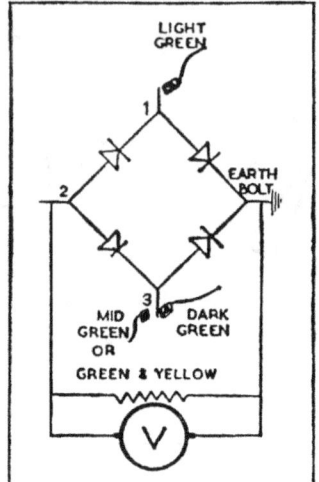

Voltmeter and Resistor Connected Across	Reading with Leads Connected as Shown
Terminal No. 2 (or centre terminal on latest type) and frame of machine	6.5 (min.) RM13 7.0 (min.) RM13/15 7.75 (min.) RM15

Procedure

Connect the alternator leads as detailed direct to the rectifier terminals No. 1 and No. 3.

(**Note.**—On the latest type rectifiers the terminals are not numbered, so connect the alternator leads to the outer cranked terminals).

Connect the test leads which must have a D.C. voltmeter with 1 ohm load shunted across, between earth (frame of machine) and terminal No. 2 (centre terminal on latest type rectifier) when the values stated should be obtained with engine running at 3,000 r.p.m.

Conclusions from these Tests

If the alternator passes its individual test, but it fails on this test it indicates that either the rectifier is faulty or it is not properly earthed.

Connecting the test leads to the centre bolt will eliminate the possibility of faulty earth connection

B.S.A. SERVICE SHEET No. 813 (contd.)

Testing the External Wiring Circuit

Using D.C. Voltmeter only
1. All cables, including battery, to be connected as normal.
2. Connect voltmeter Red test lead to earth.

Testing Charging Circuit through Ignition Switch
3. Connect Black test lead to No. 2 terminal on rectifier.
4. Switch ignition to IGN position.
5. Battery volts, i.e., six, should register on voltmeter.
6. If there is zero reading on voltmeter in the above condition, check circuit back through ignition switch, ammeter, etc., to the battery.

Testing Emergency Start Circuit (Single Cylinder Machine)
7. Connect Red test lead to earth.
8. Connect Black test lead to C.B. terminal on ignition contact breaker.
9. Open ignition contacts.
10. Switch ignition switch to EMG position.
11. Battery volts should register on voltmeter.
12. Transfer Black test lead to alternator Mid-Green lead.
13. Battery volts should register on voltmeter.

Note

These tests are to be carried out in the case of "No Charge" or "No Emergency Start" if previous tests have been carried out and all is in order.

It is important that both the ignition timing and the rotor timing is correct for efficient operation of Emergency Start.

Testing the 'Low,' 'Medium' and 'High' Charge Positions

Using D.C. Voltmeter only
1. Connect Red test lead to earth.
2. The set, including battery connected as normal, with the exception of the alternator Middle Green cable which should be disconnected at the snap connector under the saddle
3. Connect Black test lead to Mid-Green cable coming from headlamp (i.e., not coming from alternator).
4. With ignition switch in IGN position and lighting switch OFF.
5. A low voltage (i.e., 1—2) should register on voltmeter.
6. With lighting switch in PILOT, zero voltage should register on voltmeter.
7. With lighting switch in HEAD position a low voltage should register on voltmeter.

Note

Incorrect switching of these cables will cause incorrect charging rates, i.e., failure of Mid-Green and Dark Green linking together in HEAD position will result in a low charge rate with headlight switched on.

In the case of incorrect switching it is necessary to check the wiring and the switch for correct connections, etc.

B.S.A. SERVICE SHEET No. 813 (contd.)

Headlamp Switch

If both the rectifier and alternator appear satisfactory the wiring and switch contacts must be checked most carefully to eliminate any possible faults. The correct headlamp switch connections are shown in Service Sheets.

    No. 808D C12
    No. 808C C11G
    No. 808H ... ... "B" models
    No. 808J C15

Alternator Romoval and Replacement

The procedure for removing and replacing the alternator is described in **Service Sheets** No. 314 for "B" group machines and 409 for C11G and **C12,** and No. 422 for C15. **Note** that the stator should be assembled with the clip retaining the output cables on the side of the stator **next** to the engine on C11G and C12 but on C15 and "B" group machines the clip should be on the side away from the engine

B.S.A. MOTOR CYCLES LTD.,
Service Department, Armoury Road, Birmingham, 11
_{Printed in England.}

VELOCEPRESS MANUALS - MOTORCYCLE

1930'S BRITISH MOTORCYCLE CARBS & ELEC COMPONENTS (BOOK OF)
1930'S BRITISH MOTORCYCLE ENGINES (OVERHAUL & MAINTENANCE)
1930'S BRITISH MOTORCYCLE GEARBOXES & CLUTCHES (BOOK OF)
AJS 1932-1948 SINGLES & TWINS 250cc THRU 1000cc (BOOK OF)
AJS 1945-1960 SINGLES 350cc & 500cc MODELS 16 & 18 (BOOK OF)
AJS 1955-1965 SINGLES 350cc & 500cc (BOOK OF)
ARIEL UP TO 1932 (BOOK OF)
ARIEL 1932-1939 PREWAR MODELS (BOOK OF)
ARIEL 1933-1951 (WORKSHOP MANUAL)
ARIEL 1939-1960 4 STROKE SINGLES (BOOK OF)
ARIEL 1958-1964 LEADER & ARROW (BOOK OF)
BMW R26 R27 (1956-1967) FACTORY WORKSHOP MANUAL
BMW R50 R50S R60 R69S (1955-1969) FACTORY WORKSHOP MANUAL
BRIDGESTONE 90 SERIES FACTORY WSM & PARTS CATALOGUE
BRIDGESTONE 175 SERIES FACTORY WSM & PARTS CATALOGUE
BRIDGESTONE 350 SERIES FACTORY WSM & PARTS CATALOGUES
BSA BANTAM ALL MODELS FROM 1948 ONWARDS (BOOK OF)
BSA SINGLES & V-TWINS UP TO 1927 (BOOK OF)
BSA SINGLES & V-TWINS UP TO 1930 (BOOK OF)
BSA SINGLES & V-TWINS UP TO 1935 (BOOK OF)
BSA SINGLES & V-TWINS 1936-1939 (BOOK OF)
BSA OHV & SV SINGLES 250-600cc 1945-1959 (BOOK OF)
BSA OHV & SV SINGLES 250cc (ONLY) 1954-1970 (BOOK OF)
BSA OHV SINGLES 350 & 500cc 1955-1967 (BOOK OF)
BSA B31, B32, B33 & B34 1945-60 FACTORY SERVICE SHEETS MANUAL
BSA M20, M21 & M33 1945-1963 FACTORY SERVICE SHEETS MANUAL
BSA TWINS A7 & A10 1948-1962 FACTORY SERVICE SHEETS MANUAL
BSA TWINS A7 & A10 1948-1962 (BOOK OF)
BSA TWINS A50 & A65 1962-1969 (SECOND BOOK OF)
CYCLEMOTOR (BOOK OF)
DOUGLAS 1929-1939 PREWAR ALL MODELS (BOOK OF)
DOUGLAS 1948-1957 POSTWAR ALL MODELS FACTORY SHOP MANUAL
DUCATI 160cc, 250cc & 350cc OHC MODELS FACTORY SHOP MANUAL
HONDA 50 ALL MODELS UP TO 1970 INC MONKEY & TRAIL (BOOK OF)
HONDA 90 ALL MODELS UP TO 1966 (BOOK OF)
HONDA 125-150cc TWINS C/CS/CB/CA FACTORY WORKSHOP MANUAL
HONDA 250-305 TWINS C/CS/CB FACTORY WORKSHOP MANUAL
HONDA 450 CB/CL 1965-1974 K0 TO K7 WORKSHOP MANUAL
HONDA C100 SUPER CUB FACTORY WORKSHOP MANUAL
HONDA C110 SPORT CUB 1962-1969 FACTORY WORKSHOP MANUAL
HONDA TWINS & SINGLES 50cc THRU 305cc 1960-1966 (BOOK OF)
HONDA TWINS ALL MODELS 125cc THRU 450cc UP TO 1968 (BOOK OF)
INDIAN PONYBIKE, BOY RACER & PAPOOSE ILL PARTS LIST & SALES LIT
J.A.P. ENGINES 1927-1952 & MOTORCYCLES 1934-1952 (BOOK OF)
LAMBRETTA 1947-1957 ALL 125 & 150cc MODELS (BOOK OF)
LAMBRETTA 1957-1970 LI & TV MODELS (SECOND BOOK OF)
MATCHLESS 1931-1939 ALL MODELS 250cc THRU 990cc (BOOK OF)
MATCHLESS 1945-1956 350 & 500cc SINGLES (BOOK OF)
MATCHLESS 1955-1966 350 & 500cc SINGLES (BOOK OF)
NEW IMPERIAL ALL SV & OHV FROM 1935 ONWARDS (BOOK OF)
NORTON 1932-1939 PREWAR MODELS (BOOK OF)
NORTON 1932-1947 (BOOK OF)
NORTON 1938-1956 (BOOK OF)
NORTON 1955-1963 MODELS 19, 50 & ES2 (BOOK OF)
NORTON 1955-1965 DOMINATOR TWINS (BOOK OF)
NORTON 1960-1970 TWIN CYLINDER FACTORY WORKSHOP MANUAL
NORTON 1970-1975 COMMANDO FACTORY WORKSHOP MANUAL
NORTON 1975-1978 MK 3 COMMANDO FACTORY WORKSHOP MANUAL
NSU PRIMA 1956-1964 ALL MODELS (BOOK OF)
NSU QUICKLY 1953-1963 ALL MODELS (BOOK OF)
PANTHER 1932-1958 LIGHTWEIGHT MODELS 250 & 350cc (BOOK OF)
PANTHER 1938-1966 HEAVYWEIGHT MODELS 600 & 650cc (BOOK OF)
RALEIGH MOPEDS 1960-1969 (BOOK OF)
RALEIGH MOTORCYCLES 1919-1933 (BOOK OF)
ROYAL ENFIELD 1934-1946 SINGLES & V TWINS (BOOK OF)
ROYAL ENFIELD 1937-1953 SINGLES & V TWINS (BOOK OF)
ROYAL ENFIELD 1946-1962 SINGLES (BOOK OF)
ROYAL ENFIELD 1958-1966 250cc & 350cc SINGLES (SECOND BOOK OF)
ROYAL ENFIELD 736cc INTERCEPTOR FACTORY WORKSHOP MANUAL
RUDGE 1933-1939 (BOOK OF)
SUNBEAM 1928-1939 (BOOK OF)
SUNBEAM 1946-1957 S7 & S8 (BOOK OF)
SUZUKI 50cc & 80cc UP TO 1966 (BOOK OF)
SUZUKI T10 1963-1967 FACTORY WORKSHOP MANUAL
SUZUKI T20 & T200 1965-1969 FACTORY WORKSHOP MANUAL
SUZUKI TWINS 1962 ONWARDS 125-500cc WORKSHOP MANUAL
TRIUMPH 1935-1939 PREWAR MODELS (BOOK OF)
TRIUMPH 1935-1949 (BOOK OF)
TRIUMPH 1937-1951 (WORKSHOP MANUAL)
TRIUMPH 1945-1955 FACTORY WORKSHOP MANUAL
TRIUMPH 1945-1958 TWINS (BOOK OF)
TRIUMPH 1956-1969 TWINS (BOOK OF)
VELOCETTE 1925-1970 ALL SINGLES & TWINS (BOOK OF)
VESPA 1951-1961 (BOOK OF)
VESPA 1955-1963 125 & 150cc & GS MODELS (SECOND BOOK OF)
VESPA 1955-1968 GS & SS (BOOK OF)
VESPA 1963-1972 90, 125 & 150cc (THIRD BOOK OF)
VILLIERS ENGINE UP TO 1959 INC. 3 WHEELERS (BOOK OF)
VILLIERS ENGINE UP TO 1969 (BOOK OF)
VINCENT 1935-1955 (WORKSHOP MANUAL)
YAMAHA 1961-1967 YA5 & YA6 (WORKSHOP MANUAL & ILL PARTS LIST)
YAMAHA 1971-1972 JT1& JT2 (WORKSHOP MANUAL & ILL PARTS LIST)

VELOCEPRESS TECHNICAL BOOKS – MOTORCYCLE

CATALOG OF BRITISH MOTORCYCLES (1951 MODELS)
LUCAS ELECTRONICS BRITISH M/CYCLES REPAIR & PARTS (1950-1977)
MOTORCYCLE ENGINEERING (P.E. Irving)
MOTORCYCLE ROAD TESTS 1949-1953 (Motor Cycle Magazine UK)
SPEED AND HOW TO OBTAIN IT (Motor Cycle Magazine UK)
TUNING FOR SPEED (P.E. Irving)

VELOCEPRESS MANUALS - THREE WHEELER'S

BSA THREE WHEELER (BOOK OF)
VINTAGE MORGAN THREE WHEELER (BOOK OF)

VELOCEPRESS MANUALS - AUTOMOBILE

ALFA ROMEO GIULIA WORKSHOP MANUAL 1300 TO 2000cc 1962-1975
ALFA ROMEO GIULIA TECH MANUAL CARBURETED CARS FROM 1962
ALFA ROMEO GIULIA TECH MANUAL FUEL INJECTED CARS FROM 1969
ALFA ROMEO GIULIETTA & GIULIA 750 & 101 SERIES 1955-1965 WSM
AUSTIN-HEALEY SPRITE & MG MIDGET WORKSHOP MANUAL 1958-1971
BMW 600 LIMOUSINE FACTORY WORKSHOP MANUAL
BMW 600 LIMOUSINE OWNERS HAND BOOK & SERVICE MANUAL
BMW 2000 & 2002 1966-1976 WORKSHOP MANUAL
BMW ISETTA FACTORY WORKSHOP MANUAL
CORVAIR 1960-1969 WORKSHOP MANUAL
CORVETTE V8 1955-1962 WORKSHOP MANUAL
FIAT 500 FACTORY WORKSHOP MANUAL 1957-1973
FIAT 600, 600D & MULTIPLA FACTORY WORKSHOP MANUAL 1955-1969
JAGUAR E-TYPE 3.8 & 4.2 SERIES 1 & 2 WORKSHOP MANUAL
JAGUAR MK 7, 8, 9 & XK120, 140, 150 WORKSHOP MANUAL 1948-1961
METROPOLITAN FACTORY WORKSHOP MANUAL
MGA & MGB OWNERS HANDBOOK & WORKSHOP MANUAL
MG MIDGET TC, TD, TF & TF1500 WORKSHOP MANUAL
PORSCHE 356 1948-1965 WORKSHOP MANUAL
PORSCHE 911 2.0, 2.2, 2.4 LITRE 1964-1973 WORKSHOP MANUAL
PORSCHE 911 2.7, 3.0, 3.2 LITRE 1973-1989 WORKSHOP MANUAL
PORSCHE 912 WORKSHOP MANUAL
TRIUMPH TR2, TR3, TR4 1953-1965 WORKSHOP MANUAL
VOLKSWAGEN TRANSPORTER, TRUCKS & WAGONS 1950-1979 WSM
VOLVO 1944-1968 ALL MODELS WORKSHOP MANUAL

VELOCEPRESS TECHNICAL BOOKS - AUTOMOBILE

FERRARI 250/GT SERVICE AND MAINTENANCE
FERRARI GUIDE TO PERFORMANCE
FERRARI OWNER'S HANDBOOK
FERRARI TUNING TIPS & MAINTENANCE TECHNIQUES
HOW TO BUILD A FIBERGLASS CAR
HOW TO BUILD A RACING CAR
HOW TO RESTORE THE MODEL 'A' FORD
MASERATI OWNER'S HANDBOOK
OBERT'S FIAT GUIDE
PERFORMANCE TUNING THE SUNBEAM TIGER
SOUPING THE VOLKSWAGEN
SOLEX CARBURETORS (EMPHASIS ON UK & EU AUTOMOBILES)
SU CARBURETORS (EMPHASIS ON UK AUTOMOBILES)
WEBER CARBURETORS (EMPHASIS ON ALFA & FIAT)

VELOCEPRESS BOOKS & GUIDES - AUTOMOBILE

ABARTH BUYERS GUIDE
COMPLETE CATALOG OF JAPANESE MOTOR VEHICLES
FERRARI 308 SERIES BUYER'S AND OWNER'S GUIDE
FERRARI BERLINETTA LUSSO
FERRARI BROCHURES AND SALES LITERATURE 1946-1967
FERRARI BROCHURES AND SALES LITERATURE 1968-1989
FERRARI OPP, MAINTENANCE & SERVICE H/BOOKS 1948-1963
FERRARI SERIAL NUMBERS PART I - ODD NUMBERS TO 21399
FERRARI SERIAL NUMBERS PART II - EVEN NUMBERS TO 1050
FERRARI SPYDER CALIFORNIA
HENRY'S FABULOUS MODEL "A" FORD
MASERATI BROCHURES AND SALES LITERATURE

VELOCEPRESS BOOKS – RACING

CARRERA PANAMERICANA - MEXICAN ROAD RACE (BOOK OF)
DIALED IN - THE JAN OPPERMAN STORY
IF HEMINGWAY HAD WRITTEN A RACING NOVEL
VEDA ORR'S NEW REVISED HOT ROD PICTORIAL

AUTOBOOKS WORKSHOP MANUALS & BROOKLANDS ROAD TEST PORTFOLIOS

FOR A COMPLETE LISTING OF THE AUTOBOOKS & BROOKLANDS TITLES THAT WE CURRENTLY HAVE AVAILABLE, PLEASE VISIT OUR WEBSITE.
www.VelocePress.com

Please check our website:

www.VelocePress.com

for a complete
up-to-date list of
available titles

www.ingramcontent.com/pod-product-compliance
Lightning Source LLC
Chambersburg PA
CBHW080433230426
43662CB00015B/2261